Challenges in American Culture

CHALLENGES IN AMERICAN CULTURE

Edited by
Ray B. Browne
Larry N. Landrum
William K. Bottorff

Bowling Green University Popular Press
Bowling Green, Ohio 43403

The Bowling Green University Popular Press is the publishing arm of the Center for the Study of Popular Culture, Ray B. Browne, Director.

Library of Congress Catalogue Card Number: 70-133907.
Printed in the United States of America.

CONTENTS

Introduction

The designs of the creators of the American Studies Association as stated as the purpose of the *American Quarterly,* its organ, were laudable: "to aid in giving a means of direction to studies in the culture of the United States, past and present." And several early splendid works testify to the validity and vigor of this new approach. In practice generally, however—especially as the Association has grown older—these noble aims have not been carried out. The Association has failed to develop beyond a narrow emphasis.

The reasons are numerous. Undoubtedly one major cause was that those persons who professed the new discipline of American Studies had been so well trained in their own individual disciplines that they could not view this new approach except through the old-style glasses. The result was therefore merely an extension of the perspective instead of a new vision. Aging has not mitigated this weakness. In too many cases it has crystalized it. Rightly or wrongly, most persons—for reasons including those of employment—still must approach American Studies from the training of another closely or distantly related discipline—usually history or literature. Those persons therefore generally bring to their programs certain prejudices and attitudes as to what in American life needs to be studied. The esthetic preoccupation of literary study and the formal linear nature of most historical approaches result often in a largely unquestioning elitist bias.

This conventional approach often assumes that the great artist is at the vanguard of his culture or reflects in his work the most acute perceptions into the state of the culture. While this view may be valid, in practice it serves primarily as a source for historical referents and metaphors of artistic consciousness. We must argue that artistic consciousness does not necessarily include that of those classes and groups within society which maintain the culture and evoke technical and social change within it. Nor does artistic consciousness necessarily go beyond general philosophical concern with culture as fact. If we are to maintain that artistic consciousness has any relationship at all to society, we must explore the various levels of consciousness, their content, and their relationship to the culture's technical and social aspects.

Possibly a more serious objection to traditional approaches is that they neglect vast areas of inquiry in order to concentrate primarily on those which are best exemplified by written history and literature. Among these are the artifacts and non-verbal cultural products below the levels of the fine arts. Here are the store-front churches and the lore of bars and taverns, cartoons and graffiti, both legal and illegal spectator sports, television and the games and artifacts of mass existence. Sociologists and social psychologists have touched on some of these subjects, but essentially as observations in a narrower vein. The failure of American Studies is the failure to assimilate these studies and to undertake others which would benefit from a generalist's approach.

Another weakness in the conventional American Studies attitude despite the protestations of the professors, has always been, a kind of wrong-end-of-the-telescope point of view. The stated aim of the Society is to study the present as well as the past. Generally, however, for any of several reasons, the proper study of American culture to the American Studies scholar has begun in the past, and usually has ended about 1930—one is inclined to say thus culminating at a "safe" date, after which the going gets a little boggier. Professors like the comfort of the period which can be neatly boxed and tied.

Thus American Studies programs have failed to live up to their potentials because the people who studied and taught them have imposed the restrictions of their own disciplines. They would have found the mother lode richer and more rewarding if they had approached with new and eager curiosities and had used the tools of their former trade as sparingly as possible, modifying and creating anew as they went. Instead of neatly packaging their products, to change the metaphor, they should have used an open ended approach with walls to the container that were flexible. This approach would have been that now proposed by the Popular Culture as offering rewarding alternatives or supplements to American Studies programs.

Popular Culture as a term might present difficulties to many sincere persons. But it should not. Definitions may be difficult and may not even be desirable, for just possibly, as John Cawelti argues, to define the term now might in fact be to begin to narrow and hamper it, a possibility we are eager to prevent. But many people are lost without definitions. For those who desire definitions, the term "Popular Culture" can be usefully and safely defined as those elements of our lives which are not narrowly intellectual or artistically elitist. So Popular Cluture includes most of the levels of culture–the literature, arts, history, acts and attitudes–which are the works and consciousness of a people. Such an approach includes not only the historical metaphors of a society in the process of change, but also the symbols and metaphors of a society in the process of change, but also the symbols and metaphors of conflict of ideologies and life styles in our society today. We hope to be able to understand not only the historical parallels and antecedents for today's unrest, but the historical uniqueness and vitality unprecedented in the history of the culture.

Contrary to conventional American Studies approaches, Popular Culture begins with the contemporary and works backwards to origins as need arises. But always the focus should be on the *now*. Thus the relevance that students are demanding these days is obvious from the beginning. The study is made relevant by its subject matter and the approach. And no wrenching is demanded. Instead of studying Thoreau's "Civil Disobedience" and trying to tie it in with current rebellion, communes and disaffection with the world, Popular Cutlure would begin with the current state of rebellion and bring in Thoreau as relevant and useful background. Though there is obviously nothing wrong with studying Thoreau *as* Thoreau, as many people do, at least if studying him as precursor of rebellious thinking, in the Popular Culture approach, we would get to the tortured world that he supposedly was precursor to. And that can be useful. We will be using the world we live in to teach from. We simply must, as Jay Gurian so aply put it, "get past the paradox of rejecting today what we revere tomorrow." We must seize today what is today's. Time does not allow us anymore to teach only yesterday today. We are not advocating discarding the past, for we believe with Santayana that those who forget the past will be forced to relive it. But we believe that not to live in today's world is not to live fully, and in so doing to shirk the responsibility of squaring off against the world and bringing what talents we have toward settling its problems.

Northrup Frye has helped to break down the traditional barriers in cultural studies, but it seems to us that he misses the mark when he argues that "whatever is 'unstructured' is headed towards belief or concern mythology, not knowledge." The interconnected structure of knowledge that Frye and others envision assumes that all knowledge is accessible and that time is not a critical factor in the pursuit of knowledge. Had we world enough and time we could spend a century or two exploring the nature and limits of formal relationships and another on structure. But as Frederick Crews has recently pointed out, vast areas of scholarship have been virtually ignored by scholars who want to remain objective and detached, and much information will forever, it seems, remain classified or below the detachment of all but a few serous scholars.

It is time to question the distinction between scientific approaches and involved approaches in cultural studies. The relative purity of the subject matter of the natural sciences lends itself to a detachment not available to those interested in many aspects of culture. Few responsible students of the culture would argue that we should ignore methodology and objectivity but there are many areas of the culture which shift rapidly and many which can rarely be understood by the outsider. It is possible to be involved in the culture, even committed to a point of view about it and be able to do methodologically sound work concerning it. The danger is present, of course, that the work will be biased, but a larger danger is that in being detached one will make judgments about it that are ill informed. We see the same scholars who argue for objectivity making childish charges against those who are "unprofessional" in their behavior. One of the problems with American Studies is that we have been so long detached from the culture that we tend to overreact toward both extremes. If we recognize that lurking behind the overinvolved person is the True Believer, then we must also recognize that behind the extreme scientific view is the myth of Progress, the idea that if we remain detached and totally rational we will someday reach that state of Perfect Knowledge.

Meanwhile, a practical problem with the scientific view is that it tends to attach itself to clusters of thought, hierarchies of research concerns and so on which, while they may further knowledge in some areas, also attract non-scientific interests which in turn influence the direction of research. If we have seen weapons systems developing out of the sciences, social and psychological manipulation from the social sciences, we have only to see the results of a scientific study of literature and history used to create the new new myth of North American superiority under the aegis of a fully sanctioned Mandarin class. Nor is this so far-fetched. One of the reasons for the extreme division of attitudes in our society today is that we have failed to include a sophisticated awareness of the culture in our educational programs. We are mechanically appalled that our young people spend more time watching television than in the classroom but we fail to instill the critical attitude which will make them more selective in what they view. Instead, we try to lure them away from the set or condemn it outright, offering no equally interesting alternative.

The mistake in this point of view was recently reiterated by the British anthropologist Edmund Leach in his B. B.C. Reith Lectures. He insisted that the scholar must come out of his ivory tower and live in the present, "participating in history instead of standing by to watch" it. He pointed out what should be obvious about non-participation: "The cult of scientific detachment and the orderly fragmented way of living that goes with it, serve only to isolate the human individual from his environment, and from his neighbors—they reduce him to a lonely, impotent and terrified observer of a runaway world," There is, he urges, at least one consolation in being a part of history: "You should read your Homer. Gods who manipulate the course of destiny are no more likely to achieve their private ambitions than mere men who suffer the slings and arrows of outrageous fortune; but gods have much more fun!"

The importance of this attitude toward commitment was highlighted among anthropologists when the Anthropological Association at the annual meeting in 1969 passed a Resolution to make this new approach to anthropology acceptable and "legitimate."

This outlook has long been recognized by many people in the fields of literature and history, by Daniel Boorstin, Louis, B. Wright and Russel B. Nye, for example, among many. In 1959 Carl Bode published his revealing *The Anatomy of American Popular Culture 1840-1861* in an effort to urge us to "get to know ourselves."

The urgency of this need for academics to know ourselves and the world we live in was emphasized by Harold Howe, the U.S. Commissioner of Education under President Johnson, when he addressed the 1967 national meeting of the American Association of University Professors. Fully aware of the importance of the task, he spoke eloquently and truthfully of the intolerable split between town and gown in our society. He stated that young people are demanding that their education prepare them for the "incredibly complex world that makes tremendous new demands on the citizenry of a democracy." Such things as "poverty, integration, defense, transportation, space exploration, economic development, and deterioration of the cities cry out for creative, interdisciplinary thinking." Radical new attitudes are needed, he insisted, to bring the curricula up to the challenges of modern life. To paraphrase the words of William Wordsworth, the world is simply too much with us for us not to be with it. Generally speaking it always has been, but especially so during the past two hundred years with the growth of popular culture.

Popular Culture as such, as Russel B. Nye has pointed out, was an outgrowth of the Industrial Revolution, when means of mass communication began to be developed and mass society resulted. With the growth of mass society new esthetic distinctions between the "sheep" and the "goats" were developed. Thoughtful observers—and not so thoughtful observers—have long noted that the esthetic tastes of the mass society tend at times to be reduced to a lowest common denominator. But just as beauty is often in the eye of the beholder, often the difference between "high" and "low" art is in the snobbery of the observer. Perhaps "high" "esthetic" standards are permissible to the esthete. But snobbery in scholarship is just as intolerable as finickiness is in medical doctors. Scholars cannot allow the glasses of snobbery to rob them of the importance of the "popular" level of society. In the past many American Studies students have. Although they recognized that the more they knew about the milieu in which their literature was written, they could only with the greatest reluctance go beyond the "great" works, movements, the main currents of a period. They could expand to the "Main Currents of American Thought," for example, in the words of Vernon Parrington, but they were unwilling to spend any time on the "Minor Currents in American Development." "American Life and Letters" is a course taught on a few campuses in this country, but it has always lived on the edge of respectability with faculty though generally it has been popular with students. Generally, instructors, though greatly respectful of and amused by Dr. Johnson, have tended to forget one of his wise observations when asked by Boswell how insignificant an event must be before it is unworthy of being considered important in the biography of a man. If, as Dr. Johnson replied, no event is too insignificant in a man's life, how infinitely more significant are all events in the life of a society or nation!

Instead of brooding on Dr. Johnson's remark, however, many of our students have too slavishly followed the arguments of such pundits as Dwight Macdonald and Edmund Wilson that anything that was widely disseminated must be esthetically inferior. The esthetic value is actually, however, beside the point. T.S. Eliot felt, with great apprehension, that popular literature has much more influence on the reader than "great" works have. Perhaps he was right, for surely popular literature (and all forms of popular culture) have a thrust and power all their own, and we ignore them at great peril. The student of American Studies, no matter how much committed to the esthetically satisfying in personal tastes, should be open to examine all aspects of the culture he studies. It is a weakness and misdirection to think that we must approve of what we study, as much so as to insist that the medical researcher approve of the diseases he tries to find cures for. Both student and doctor should be openminded, and remember that Dr. Johnson advised catholicity.

We understand more of English literature, undoubtedly, because of C.H.B. Quennell's three-volume study of everyday things in England, more of Addison and Steele because of R.M. Wiles' study of eighteenth century English provincial newspapers, more of Melville because of the whaling museums at Mystic, Connecticut, and New Bedford, Massachusetts, and so on. As Richard Altick, in his delightful *The Art of Literary Research,* puts it: "The three disciplines—the history of literature, of ideas, and of the conditions and habits that set the tone of everyday life in any given period—are inseparable." But the mind of man is so peculiar that we despise the common things of our own time while spending any amount of time and money trying to locate even shreds of commonplaces of earlier times. Great museums spend large sums on artifacts of long ago while kicking into the gutter those of today. We prize the graffiti of earlier periods while merely painting over our own today. We revere the snatches of songs imbedded in Shakespeare's plays while despising our own popular music. Archeologists, as Fred Schroeder has suggested, must dream of finding in Greece a *Searsopolis Roebuckeles Katalog,* or its equivalent in the ruins of other past civilizations.

Popular culture demands to be studied. The greatest creators of art are those who most nearly picture the entire spectrum of existence. Herman Melville's strong hawser of art and truth, for example, is interwoven with a dozen strands of popular culture. One cannot begin to understand his works without careful research into the popular culture elements. So, too the works of Mark Twain. Henry Nash Smith feels that new critical evaluations of Twain's works must be built on further studies in the folklore and popular culture that shaped them.

Popular culture has trusts and urgencies far more important than those concerned with esthetic qualities and literature. Popular culture is the voice of the people, and the voice is becoming louder and louder. Regardless of whether the student respects or despises these voices, they will be heard. Popular culture is the voice of society, the barometer that can act as a Richter scale revealing where the next earthquake will be and what its intensity.

Understanding the voices is difficult, and life is short. Obviously no man can be a specialist in all areas of society. But the student of today can be more flexible, more understanding, more comprehensive than he has been in the past. In the broad field of American Studies, at least, there is urgent need for the generalist-specialist, the person who can demonstrate the viability of the humanities in general. American Studies should be more supra-disciplinary than interdisciplinary. It should attract those students who are both specialists and generalists.

Not all students in American Studies today admit the need for broadening the base of their work. It would seem, however, that events in the last few years would invalidate such a negative attitude. Scholars, students, citizens—all are demanding that something new be added to the old curriculum, to overcome what Frederick Crews has called the taciturnity of the scholarly mind toward the world around us. Those people who resist change—who deny the obvious—do themselves, the curriculum in general and American Studies in particular a disservice. There can be no danger in broadening the base of study. To fail to do so is dangerous.

Carol Bagley has argued that Popular Culture can save American Studies from itself. Perhaps it is an overstatement that American Studies must be "saved." But it is clear that the study of Popular Culture has a great deal to offer American Studies. The differences that seem to exist between the two are real only in the eyes of the beholder. They are surely two elements—not levels—in the same structure, the only difference being that Popular Culture is the more comprehensive. The closeness of the two has been demonstrated many times, in literary scholarship, and very convincingly in the second national meeting of the American Studies Association, in Toledo, Ohio, in the fall of 1969, where some 90 papers were delivered, half of them being in "conventional" American Studies subjects and half in Popular Culture. Twenty five of those papers are included in this volume.

There is no difference between American Studies, properly defined, and Popular Culture. Both seek an understanding of the full and real society, both past and present, and both do, or should, realize that the mansion of truth and understanding has many rooms, on several levels. There is an upperstory, without doubt, where only some can climb. The ground level, easier of attainment, is more heavily populated. There is also a basement. But we should not forget that the basement of our society is like the basement of a house. It may contain explosives which might be ignited; there might be termites there eating at the foundation. More important, there might be stored or created there great ideas and thrusts that may rise. We therefore reinforce Jay Gurian's plea about the needs of American Studies (-Popular Culture programs): "We begin where most disciplines end—we open up further as they close around their discoveries. But we must do more to keep the end open, to let the uncomfortable, the noisey, the uncatalogued, the unsanctified, the immediate, into our enterprise."

Otherwise, one is forced to prophesy, the lack of nourishment which has weakened most other "new" disciplines must surely weaken ours, and a noble hope will have been stunted by its keepers. America, society—mankind—asks for more.

Richard Caton Woodville and Early American Genre Painting

by

Francis S. Grubar

If, as Wolfgang Born once noted,[1] still life is the chamber music of painting, then genre must surely be the pop and folk expression of a given period, interpreting as it does the manners and mores, humor and pathos of familiar, ordinary, daily existence, usually in an anecdotal, unheroic, and sometimes impressive artistic form. It has an ancient legacy, probably dating back to prehistoric hunting scenes and religious rituals. Throughout most periods in art history, genre expression in some form can usually be found.

Genre, therefore, has been of some concern to man in his artistic efforts. This is particularly evident in periods of stress and change. A good genre artist is tuned closely to the pulse of his period and can be expected to react visually in a believable, matter-of-fact-manner while depicting accurate interpretations of contemporary or past life. Thus, in addition to its artistic value, the work of genre artists may also provide significant data for other disciplines.

Increasing research has already developed evidence that our genre school played a significant role in the development of American art, yet a serious study of the whole movement still awaits publication. While portraiture received the major emphasis in our Colonial art, examples of anecdotal genre are found occasionally on wall paper and embroidery designs, shop and tavern signs, graphic material, ceramics and folk sculpture, and some paintings and drawings. Even in our portrait painting, the grand manner of Europe was sometimes transformed into a spirit more genre in nature.

Perhaps the first true genre painting by an American Colonial artist is *Sea Captains Carousing at Surinam*, now in the collection of the City Art Museum, St. Louis. Painted during the 1750's by the Boston artist, John Greenwood, who spent some five years in Surinam, its boisterous, Hogarthian atmosphere in a bar room interior anticipates the genre themes of Richard Caton Woodville and others a century later. It recalls, as well, earlier "low-life" scenes by 16th and 17th century Lowlands Little Masters.

However, this painting was unusual and exceptional for its period. The agrarian, aristocratic structure of Colonial society apparently offered little incentive for developing a significant effort in this vein. The first manifestation of a genre movement had to await the growth of a national spirit and pride in the young country. These elements appear with rising vigor in the early decades of the 19th century.

Among the earliest genre artists at this time was John Lewis Krimmel, a short-lived German artist who arrived in Philadelphia around 1810 and pictured the life of that city in a series of small, finely executed paintings. Another artist was Henry Sargent, from Boston, who produced two intriguing interior scenes in the 1820's, *The Dinner Party* and *The Tea Party*, both in the Boston Museum of Fine Arts.

By 1830, William Sidney Mount had found his artistic direction in genre painting and, over the next three decades, offered leadership and inspiration to a number of excellent genre painters who flourished in the 1840's and '50's. Richard Caton Woodville was particularly receptive to Mount's work during Woodville's formative years in Baltimore.[2]

According to the parish records of St. Paul's Church, Richard Caton Woodville was born in Baltimore on April 30, 1825, the eldest

son and second of five children of William and Elizabeth Woodville. He was named after his great-uncle Richard Caton, a cotton merchant, geologist, and son-in-law of Charles Carroll of Carrollton, the last surviving signer of the Declaration of Independence.

Woodville's early life in Baltimore was doubtless a pleasant one in the thriving commercial center, known also for its social amenities. At the age of eleven, he was enrolled in St. Mary's College, Baltimore, at that time considered one of the finest boys' schools in the area. Along with his academic studies, he probably received his first instruction in drawing there. A small watercolor, *Battle Scene with Dying General*, probably copied from a contemporary print, was done in 1836, according to an inscription on the reverse.[3]

As a teen-ager, Caton (he was usually referred to by his middle name), produced a number of incredibly precise miniature sketches during the next few years, indicating a remarkable sensitivity for the possibilities of line. The richest source for these is found in a scrapbook compiled by Woodville's boyhood chum, Stedman R. Tilghman, which contains among other personal souvenirs, nineteen sketches by Caton of Sulpician monks at St. Mary's, doctors, medical students and patients at the University of Maryland and Baltimore Almshouse, spanning the years 1838-1845.[4]

His family probably objected to any artistic aspirations Woodville may have had at this time for his name was discovered among the medical students registered at the University of Maryland for the 1842-1843 session. Possibly his sketching activities did not meet with the faculty approval, or perhaps Caton was able to convince his family that a medical career was not his aim in life—at any rate, his name does not appear on subsequent records at the University.

The following year, in May of 1844, Caton did *Soldier's Experience*, a watercolor now in the Walters Art Gallery, which is the earliest located painting bearing the unmistakable Woodville genre stamp. A meticulous attention to detail, an acute rendering of a contemporary room interior, and the warm human sentiment permeating the whole, are characteristics which appear consistently throughout his American scene paintings. Five years later in Düsseldorf he used this work as a basis for his more elaborate oil painting, *Old '76 and Young '48*, also in the Walters Art Gallery.[5]

On January 3, 1845, Caton married his childhood sweetheart, Mary Theresa Buckler. In May, the newlyweds sailed for Europe, settling in Düsseldorf, where Caton studied and painted for the next six years, primarily under the supervision of Carl Ferdinand Sohn, a professor of painting at the Düsseldorf Academy.

Although he occasionally painted a romantic genre scene of earlier days or did portraits of friends, family or himself, Woodville became best known for his representations of the American scene. Ironically, all of these were probably painted in Europe, either in Dusseldorf, Paris or London, possibly from sketches made in Baltimore prior to his departure or on one or the other of the two short trips he made back to America in the 1850's. It seems quite clear from the few facts known of his later career that Caton had decided to join the ranks of American expatriates in Europe.

One institution which aided in promoting Woodville's reputation in America was the American Art-Union, which acquired his *Card Players* (now in the Detroit Institute) in 1847 and managed to have something by the young artist in most of its annual distributions until the unfortunate legal judgment passed against it caused its end in 1852. Woodville was not a prolific artist. His slow, painstaking manner and early death resulted in few major efforts. Yet these became well known to thousands who saw them exhibited in the galleries of the Art-Union in New York; many more who had not had the opportunity of seeing the originals, still became familiar with his approach through the large number of steel line engravings and lithographs published after his work. *The Cavalier's Return* (1847, New York Historical Society), *War News from Mexico* (1848, National Academy of Design), *Politics in an Oyster House*, 1848, *Old '76 and Young '48*, 1849, and *The Sailor's Wedding*, 1852. (all three in the Walters Art Gallery), and *Waiting for the Stage* (the Corcoran Gallery of Art), were probably as familiar to Americans of that period as the work of Benton, Curry, Burchfield, Hopper and Wood was to the generation of the 1930's.

Painted in Paris shortly after his departure from Düsseldorf early in 1851, *Waiting for the Stage* (see Plate 1) reflects the degree of synthesis Woodville was able to achieve after his exposure to European training. The sound draughtsmanship, precise composition and American subject matter come through as strongly as ever, but there is a greater color subtlety as well. This small oil on canvas, measuring only 15" high by 18½" wide, is initialed and dated in the lower right hand corner "R.C.W. 1851/Paris." In the lower left hand corner is the familiar red cuspidor, almost a Woodville signature in itself. Since the publication of my article on this painting,[6] I have been able to identify the young bearded gentleman as Dr. Christopher Johnston, an acquaintance from Baltimore, who visited Caton in Paris at this time. It was not unusual for genre painters of Woodville's generation to include friends and relatives in their little dramas. Apparently the painting was an immediate success. Before the end of the year the famous French art dealers, Goupil and Company, published a lithograph after the painting, but with the title, "Cornered."

The sparse facts on Woodville's last years suggest a note of tragedy. There had been a separation in his first marriage before 1850, Mary Theresa returning to Baltimore with the two children. Caton's second marriage was with a talented art student he had met at Professor Sohn's studio in Düsseldorf–Antoinette Schnitzler, daughter of an Austrian architect and Russian mother. From Paris, the couple moved to London in 1852, where they lived until Caton's premature death in 1855. Woodville family tradition maintains that a serious physical affliction was the cause of his early death, but there is no agreement as to a specific cause. Obviously he was under medication since his death certificate states that he died from an overdose of morphia, medicinally taken.

Strangely enough, the only contemporary published notice known of Richard Caton Woodville's death is a letter from William Michael Rossetti, the art critic and brother of Dante Gabriel Rossetti, leader of the Pre-Raphaellites, to *The Crayon* magazine of art in New York. Only thirty years old when he died, almost in obscurity, Woodville's work survived to serve as a continuing inspiration for a number of artists who followed in his direction. There can be no question of his position among the first rank of 19th century

American genre artists.

NOTES

[1]Wolfgang Born, *Still-Life Painting in America* (New York, 1947), p. 3.

[2]Two paintings by Mount were in the Robert Gilmor collection, *Country Lad on a Fence*, painted in 1831, present location unknown, and *The Long Story*, signed and dated 1837, now in the Corcoran Gallery of Art, Washington, D.C. See Bartlett Cowdrey and Hermann W. Williams, Jr., *William Sidney Mount 1807-1868, An American Painter* (New York, 1944), p. 15, and Anna Wells Rutledge, "Robert Gilmor, Jr., Baltimore Collector," *The Journal of the Walters Art Gallery,* XII (1949), pp. 31, 39, n. 65.

[3]In the collection of a Woodville descendant, Mrs. Gordon Callender, Mont St. Hilaire, Quebec, Canada. See my exhibition catalogue, *Richard Caton Woodville, An Early American Genre Painter* (The Corcoran Gallery of Art, Washington, D. C., 1967), n.p. for illustration.

[4]The Dr. Stedman R. Tilghman Scrapbook, Maryland Historical Society. Illustrations of some of these sketches may be found in the Woodville catalogue (n. 3), and in my article, "Gentlemanly Genre," *Art News*, 66 (May, 1967), p. 32. I intend having all of Woodville's located work illustrated when the book on this artist is published.

[5]Both are reproduced in the Woodville catalogue, n. 3.

[6]Francis S. Grubar, "Richard Caton Woodville's WAITING FOR THE STATE," *Corcoran Bulletin,* 13 (October, 1963), pp. 10-14. The new evidence supporting my identification will appear in the Woodville book.

Waiting for the Stage, 1851
by Richard Caton Woodville

Plate 1

The Corcoran Gallery of Art
Washington, D.C. Used by permission.

Photograph of Richard Caton Woodville c. 1852-5

Plate 2

Mrs. Richard Marquart, Suffern, New York

Waiting for the Stage, 1851
by Richard Caton Woodville

Plate 1

The Corcoran Gallery of Art
Washington, D.C. Used by permission.

Photograph of Richard Caton Woodville c. 1852-5 — Plate 2 — Mrs. Richard Marquart, Suffern, New York

America's Two Poster Movements

by

Michael Gordon

We are currently witnessing an interest in poster art of such proportions that one is tempted to characterize the poster as *the* art form of the 1960's. Every college and paperback bookstore seems to have its share of psychedelic posters with their strangely pleasing Day-Glo colors, as well as the ubiquitous personality posters whose over-blown photographs include everyone from Mao to the Rolling Stones. Galleries have sprung up which deal in signed and limited edition posters by artists as diverse as Marc Chagall and Red Grooms, and the posters they sell are commissioned works announcing everything from film festivals to public school centennials. Museums are devoting entire shows to poster art and feature stories on the posters are appearing in national magazines.[1]

What makes the current popularity of the poster of particular interest is that this is not the first time it has happened. In the 1890's this country, as well as several in Europe, saw an efflorescence of poster art and public interest in it of such magnitude that it was commonly described as the "poster craze."[2] In 1896, in the United States alone, it was estimated that there were over 6,000 poster collectors.[3] During this decade, magazines and newspapers held poster contests, poster shows were common occurrences and hostesses even gave parties to which guests were expected to come dressed as figures in recent posters.

In view of the fact that the present interest in poster art in this country represents a renaissance rather than an innovation, two questions arise. First, what was responsible for the poster movement of the 1890's; second, why was there a period of more than sixty years after this initial burst of enthusiasm during which the poster was relegated to an obscure corner in the art world? This paper will attempt to shed some light on these questions.

The poster has a long history.[4] The Louvre, in its collection, has a papyrus dated 146 B. C. which offers a reward for two slaves who had escaped from Alexandria—clearly an early poster. In the form of mural inscriptions and sign boards the poster can be traced back even further. In the 17th and 18th centuries posters were being used widely for propaganda purposes; so much so that for a time in the 17th century and again in the 18th century the French government attempted to control the printing and posting of them.[5] Nevertheless, the poster did not emerge as a significant art form until the 19th century. Art historians seem to feel that the reason for this is that before this time artists did not have the technical means to exploit this medium.[6]

While not given to use of terms such as "necessary" and "sufficient" conditions, essentially what these art historians are saying is that lithography was a necessary condition for the emergence of the art poster.

> The process of color lithography was ideal for this kind of poster work; the artist could work; unrestrained by technical problems, almost as if he were working on paper, and he need not restrict himself to using the available type face if he felt that his own handlettering would be more harmonious and effective.[7]

Lithography, then, provided the artist with a freedom of expression that could not be found in any of the other then existing printmaking techniques.

Alois Senefelder, a German printer, discovered lithography in the last half of the 1790's.[8] Senefelder's innovation was enthusiastically greeted by the art world. Gericault, Delacroix, Daumier, and Goya all worked in black and white lithography, but by 1850, Goldwater claims, much of the original interest had been dissipated.[9] Artists working in this medium were replaced by craftsmen whose concern was merely to reproduce existing works of art.

The development of color lithography in the 1830's, attributed to Engellman, a Frenchman working in Paris, did not do much to reinspire an interest in lithography on the part of serious artists. A partial explanation of this is to be found in the fact that while Engellman took out the patent for what he called chromolithography in 1837 the process was by no means completely satisfactory at that time. Color lithography was perfected in England during the 1850's and 1860's. In any case, by 1870 this was a technique whose potential was ripe for exploitation.

In itself, lithography could only provide the artistic possibility for the poster, but the poster had to lend itself to inexpensive production if businessmen were to consider it as an advertising medium. With this in mind the importance of the development of inexpensive and efficient printing techniques becomes obvious.

In the second decade of the 19th century, steam power was successfully applied to a printing press. At this time Friedrich König, a German, developed a press that could print 1,100 sheets an hour in contrast to the 300-sheet maximum of hand-run presses. These were conventional printing presses. Lithographic presses presented certain unique problems involved in producing a cylindrical lithographic printing machine, and it was not until a decade or so later that Engues, a Frenchman, developed a rotary lithographic press which gained popularity.[10]

One might say, then, that with the development of effective color-lithography techniques and the rotary lithographic press the "necessary" conditions for the emergence of mass poster use existed; nevertheless, it remained for one man to exploit these techniques in such a way that something truly original could be said to have been produced. This man was Jules Cheret.

Cheret was born in France in 1836. During the 1860's he worked as a lithographer in London; a time during which, the reader will recall, color lithography was being perfected in England. He apparently not only mastered this technique but "also saw and no doubt, helped to produce those small placards for theatres and for any recruiting which were beginning to be popular."[11] He returned to France in 1867 and began to produce posters by means of color lithography; the first was one for the play *La Biche au Bois,* in which Sarah Bernhardt, whose career was then only beginning to rise, appeared.[12] Cheret's poster work was by no means an overnight success. Laver maintains:

> Cheret's discovery [of how to make successful color posters] did not bear fruit immediately . . . it was not until towards the end of the 'eighties that the hoardings of Paris suddenly bloomed into all the colors of a flower show.[13]

Further evidence for Laver's statement is found in a catalog for an exhibition held in 1896, in which it is claimed that while the first poster show was held in Paris in 1884.

> . . . there were no posters worth mentioning on view. The first serious exhibit was made by Jules Cheret in the Galleries of the "Theatre de l'application" in 1889. The illustrated posters exhibited on that occasion excited the greatest admiration among the Paris critics and public and for his work Cheret received the cross of the Legion of Honor.[14]

That poster collecting was firmly established in Paris by 1891 is indicated by the fact that in the fall of that year, a Parisian print dealer, Edmond Sagot, published a catalog of posters which he was offering for sale. The fact that a catalog was issued at that time suggests that a certain amount of public interest in poster collecting had already manifested itself.

During the course of the decade public interest in the poster grew tremendously, and Cheret remained the most popular of the poster artists. So great was the market for his posters that stories were circulated in Paris about a young boy who removed a Cheret poster after it was put up in order to sell it to feed his starving family.[15]

Cheret was the first artist to exploit this medium successfully on a large scale, but he was followed in the 1890's by men such as Lautrec, Steinlen, and Grasset. The work of these men had considerable impact on the poster movement both in France and abroad.

The question still remains, why did the poster catch on so strongly in France? Furthermore, why do we get the tremendous public interest in it? In answer to the first part it should be noted that at least two commercial enterprises took strongly to the poster as an advertising medium: the music hall and theater, and the publishing industry as well as numerous other industries on a smaller scale. Goldwater argues that the success of the poster in France was a response to "the sudden glory of the music-hall itself."[16] The public interest in the form of poster collecting has been explained by one student of the phenomenon in the following words:

> The poster movement began in France. It grew out of the vogue for print collecting which reached its height around the middle of the century. The first collections contained mostly posters issued in conjunction with the publication of new books....Then, with the posters of Jules Cheret, what had been but a branch of print collecting was transformed into a new kind of connoisseurship.[17]

In this country, the story of the poster movement is somewhat different.

While it has been claimed that the work of Currier and Ives had an important influence on Cheret while he was working in London in the 1860's, the art poster was initially an import to the United States.[18] This is best seen by looking at the posters shown in this country's first poster exhibit. In November of 1890, The Grolier

Club of New York sponsored a show of "illustrated bill posters."[19] Of the 100 items in the show 45 were the work of Cheret; only seven posters were done by American artists, and these seven were stylistically rather different from their European counterparts. For one thing, only one of the seven posters was a signed work (i. e., signed in the block), indicating the status of the poster as art at the time. They were all theater posters with rather realistic renderings of scenes from the plays they advertised. Posters of this kind had been produced in this country since the 1870's, if not earlier.[20]

When posters in the new tradition began to appear in large numbers around 1894, they showed the influence of European work, but they had a distinctively American quality about them. Penfield's posters for *Harper's* suggest what we know—that this artist had seen and been impressed by the work of Cheret, Steinlen, and Lautrec,[21] but that the subject matter and treatment have an original quality which makes them transcend the label of mere derivative art. Similarly some of Bradley's work (e. g., his first poster for *The Chap Book* in 1894) has a Beardsleyesque quality about it, but the vast majority of it bears little resemblance to that English artist's work, or that of any other English or Continental artist for that matter.

It is difficult to put precise dates on the duration of the poster craze in this country. Most writers who have discussed this period see the years between 1894 and 1896 as those when interest was most intense. While there are no serious grounds for doubting these estimates, there are several ways of further approximating these dates that have not previously been used. One can, for example, enumerate the distribution of articles listed under the heading of "posters" in the *New York Times' Index* and the *Reader's Guide to Periodical Literature.* The *Times* presents the following pattern:

Table 1

Year	1890	1891	1892	1893	1894	1895	1896	1897	1898	1899
No. of articles	1						17	2		2

There are no articles listed in the five year period preceding 1890 and the article which appeared in 1891 (July 27) deals with posters and poster collecting in France. There are also no articles on the poster in the five years following 1899. Appropriately enough the last article to appear on the poster in the *Times* (July 8, 1899) was entitled "The Passing of the Poster Craze." The *Reader's Guide* lists twelve articles.

Table II

Year	**1890**	**1891**	**1892**	**1893**	**1894**	**1895**	**1896**	**1897**	**1898**	**1899**
No. of articles			**1**		**1**	**6**	**4**			

These two sources would also place the height of poster interest in the years between 1894 and 1896.

Two magazines were published here in the 1890's directed solely at the poster collector: *The Poster* and *Poster Lore.*[22] Both were published during the first half of 1896. Their publication histories suggested that enough public interest was generated before 1896 to create the impression that magazines of this kind could be successful, but either this was a misconception or the poster craze was already moribund by the last half of 1896.[23]

The poster exhibition or show is clearly another indicator of public interest in this medium. Unfortunately, we do not have available a complete list of all shows held in this country in the 1890's. However, using the dates of poster show catalogs in the New York Public Library as well as the shows mentioned in newspaper and magazine articles of the time we can get some further idea of the period when interest was most intense. The Library has seven catalogs of American shows in its collection: 1890, 1; 1895, 3; 1896, 2; 1897, 1. *Leslie's Weekly* for March 25, 1895 tells us that:

> There have been no less than seven collections shown in New York and vicinity this winter. . . .

The Poster for April, 1896 mentions shows recently being held in cities, including Minneapolis, Milwaukee, New York, Bangor and

Philadelphia. In 1899 there was one show in New York but apparently none in 1898.[24]

Looking at all the above indices it appears that the time between the beginning of 1895 and the second half of 1896 was when the poster craze was at its height. By 1897 one writer was commenting:

> Poster collecting in this country, which began only a few years ago, can scarcely be said to have diminished. It has constantly grown more intelligent, however, *and has less than formerly the character of a passing fad.* (emphasis added).[25]

A year later Charles Latimer claimed "... the poster 'craze' died out in the United States about a year after it began."[26] And in 1899 an acknowledged expert on the poster wrote:

> That the fine frenzy regarding posters which raged in America some two years is now, as far as the faddish part of the public is concerned, a thing of the past, there can be no denying.[27]

What these writers were saying is that by the end of 1896 the mass interest in the poster was waning though there was still some interest left in poster collecting.

To understand the development of the poster movement in this country we must appreciate the contribution made to it by the publishing industry. As Bunner has indicated:

> ... it may be stated as a general proposition that art in postermaking has, in this country, found its best inspiration, in most cases, from literature.[28]

In 1889 *Harper's* commissioned Eugene Grasset, the well-known European poster artist, to do a poster for its Christmas issue. In the years that followed, *Harper's* also used posters by other artists as well as Grasset. These posters must have been successful for in 1893, *Harper's* was having its talented art editor, Edward Penfield, turn out posters on a monthly basis. The demand for the posters occasionally was greater than that for the magazine they advertised.[29] Other literary magazines of the day, such as *Scribner's* and *Lippincott's*, also experimented with the use of posters in those early years of the 1890's, and by 1894 the use of the poster as an advertising medium by such magazines became a fairly common practice.

These national literary magazines were not alone in their use of posters. The small avant-garde periodicals that proliferated widely after *The Chap Book's* success in 1894 also made great use of the poster. In point of fact, all branches of the publishing industry from papers to limited edition books used this medium throughout the period. In the case of limited-edition books the publisher would have the illustrator of the book also execute a poster for it; the poster, numbered to match the book, was presented as a gift to the book's purchaser.

The first poster contest in this country or in Europe was sponsored by an American periodical, *Century Magazine,* late in 1895. This contest, which was held in Paris, proved to be so successful that in April of 1896 the same magazine sponsored a contest for a poster to advertise its mid-summer issue, but it was held in the United States and was won by an American poster artist, J. C. Leyendecker. The idea of the poster contest caught on not only among publishers but among other industries as well, and for a time the poster contest became a fairly common event in this country.

After the publishing industry, the other major exploiter of the poster in the United States was the bicycle manufacturer. Almost every major artist of the time did at least one poster for Victor, Columbia, or one of the other bicycle firms. Since bicycling in the 1890's also had a faddish quality about it, when the Pope Manufacturing Company, makers of Columbia Bicycles, held a show in 1896 of designs that had been submitted for a contest it had sponsored at the Metropolitan Bicycling Academy, the *New York Times* said: "The cycling craze will for weeks give way to the poster craze. . ."[30] This combination of cycling and posters was so irresistible that unusually large crowds turned out in all three cities where the exhibit was held, despite the fact that there was a charge for admission. Other industries also made use of the poster, but the publisher and the bicycle manufacturer were the leaders.

During the time when public interest in the poster was at its highest it manifested itself in some rather interesting ways. Perhaps the most unique was the poster party. In 1896, one writer said of it:

> The "Poster Party" promises to become a social fad. In issuing the invitations the hostess requires each woman to come in the costume of the figure on the poster of a certain newspaper or magazine that she names, being careful to have no two alike. The men she requests to represent well known literary men. . . During a recent poster party each woman in turn was called on to pose in correct representation of the poster figure she portrayed, and guesses were made and written upon cards as to what newspaper or magazine she represented.[31]

Poster buffs sent their friends Easter cards in the form of miniature posters. Stores, such as Brentano's, opened special departments to cater to the demand for posters, poster cataloging systems were sold and there was even talk of putting together a national poster collectors directory.[32] To be sure, despite its popularity poster collecting was not the pastime of the poor; the price of posters,which ranged from a quarter to so much as eighty dollars, made this a hobby only the relatively affluent could afford.

Like all fads, the poster craze, as we have already indicated, soon burnt itself out, but the poster was to remain a permanent part of the American landscape. Nonetheless, many years were to pass before the poster was again to be given serious consideration as an art form.

Artists of the stature of Lautrec and Bonnard in France and John Sloan in this country did create posters, but this represented a very small part of their work. All the important poster artists of the 1890's, e. g., Cheret, Bradley, Mucha, etc., were essentially commercial artists whose work was almost totally in the area of illustration and poster making. With the exception of a few German Expressionists this pattern holds until the 1940's when a number of important artists working in France began to make posters.[33] French museums had begun to use posters to advertise shows as early as 1927, but it was not until the second half of the 1940's that artists such as Picasso, Leger, Matisse and others began to take a serious interest in this medium.[34] Many of them worked in collaboration with the famous lithographic house of Mourlot. A significant number of the posters produced by these men did not, however, contain original designs, but rather often depicted paintings and drawings included in the show they announced. This format continued to characterize most posters done in Europe as well as in this country up until the 1960's.

The question we now turn to is why, in the 1960's, this country saw a rebirth of poster art and a concomitant development of public interest in it. Before attempting to explore this matter, the point should be made that what we have seen in this decade involves two distinct though somewhat interrelated phenomena: the fine-arts poster and the psychedelic poster. These must be dealt with separately. The former, at least initially, appears to be the child of a grant of $100,000 made by the Albert A. List Foundation, in 1963, to Lincoln Center, establishing the Lincoln Center Poster Program Fund.[35] The Lincoln Center program works in the following manner. An artist is selected to design a poster for a particular event; if he accepts, he is given a stipend of $1,000, and his materials are paid for by the Fund. He supervises the entire production of an edition of 110 posters, all of which are signed and numbered. Five of these are kept by the artists and the rest are sold to the public through various distributors. The long-run edition, unnumbered and unsigned, is used to advertise the event it announces and copies of it are also sold to the public. The Lincoln Center program was expanded by the List Foundation in the form of the List Art Poster Fund to offer similar services to other organizations. Included among the many organizations it has created posters for, are the Corcoran Gallery, the São Paolo Biennalle and the Jewish Museum. The artists who have produced these posters are some of the country's most eminent. They include Leonard Baskin, Robert Motherwell, Larry Rivers, George Segal, and Roy Lichtenstein. In the fall of 1967 Vera List along with Portia Harcus and Barbara Krakwo formed HKL Ltd. to publish and distribute List Art Posters.

The significance of the List Fund Grant is twofold. For one thing, it encouraged important artists to try their hand at original poster design, rather than merely adapting an already existing piece of work to the demands of the poster. It also exposed at least part of the public to posters executed by these very talented artists.

The success of the List Fund can be seen by the similar programs that have sprung up in its wake. Poster Originals Ltd. is a firm which began by selling European and American posters in limited and long-run editions, including the List Posters, and not long after began to collaborate with organizations desiring to have a poster commissioned for a forthcoming event. This firm works out the various problems involved in the production and distribution of the poster. The organizations that have used its services include the Museum of Modern Art and the Temple University Music Festival.

Another notable poster program is the one directed by the *Paris Review.* A grant to this periodical from Mrs. Henry J. Heinz enabled them, starting in 1965, to enroll the services of artists such as Marisol, Indiana and Nevelson to produce posters in numbered and signed editions of 150.[36] This program differs from the other two we have discussed in that these posters are not actually used to advertise the commissioning agency, since no long-run edition is available. It appears to have been undertaken less as a promotional campaign than as an aesthetic venture.

It would be an oversimplification to say that these programs have been solely responsible for the new fine-arts poster. Clearly the whole Pop Art movement has had the effect of giving aesthetic legitimacy to art forms previously held in disregard, and other forces have been operating as well. Nevertheless, it is unlikely that many artists would have worked in the poster medium, or, obviously, received the public exposure of their work, had it not been for such programs as these. Moreover, the increasing desire and willingness of various institutions to use commissioned posters is also probably an outgrowth of them. Chicago, for example, not long ago, hired the Container Corporation of America to design a series of posters proclaiming that city's various attractions.

Another important force in the recent fine-arts poster movement is the art gallery, or rather a select group of them. The Leo Castelli Gallery, for example, began using poster-like mailing pieces soon after it opened in 1957. In 1963, the artist Jack Tworkov signed some of these being used for a show of his and they were sold unfolded. This "poster" did not sell very well; however, later in the year a poster mailing piece issued for a Lichtenstein show and made up in a signed, limited edition of 200, was commercially successful. The Lichtenstein poster was doubly important because not only did it sell well but it was the first to be printed by the Castelli Gallery in a manner which distinguished it from the mailing piece—it had margins while the mailing piece did not.[37] Since 1963, Castelli has, for several shows each year, continued to issue poster editions of its mailing pieces. At the present time, the gallery generally produces these posters in unsigned editions of between 200 and 400 posters. Other galleries that have figured importantly in the fine-arts poster movement included the Andre Emmerich and Rose Fried and Sidney Janis galleries.

The history of the psychedelic poster is markedly different from that of the art poster. While the information we have about its origins are limited, what we do have suggests that its beginnings are connected with the Hippie Movement and more specifically the rock music associated with it. By 1965 San Francisco was established as the Hippie Mecca, as well as a center for much of what was new in American music. San Francisco's contribution to American music is acid-rock, and this music has played a role vis-à-vis the psychedelic poster similar to that played by literature in the poster movement of the 1890's. Wes Wilson, generally acknowledged to be one of the most important San Francisco poster artists, claims that the first psychedelic poster was one done by him in 1965 to advertise a dance.[38] In any case, by February of 1966, Wilson was doing posters on a weekly basis to advertise dance-concerts at Bill Graham's Fillmore Auditorium. These were the first psychedelic posters to be produced on a regular basis. The Avalon Ballroom, San Francisco's other Carnegie Hall of rock, also began to use posters in 1966, many of them being the work of Victor Moscoso.

The story of the Fillmore's use of these posters provides an interesting picture of the development of public interest in the psychedelic poster movement.[39] Before opening the Fillmore, Graham was associated with the San Francisco Mime Troupe, a group which had occasion to have promotional work done for it by the printing shop in which Wes Wilson was a co-owner. Wilson's posters had by late 1965 already begun to attract attention in the Bay area, and thus it was not surprising that Graham asked him to do the first Fillmore posters. These posters printed in editions of no more than 1,000 were, at first, posted on telephone poles, walls and construction sites by Graham and his wife, an accomplished poster artist in her own right, who travelled around the Bay Area on their motor-scooter. After three or four months they noticed that the posters were rapidly disappearing and that storekeepers who had originally declined to put the posters in their windows were beginning to ask for them. By the summer of 1966 people had become so expert at the art of removing posters and interest in them was so great, that it became necessary to double the sizes of the printing runs to 2,000. Prior to this time the posters, other than the ones which were posted in the streets, were given to those attending Fillmore concerts. A poster advertising the following week's show was either placed on all seats or handed out at the end of the concert. Graham at that point, while continuing to give his audiences posters, began to use boutiques and record stores as retail outlets for the posters.[40] As the demand for the poster continued to increase, Graham began to reprint posters that were already out of print and also began to number them.[41] At present, one can if one wishes, purchase the whole series, which numbered 128 in all as of July, 1968. This is occasionally done by collectors. Ultimately he began to sell these posters nationally. In February of 1967 alone, he sold 112,000 and the demand for posters is now so great that they are printed in runs of 20,000.[42] Apart from Wilson, the artists who have done work for the Fillmore include Mouse, Griffith, Maclean and Conklin.[43]

The Fillmore and Avalon posters and more recently the Fillmore West posters represent a major if not *the* major stream of the psychedelic poster movements.[44] Similar posters have also been done to advertise peace rallies, art shows (i.e., the now classic "Joint Show" posters), and concerts. There also exists another species of psychedelic posters which differs from those discussed above in that they are, however contradictory the term may sound, pure posters. They are not produced to sell anything except themselves and frequently contain humorous references to drugs such as "Better Living Through Chemistry", "God Grows His Own", etc. One producer of this type of poster, American Newsrepeat Company, makes a poster which has the words "no smoking" on it. This poster is given away free of charge. As a group these posters are less apt to borrow forms from previous artistic movements and rely to a greater extent on photomontage and other similar techniques. Often these posters are unsigned, indicating the non-art view held of them by their producers.

What distinguishes the psychedelic poster from the fine-arts poster, apart from obvious stylistic differences, is the fact, that, because of the price and subject matter, it is truly a form of popular art. Even the long run edition of the fine-arts posters seldom sell for less than five dollars, and the Chagall poster used to announce the opening of the new Metropolitan Opera House sold in the unsigned, long-run edition for twenty-five dollars. At a dollar or two the psychedelic posters easily find their way into apartments and dormitory rooms. In terms of their ubiquity they are only second to the photographic posters.

The work of major psychedelic poster artists—Wes Wilson, Moscoso, Griffith, Mouse, Max and Maclean—shows a great deal of individuality despite a shared preference for bright color. Wilson's work, with its elongation and flowing lines, suggests that the renewal of interest in Art Nouveau was one of the forces responsible for the psychedelic poster. Max's posters with jazzed up color, also have a turn of the century feeling about them while Griffith's work seems to hark back even further into the art history of this country with its evocation of old circus and patent medicine posters. That these posters are being taken seriously as art is indicated by the fact that they are being bought by Museums. In the Museum of Modern Art's recent poster show "Word and Image" the works of Wilson, Moscoso, and Max were well represented.[45]

Having looked at the poster movements of the 1890's and the 1960's we shall now, by way of a summary and conclusion, try to put them into an analytical framework. We have maintained that the movement of the 1890's initially grew out of technological developments which allowed the poster to be used successfully as an advertising medium. The public response to it was the product both of its novelty and the fact that print collecting was already established as a hobby.

The more recent poster movement, or movements, have, as we have shown, different antecedents. For the sixty or so years during which interest in the poster was negligible there was no lack of technological means, and artists did occasionally dabble in poster art. What was lacking was sponsorship. As Kauffer has noted: "The poster is more strictly *commissioned* than most other work."[46] Until art galleries and poster programs began inviting artists to create posters there was little else motivating them to do so. That is to say, the current interest in the poster cannot be interpreted as part of any imminent unfolding of art history, though it seems to be related to the Pop Art movement. Without the various sponsorship programs it is unlikely that so many eminent artists would have become involved in poster making.

The psychedelic poster's history more clearly resembles that of the poster of the 1890's than it does the current fine-arts poster. Aesthetic considerations were clearly secondary to promotional ones.[47] Unlike the directors of the *Paris Review*, the promoters of the San Francisco dance-concert houses appear to have been less concerned with supporting the arts than they were with having people know what was going on next weekend at the Avalon or Fillmore. As it happened these men had enough taste, and foresight as well for that matter, to choose artists whose work was both successful as advertisement and significant as art. The fact that these posters caught on throughout the country, at least in urban areas, must be seen as being in part the result of the tremendous amount of publicity that the Hippie Movement, its music, and drugs, were receiving in the national news media. One should not, of course, overlook the intrinsic attractiveness of these posters. They are both beautiful and eye catching: nonetheless, this in itself probably could not account for their success.

What of the future of the posters we have discussed? The current interest in poster art has resulted in a revival of interest in the posters of the 1890's, so much so that posters by American artists such as Bradley and Penfield which were sold for a few dollars a few decades ago are now bringing as much as 50 or 200 dollars, and others by European masters such as Lautrec or Mucha sell for well over a thousand dollars. The fine-arts posters which are now being produced seem guaranteed a place in the art dealer's catalog if only because of the calibre of the artists who are doing them. The availability of willing sponsors will probably determine whether or not these artists continue to make posters. Finally, it is probably safe to assume that there will be a market for psychedelic posters as long as there is an interest in the Hippie Movement and its adjuncts, acid rock and drugs. As we watch this interest expire, these posters, despite their artists' merit, will probably be relegated to the design collections of museums, only to be shown when retrospective shows of poster art are mounted.

NOTES

[1]Perhaps the most important recent poster show was the one held in 1968 at the Museum of Modern Art. This show contained more than 200 posters dating from 1879 to 1967. Among the magazines which have done stories on the poster the following are included: *Life,* September 1, 1967; *Time,* April 7, 1967 and June 7, 1968; *Newsweek,* March 6, 1967; and the *Saturday Evening Post,* March 23, 1968.

[2]The terms poster "craze" or "mania" are frequently encountered in the journalistic literature of the 1890's.

[3]*The Poster,* I (January, 1896), p. 9.

[4]Several histories of the poster are available. See, Charles Price, *Poster Design* (New York: George W. Bricks, 1922), Charles Hiatt, *Picture Posters* (London: George Bell, 1896) and W. S. Rogers, *A Book of the Poster* (London: Greening, 1901). A very important book dealing with the American poster

movement recently came to the author's attention: Edgar Breitenbach, *The American Poster* (New York: American Federation of Art, 1967).

[5]Ervine Metzl, *The Poster* (New York: Watson-Guptill, 1963), p. 29.

[6]See, for example, Robert J. Goldwater, "L'Affiche Moderne, A Revival of Poster Art after 1880", *Gazette des Beaux Arts,* XXII (December, 1942), pp. 173-182.

[7]Alan M. Fern, "Graphic Design", *Art Nouveau,* ed. Peter Selz and Mildred Constantine, (New York: The Museum of Modern Art, 1959), p. 33.

[8]The exact date of Senefelder's discovery, i. e., that crayon on stone could be used to make prints, is a subject of mild controversy. Some historians put the date at 1795, others at the end of 1798 or the beginning of 1799. For an excellent general history of lithography see, Wilhelm Weber, *A History of Lithography* (London: Thames and Hudson, 1966).

[9]Goldwater, *op. cit.,* p. 174.

[10]A factor which we have not discussed but which also may have contributed to the mass use of posters in the late 19th century is paper. In the first few decades of this century paper was produced for the most part from rags, making it a fairly expensive commodity. In 1840, Friedrich Gottlob Keller, a weaver, developed a process for manufacturing paper from wood pulp. This reduced the cost of paper production significantly. As a result of Keller's discovery "Commercial printing–such as posters, circulars, and sale catalogues–and popular newspapers and magazines–in brief, all ephemeral reading matter–were henceforth universally printed on wood-pulp paper." S. H. Steinberg, *Five Hundred Years of Printing* (New York: Criterion Books, 1959), p. 203.

[11]*XIX Century French Poster,* with an introduction by James Laver and a preface by Henry Davray (London: Nicholson and Watson, 1944), p. 9.

[12]Bernhardt was literally an important figure in the French poster of the late 19th century. She was responsible, to a large extent, for Alphonse Mucha's career and was the subject of many of his posters. For a discussion of the role she played vis-à-vis Mucha, see, Brian Read, *Art Nouveau and Alphonse Mucha* (London: Her Majesty's Stationery Office, 1963).

[13]*XIXth Century French Posters, loc. cit.*

[14]*Catalogue Exhibition of Modern European Posters* (New York: Meyer Brothers). This catalog is not dated; however, references to this show in periodicals of the time establish it as having taken place in 1896.

[15]Reference to this story can be found among other places in Donald Warren "Notes of a Poster Collector in Paris", *The Chap Book,* I (October 10, 1894) p. 252. The problem of posters being stolen from the walls and kiosks of Paris became so great that it was claimed in the *New York Times* (January 30, 1897) that posters were being stamped with the imprint "this poster can be neither given away or sold; anyone in whose hands it is found will be subject to prosecution," p. 4 of the Saturday Supplement.

[16]Goldwater, *op. cit.,* p. 182.

[17]Robert Koch, "The Poster Movement and Art Nouveau," *Gazette des Beaux Arts* I (November, 1957), pp. 285. The first historical study of the poster was published in 1884 by Ernest Maindron in the *Gazette des Beaux Arts.* Two years later this article was followed by a rather comprehensive illustrated monograph on the poster by the same author: *Les Affiches Illustrees* (Paris: H. Launette and Cie, 1886).

[18]Metzl, *op. cit.,* maintains that the *Currier and Ives* prints which were imported to England and the Continent in the second half of the 19th century "showed Europe how to produce lithography in several colors, and how to do it fast," pp. 37. He claims further that these prints "attracted attention" from Cheret when he was working in England. The only problem with Metzl's statement is that *Currier and Ives* did not produce any prints by means of color lithography until 1889, by which time Cheret had already returned to France and established a reputation for himself as a poster maker. See Harry T. Peter, *Currier and Ives* (Garden City, New York: Doubleday, Doran, 1942), p. 15.

[19]*Catalogue of an Exhibition of Illustrated Bill-Posters* (New York: the Grolier Club, 1890).

[20]An excellent discussion of posters of this type can be found in F. Weitenkampf, *American Graphic Art* (New York: Macmillan, 1923).

[21]Posters by these artists were in the personal collection of Edward Penfield. The author was able to see this collection through the courtesy of the artist's son, Mr. Walker Penfield.

[22]Other magazines such as *Echo* (published in Chicago from May, 1895

through July, 1896) had columns devoted to the poster.

[23]While interest in the poster began in France, that country did not have a poster periodical until 1897 when *Estampe et L'Affiche* began publication (it ceased publication in 1899), though from 1896 through 1900 a series of reproductions of superb quality were sold on a subscription basis. The series was known as *Les Maitres de L'Affiche.* Great Britain had two poster periodicals: *Poster Collector's Circular* (January-May, 1896) and *The Poster* (1898-1901), in 1898 the name of this periodical was changed to *The Poster and Art Collector.*

[24]In 1896 there were also shows in Denver, Chicago and Richmond. The other sources referred to are Weitenkampf, *op. cit.,* and various numbers of the American periodical, *The Poster.* It is of interest to note that the Sunday magazine of *The Philadelphia Inquirer* for March 1, 1896, p. 1, noted that poster enthusiasm was not yet as great in Philadelphia as in other cities.

[25]*The Quadrangle Club Catalog of an Exhibition of American, English, Dutch and Japanese Posters from the Collection of Mr. Ned Arlen Flood* (Chicago, 1897), p. vii.

[26]*The Poster and Art Collector,* I (August-September, 1898), pp. 115-116.

[27]Percival Pollard, "American Poster Lore," *The Poster and Art Collector,* II (March, 1899), p. 123.

[28]H. C. Bunner, "American Poster, Past and Present," *The Modern Poster,* ed. Arsene Alexandre, *et al* (New York: Charles Scribner's Sons, 1895), pp. 99-100.

[29]Edgar Breitenbach, "The Poster Craze," *American Heritage,* XIII (February, 1962), p. 28.

[30]*New York Times,* March 13, 1896, pp. 6. This contest was so successful that Pope received more than 1,000 designs, many more than had been prepared for. An excellent discussion of bicycling at the turn of the century is to be found in Sidney H. Aronson, "The Sociology of the Bicycle," *Social Forces,* XXX (1952), pp. 305-312.

[31]*The Poster,* I (March, 1896), p. 38.

[32]At the height of the poster craze it was claimed that there were twenty firms in this country involved in poster making and these firms had a capital

investment of almost $3,000,000. *The Poster,* I (February, 1896), p. 16.

[33]Of the involvement of German Expressionists in poster art Hellmust Rademacher has written: "Only a few expressionists, Hechel, Kirchner, Pechstein and Kokoschka produced posters, and then only singly and for special occasions." *Masters of German Art* (Edition Leipzig, 1966), p. 24.

[34]This phase of the history of the poster is dealt with in the introduction to Ferdinand Mourlot, *Art in Posters* (New York: George Braziller, 1959).

[35]From soon after its inception through 1966 the List Art Poster Program was directed by the American Federation of Art but is now again administered by the List Foundation.

[36]The information on the *Paris Review* poster program was obtained through personal correspondence with the program's director, Mr. Peter B. Ardery.

[37]It was not until 1966 that Castelli began printing the limited edition of the poster mailing pieces on special paper stock. All information contained in this paragraph is based on an interview with Leo Castelli and Ivan Karp, New York, September, 1968.

[38]Letter to the author, January 3, 1968.

[39]Much of what follows is based on an interview with Bill Graham, New York, June, 1968.

[40]The store specializing in psychedelic posters did not come into existence in the Bay area until the middle of 1967.

[41]Numbering here does not refer to posters in the same edition, but rather to posters in the series. Thus the first poster used to advertise the Fillmore is No. 1 and the most recent No. 128.

[42]The figure of 112,000 posters is taken from an article that appeared in *Time* (April 7, 1967), p. 69.

[43]Graham uses mailing pieces in the form of posters, and his tickets also are miniature posters.

[44]The Fillmore closed in the summer of 1968 and the Avalon closed in

fall of the same year. The Carousel, which was opened by Graham in the spring of 1968 was renamed the Fillmore West when the Fillmore was closed. It should be noted that the Avalon was not operated by Graham and that since this paper was written Graham has stopped using posters.

[45]Moscoso, alone, had six posters in the show.

[46]McKnight Kauffer, *The Art of the Poster* (London: Cecil Palmer, 1924), p. x.

[47]Graham, however, maintains that he will not use a poster artist unless he likes his work.

Joseph Stella and Hart Crane: The Brooklyn Bridge

by

Irma B. Jaffe

The alliance between painting and poetry has long been a subject of fascination for writers and readers of cultural history. Often this interest has focused on problems of defining the special characteristics, and delimiting the province of each. But the challenge of tracing actual connections between poet and artist, between specific works of poetry and art, has also enlisted the detective instincts of historians of these matters, and it is such a connection with which I am concerned in the following discussion of the relationship between the painter Joseph Stella and the poet Hart Crane.

The two men have been linked by a number of writers because of their common interest in the Brooklyn Bridge. In a letter to Lloyd Goodrich, then Associate Director of the Whitney Museum,[1] Professor Henry W. Wells of Columbia University remarked that in many years of studying literature in relation to the arts he had never encountered a single page that had inspired so many fine pages as Joseph Stella's account of his Brooklyn Bridge pictures.[2] This page, he goes on to say, was the core of Hart Crane's famous poem, *The*

Bridge. Wells, supposing that Stella and Crane were close friends, suggests that a study of the relationship between the two men should be undertaken. Another writer, David Steinberg, a journalist for the *Newark Ledger* at the time of the Joseph Stella retrospective exhibition at the Newark Museum in 1939, wrote in connection with the monumental five-panel painting, *New York Interpreted,* "The fifth panel, 'Brooklyn Bridge,' is the undisputed source of Hart Crane's most famous poem *The Bridge*." Brom Weber, in his biography of Crane, reviews some general evidence that would tend to suggest the possibility that Crane had been led to his concept of the bridge by Stella's painting.[3]

Four questions arise in discussing the relationship between Stella's painting and Crane's poem. *Which* work of Stella's is pertinent to the problem; when and how could Hart Crane have seen this pertinent work; when did he first know of Stella's essay; and did the men actually know each other?

Joseph Stella executed six paintings centering on the Brooklyn Bridge. Three of them were done in the nineteen thirties, one in 1929, too late to play a role in our story. His first bridge painting, however, was finished in 1919, and was exhibited for the first time at the Bourgeois Galleries in New York in April 1920. It was reproduced in the October 1921 issue of *The Arts,* in the first issue of *Broom,* November 1921, and in *The Little Review* of Autumn 1922, the "Stella Number." These are the reproductions referred to by Brom Weber.

Hart Crane read these periodicals. He was intensely interested in the painting and literature of his contemporaries. It is possible that this *Bridge* by Stella directed his imagination to the potentialities of the Bridge as poetic material. But it must be remembered that Crane was living in Cleveland at the time, and would not have had the Brooklyn Bridge itself as a constant and dramatic part of his environment, as it was to become when he moved to Brooklyn early in the Spring of 1923. In fact, the first idea of the poem does not appear to have formed in Crane's mind until January 1923, for on February 6 of that year he wrote to his friend Gorham Munson, with whom he was in constant correspondence, ". . . I am ruminating on a new longish poem under the title of *The Bridge.*"[4]

As it happens, the five canvasses that constitute Joseph Stella's great portrait of New York City, *New York Interpreted,* had their inaugural showing in the galleries of the Société Anonyme during January 1923. At the center of this polyptych is the dark-toned panel titled "Skyscrapers," based on the famous triangular shaped Flatiron Building in New York where Broadway and Fifth Avenue converge at 23rd Street. (Stella likened this image of the building to a ship's prow—a symbol of victory, he called it, which he possibly associated with the Victory of Samothrace represented as alighting on a ship's prow. He had seen that work in the Louvre when he visited Paris in 1911-1912.) Flanking "Skyscrapers" are two paintings titled "White Way" referring to the theatrical section of Broadway, harshly bright to express the garish brilliance of the entertainment world. At the far left is "The Port," while the opposite end position is occupied by "The Bridge," undoubtedly the single most famous painting in Stella's oeuvre.[5]

There was considerable publicity attending the exhibition of *New York Interpreted,* and extraordinary interest in this work. The most eminent American art critic of the period, Henry McBride, began his monthly article for *The Dial* of April 1923, with the comment, "So far, more people have asked me what I thought of Joseph Stella's new work at the Société Anonyme than have inquired into any other event of the season." In the light of Crane's comment to Munson at this very time that he was thinking about a new poem under the title of *The Bridge,* it would seem that there could well be some connection between the exhibition and Crane's new inspiration. There is, however, a hitch. Crane, as has already been remarked, was not living in New York at the time of this exhibition, and it is not likely that he could have made a brief visit to the city during the time of the exhibition, given the dates of his letters from Cleveland, and their contents. Did the poet and artist know each other well enough that Crane could have seen the work in progress in Stella's studio during some previous visit? We shall see that this possibility must be discarded. There is however one way, and I believe the only way, that Crane could have had visual knowledge of *New York*

Interpreted. At the time of the exhibition the Société Anonyme published a brochure with an introductory text by Katherine Dreier (the patron and prime mover of this first museum of modern art) with all five panels of the polyptych illustrated. Crane maintained close friendships in New York and it is plausible to suppose that he received a copy of this pamphlet from one of his friends. In the light of the date of Crane's letter to Munson, February 6, 1923, that he was planning a new poem under the title of *The Bridge* we are tempted to see the link between painting and poem formed at this time in this way, and to conclude that it was the Bridge of the polyptych that interested the poet.

That such a link existed seems further born out, indirectly, in a letter of Crane's to Otto Kahn who was aiding him financially at that time. On September 12, 1927 he wrote to his patron, "Thousands of strands have had to be searched for, sorted out and interwoven. In a sense I have had to do a great deal of pioneering myself. . . For each section of the entire poem has presented its own unique problem of form, not alone in relation to the other parts. *Each is a separate canvas, as it were, yet none yields its entire significance when seen apart from the others* (my emphasis). This passage is followed by the comment, "One might take the Sistine Chapel as an analogy."[6]

True, one might. But might one not take the five panels of *New York Interpreted* as a closer analogy in view of the subject matter, the imagery Crane projected in his ideas about his work—quite the aesthetic problem one sees that Stella had to face—and in the multipartite organization of the poem? It is interesting to recall that Crane had never seen the Sistine Chapel, the paintings of which are, of course, not on canvas. Otto Kahn would no doubt have been deeply stirred by the grandeur of Crane's concept being linked to Michelangelo's ceiling, and it was reasonable for the poet to suggest this analogy: the fact of the reference cannot be taken as any evidence that the Sistine Chapel was a formative influence in Crane's poem, and we may still cling, for another moment, to our speculation that Stella's painting was the real source of Crane's inspiration.

Ironically, our grip on this plausible circumstance is weakened by the one piece of evidence that obligingly informs us as to the other questions we have in mind—which Bridge painting is at issue, the personal relationship of the two men, and the poet's first knowledge of Stella's essay that Wells assumed was so significant for the poem. "The Bridge" was a long time in preparation—six years—for it was not until 1929 that it was ready for publication. Late in 1928 Crane had gone to Europe. In Paris he met "the amazing millionaire Harry Crosby. . ." he wrote to Malcolm Cowley, who ". . . is going to bring out a private edition of *The Bridge* with such details as a reproduction of Stella's picture in actual color as frontispiece."[7] Crane then wrote Stella, requesting permission for the use of his painting for this purpose.

> Dear Mr. Stella: Sometime before leaving America Charmion Habicht showed me a copy of your privately issued monograph called "New York," containing your essay on Brooklyn Bridge and the marvelous paintings you made not only of the Bridge but other New York subjects. This has been the admiration of everyone to whom I have shown it. And now I am writing you to ask if you will give permission to an editor friend of mine to reproduce the three pictures—"The Bridge," "The Port," and the one called "The Skyscrapers." He would also like to reprint your essay.
>
> I have also a private favor of my own to ask of you. I should like to use your painting of the Bridge as a frontispiece to a long poem I have been busy on for the last three years—called *The Bridge.* It is a remarkable coincidence that another person, by whom I mean you, should have had the same sentiments regarding Brooklyn Bridge which inspired the main theme and pattern of my poem.[8]

Since Crane refers in the first paragraph to *New York Interpreted,* it is clearly the Bridge painting in this work that interested him. From the tone of the letter it is clear that the two men were certainly not closely acquainted, and it would even seem that they did not know each other although they had mutual friends, Gaston Lachaise and Edgar Varèse, for example.[9] The essay that Wells assumed had inspired Crane's poem seems to have come to his attention only in 1928, when, as we know from the letter to Otto Kahn, a good deal of the work had already been done. But the most unsettling inference to be drawn from this letter is that Crane had but recently become aware of Stella's work on the Bridge theme and that he viewed the similarities as "coincidence."

It is puzzling. Can we accept at face value the content of this letter? As Brom Weber quite reasonably points out, Stella's Bridge paintings had appeared in literary magazines that Crane read—those, in fact, in which his own work was published. The poet was deeply concerned with the advanced art movements, and Stella was a leading figure in the art world of the twenties. In 1924 Henry McBride wrote, in the *New York Sun*, "everything Stella does must be seen by all those who wish to keep in the current of modern feeling." Stella's Bridge paintings were already famous, and it is difficult to think that Crane could have remained unaware of them. And our attention is drawn, as we puzzle over this letter, to the curious reference to *three* years during which he had been busy on his poem. We know, of course, that it was *six* years earlier that he had begun this *magnum opus*. Can we conclude that Crane's memory is not to be entirely trusted in this connection, and that even the original stimulus had been somehow forgotten? We must respect the possibility of the "remarkable coincidence," but this observer is strongly persuaded that Stella's soaring *Bridge* did play an inspirational role in the genesis of Crane's poem.

The opening lines of the end section of *The Bridge,* "Atlantis," occupying the same position in the poem that the "Bridge" takes in *New York Interpreted,* express with exquisite precision the visual effect of the painting, with its prominent cables, its wiry linearity, its dark tonality struck with light flickering over its scumbled surface:

> Through the bound cable strands, the arching path
> Upward, veering with light, the flight of strings,—
> Taut miles of shuttling moonlight syncopate
> The whispered rush, telepathy of wires.

Up the index of night, granite and steel—
Transparent meshes—fleckless the gleaming staves—
Sibylline voices flicker, wavering stream
As though a god were issue of the strings. . .[10]

Both the painter and the poet saw in the Bridge the symbol of the New World that is at the heart of American mythology. Each used the Bridge as a metaphor of transition from night to day, that is, from past to future. Crane writes, "Bridge, lifting night to cycloramic crest of deepest day . . ." while Stella tells us in "Brooklyn Bridge (A Page of My Life)," the essay to which Crane referred in the above quoted letter, "a new light broke over me . . . a new clarity proclaimed the luminous dawn of a new era." The poem and the painting are charged with metaphysical meaning and yet are anchored in concrete observation. There is inherent in these works a religious symbolism, only lightly touched on by Crane, profoundly important in Stella's work. Crane addressed the Bridge, "O harp and altar;" Stella painted his polyptych in the form of Renaissance altarpieces, the central section taller than the four flanking wings, with each panel bordered along its lower margin by a predella. But religion is identified with science and machinery which, for Crane and for Stella, had to be absorbed into contemporary art as naturally as the human figure and landscape had served the imagery of the humanist tradition, and the two works thus express contemporary awareness in a context of timeless and universal experience: each artist feels himself in transition, identified with the central aspirations of his time.

Crane and Stella both associated their art with that of music. Crane quotes Plato in the epigraph to Atlantis, "Music is then the knowledge of that which relates to love in harmony and system," and the references to sound are significant in the entire section. Stella thought of New York as "a symphony that is free in the vastness of its reverberations yet sharp and precise in its development."

Each man was deeply responsive to the other's medium of expression. Crane's interest in painting and painters has been extensively remarked on: Stella's knowledge of poetry has not been brought to public notice. In the opening paragraph of his autobiographical notes he recalls how he arrived in New York "well informed about the true painting," and with the greatest admiration for Walt Whitman," from whose works he could quote at great length as well as from Dante, Shakespeare, Baudelaire and Poe, his friends still remember. In 1929, in an interview with the Italian writer Bruno Barilli in Milan, he compared Poe and Whitman, "Two poets, two Americans, quite different from each other. . . the poetry of Poe has more truth. I see Poe everywhere in America in the sad countryside of abandoned shanties, in the sordid, lonely neighborhoods of the big cities, like Brooklyn. . . Poe cannot be translated. In what Italian or French form could one cast *The Raven*? Poe is pure, lucid, profound, and mathematical. Calm and fatal. You must read *The Maelstrom* in English. Never has language achieved such dizzying clarity, such immutable precision. In America you feel the frightful loneliness, the black melancholy the moment you arrive. Poe could only be American."[11]

The differences in the approach of the two artists to their theme, and their treatment of it, lie in their relation to the American past and the whole American land. In Hart Crane's poem we find his specific identification with this country's history—and with its mountains, valleys, and rivers. The Bridge, for Crane, reached back to Pocahantas, to Columbus, and then back to Troy, and "It leaps from Far Rockaway to the Golden Gate."

For Stella, too, the Bridge serves as self-identification; but from a viewpoint focused by his consciousness as a European as well as an American, he saw the span "traced for the conjunction of worlds."[12]

The accent of Crane's contemporary speech echoing in the corridors of time is the American accent of human optimism, of earnestness and of rational doubt.

> Walt, tell me, Walt Whitman, if infinity
> Be still the same as when you walked the
> Beach near Paumanok—

Stella, in contrast,

> felt. . . as if on the threshhold of a new religion
> or in the presence of a new divinity.[13]

A feeling of optimism does indeed generally characterize Crane's poem, realized in part through his use of space. Not only in lines such as "And one star, swinging, takes its place, alone, /Cupped in the larches of the mountain pass," or "Stars scribble on our eyes the frosty sagas/ The gleaming cantos of unvanquished space. . ." but the whole atmosphere of the work evokes the sense of vastness, that spaciousness that has often been noted as a characteristic of American sensibility. Stella's painting, on the contrary, is dense with ambiguous feeling. The bridge and the city beyond are imprisoned behind the vertical bars that lie on the surface, and are caught in the web of wires and cables. The sky is blocked off by the buildings seen through the pointed arches of the bridge towers. In many of his private writings in Italian Stella described his feelings about New York.[14] "The sickness of the city is this: closed in as one is among the buildings, the sky and the countryside blocked off, we are beset from morning to night by the multifarious crowd that weighs down on us, suffocating us like an obsession, like a nightmare." In other passages his pessimism lifts and he sees our bridges "hang like aerial highways through the chimeric fortunes of the future." Both men use the cyclopean image in these works, but it is possible that Stella's prose-poem about his painting was written after Crane's poem, so that we have the original influence from the painter to the poet now reversing its direction: "From Cyclopean towers across Manhattan waters/ —Two—three bright window-eyes aglitter. . ." Crane wrote. Stella described the city as "an immense Kaleidoscope—everything in hyberbolic, cyclopic, fantastic."

Through Crane's poem there is an endless sense of movement—people on the move, and rivers flowing. Stella's painting is devoid of human figures; the only water is that of the dark, still harbor, and the movement in *New York Interpreted* is throbbing rather than flowing. Cables and wires in Crane's poem are like veins and arteries carrying the sap of life through the body of the image. In Stella's painting the cables and wires bind the image like cords wrapped around a shrouded form.

Nevertheless, each in his way, Crane lyrical, Stella heroic, each found in the Bridge

> the shrine containing all the efforts of the New Civilization of America—the eloquent meeting point of all the forces arising in a superb assertion of their powers. [15]

NOTES

[1]Dated March 24, 1949, the letter is in the "Joseph Stella" file in the Whitney Museum of American Art.

[2]Wells refers to Stella's essay, "The Brooklyn Bridge (A Page of My Life)," published privately by Stella in the mid-twenties. Through Hart Crane's interest, the essay appeared in *Transition,* number 16-17, June, 1929.

[3]Weber, Brom, *Hart Crane.* New York: The Bodley Press, 1948, pp. 317-318.

[4]Weber, Brom (ed.) *The Letters of Hart Crane.* New York: Hermitage House, 1952, p. 118.

[5]Brooklyn Bridge as a motif did indeed have a very special place in Stella's mind and sensibility. Born and raised in the small medieval village of Muro Lucano in the mountains near Naples, he arrived in the United States in 1896 in his nineteenth year. The impact of New York, bustling, building, already vertical and growing perceptibly before one's eyes, was understandably enormous. But it was the Brooklyn Bridge above all that caught and held his imagination; years later, in his autobiographical notes, he relates, "In 1918 I seized on the . . . American theme that inspired me so much inspiration since I landed in this country, the first erected Brooklyn Bridge."

[6]Weber, *Letters,* p. 305.

[7]*Ibid.,* p. 335.

[8]*Ibid.,* pp. 333-334. The artist Charmion Habicht is better known as von Weigand.

[9]Brom Weber remarks that Crane in a subsequent letter to Stella remembered meeting him sometime in the 1920's. Weber, *Hart Crane,* p. 317.

[10]Frank, Waldo (ed.). *The Complete Poems of Hart Crane.* New York: Doubleday Anchor Books, 1958. All following quotations from Crane's poem are from this edition.

[11]*L'Ambrosiano,* Milan, September 8, 1929.

[12]Stella, "The Brooklyn Bridge. . ."

[13]*Ibid.*

[14]A full discussion of the symbolism of *New York Interpreted* is found in my book, *Joseph Stella,* published by Harvard University Press in the current year. I have had Stella's papers at my disposal through the courtesy of the painter's nephew and estate executor, Sergio Stella: the following three quotations are my translation from unpublished writings found among these papers.

[15]Stella, "The Brooklyn Bridge. . ."

Ideas Behind Avant-Garde Art

by

John W. Rathbun

It has been the usual misfortune of avant-gardes to be ignored, tolerated, domesticated, or contained by their hosts as if they were some kind of malignancy. Today's avant-garde is so much a part of the public consciousness that the puzzle is whether it will be domesticated—like Emerson and his group—or contained—like the Greenwich avant-gardists of the twenties. The puzzle is complicated by the fact that we now know more about the nature of the avant-garde. It is not limited to artists exploiting their craft to advance the frontiers of cultural experience. Nor is it progressive. And it is certainly not in the vanguard of society. It is, instead, as Poggioli and Weightman have recently argued, a more or less autonomous part of modern western society, dedicated in large part to challenging the values and objectives of that society, and characterized by a number of metaphysical ideas that have their origin in philosophical romanticism.

When closely examined, these "ideas" can probably be more adequately described as attitudes, perhaps even fashionable cliches adopted with the same mindless want of thought that obtains in the culture avant-gardists commonly criticize. Key concepts, phrases, or words are embraced with a passion that establishes their advocates as members of a quality sub-culture, whether or not they put pen to paper or fingers to the keyboard. Today, for instance, all self-respecting avant-gardists are authenticity minded, by which is meant a genuine, authoritative selfhood to which all men should aspire. The secondary and tertiary words—words like brotherhood, love, creativity, freedom, peak experience—serve either as attributes of authenticity or as a means for achieving authenticity. In the present state of our numbed society, when a man becomes an authentic person, that is, when he can trot out the favored attitudes and prejudices, he can join a fairly elite group and stand like a Triton amongst the rest of us minnows. Unfortunately, such a man frequently seems to embrace an ideology rather than a rational body of thought. Artists seem peculiarly prone to this malady. When one compares their written or reported statements to their art, the statements appear curiously flat, even conventional, while the art seems full of wit and enthusiasm and sometimes even profundity. There are, of course, exceptions. Ad Reinhardt and Jasper Johns abound in specific insights that strike one as startingly true, and the same can be said for other artists. But the reverse is distressingly prevalent. The verbal facility of artists is simply not equal to their artistic practice.

In some respects, the avant-garde artist starts where most thoughtful men in this culture start. Like most of us, he has a sense of rootlessness and of a heavily circumstantial isolation. Uncertainty and anxiety are conditions of life, the origins of which are speculatively unproductive and the conclusions of which are beyond imagination. Consequently value becomes an individual concern. But more than most of us, the artist has to do something with all this. He must constantly meet the new while avoiding the expedient. He finds the concept of beauty an alien notion, the relation between subject and form an enormously complex matter, the "real" a shifting, kaleidescopic puzzle, the need to encompass experience distressing and bewildering. He is situated right at the center of his own moral universe, responsible only to his own integrity and to his own talent. He may maintain a humanist orientation, but he is not likely to stress values of dignity, grace, and intelligibility that were constituent parts of the older humanism, because, as Don Judd said in 1965, "it is impossible and not even desirable to believe most generalizations." Given this "void between one's lonely self and the world," as Motherwell phrases it, the artist frequently embraces an enlightened subjectivity in order to discover an essentially good "inner nature" common to all mankind. And in this inner nature, he hopes, values may be found that have wider dimensions than the public philosophy.

The extreme emphasis on subjectivity explains why avant-garde artists so often think of themselves as revolutionaries. Not only do they engage, and frequently discard, previously existing artistic forms and limitations, a familiar position, but through their art they contest public policies and attitudes, scarcely a revelation either. The fashion in which they cast their social criticism is interesting, however. The entire tone takes on a militant and prophetic note which identifies such artists, as Richard Pusette-Dart, Balcomb Greene, and others have said, as "moral" men possessing "an undetachable moral sense." Their work, therefore, is thought to have moral applicability, even though presented in different forms. Barnett Newman, for example, views art as a continuing defiance of man's fall which seeks to bring man again into Edenic existence, while Morris Graves contends that art acquaints man with his "cosmic significance," and Stephen Durkee differs from the other two in suggesting that art encourages self-reform as a means for opposing disharmony and evil.

Such statements, conventional enough in art history, are perplexing when cast against the work they are intended to illustrate. It is difficult to see how the highly abstract non-referential art of either Newman or Durkee meets their stated intentions. One means of arriving at a correlation is to focus on how these artists think that the moral sense is translated into a work of art. Not all artists accept the theory of transformation (Rauschenberg and Lichtenstein reject it), but both Newman and Durkee, as well as Stankiewicz, Johns, Oldenberg, and others think that art transmutes the character, condition, or nature of original experience. In effect, then, an art work may possess its "own integrity and intensity," as de Kooning puts it, and alone excite an "emotion or an idea" in the spectator's mind.

The concomitant thought follows, that the experience of art can peculiarly stir sensation and rational emotion as these are distinguished from intellect and will.

Furthermore, works of art that embody the moral sense may have a transcendent property that makes them superior in excellence and degree to those that enjoy wide public esteem. They also have the power of altering conventional perception, which can make possible the apprehension of higher forms of reality, usually of a moral or spiritual nature. Jack Youngerman's statement that he looks for "eloquent shapes" to provide "some *revelation*" implies not only the stimulation of new awarenesses but as well a hope that the spectator will emerge with new mental and spiritual perspectives. Dan Flavin, who experiments with electric and fluorescent lighting in his sculpture, explicitly tries to move beyond "modern technological fetish" to get at what he calls spiritual and visual expressiveness. And the young group of New York artists who formed the Park Place Gallery and generally worked with geometric shapes and spatial ambiguities, tried, in Dean Fleming's words, to move the reference beyond the canvas: "We want to make people realize that what they see has a transcendent nature and a multiplicity and that they themselves are capable of this change inside their own psyches; and the experience of that change can be ecstatic." Such exalted objectives naturally breed their own denial. In Warhol's disenchanted romanticism, art is perversely reduced to a dispassionate, static activity in which the very sense of being bored is the sole assurance of one's humanity.

All of this implies that while artists may have abandoned the narrative element they still retain the literary. The work of art is to be experienced, just as the poet says that "A poem should not mean But be." But in the *act* of painting there can also be a kind of stasis, or being-ness, something complete in itself and satisfying. In its extreme form, the act of painting is similar to Zen *wa-tzu,* that is, the cultivation of personal preparation and serenity of mind to formalize activity—the position of a Mark Tobey. The resolute denial of painting as any kind of worthwhile act is found in Warhol and Billy Al Bengston, men who see nothing special in art, who reject the whole idea of mystique in painting, and who simply feel, because they are burdened with a particular skill, that they are doomed to painting when they would immensely prefer to overhaul motorcycles.

The majority of artists range between these polar positions. They may agree with Clyfford Still that artists are "committed to an unqualified act," but they also share Reinhardt's skeptical view that "the fine artist need not sit cross-legged." To the extent that the canvas became the object in action painting (rather than outer "nature," so called), painting could become a creative process in which the end was the act of painting itself. The attitude persisted beyond the slump in popularity of action painting. Rauschenberg takes the act of painting to be a "fact" or an "inevitability," and Jose de Rivera says that "Art for me is a creative process of individual plastic production without immediate goal or finality." Wesselman also thinks that the act of painting is "audacious," and Lichtenstein strikes the moderate note in saying that "Interaction between painter and painting is not the total commitment of Pop, but it is still a major concern—though concealed and strained." In stressing art as an act, problems of design, of metaphor and symbolic statement, of form, become the conditions of the artist's involvement, and eased out completely are such extraneous concerns as marketing the work or finding its public.

In stressing the complete self-integration of art, its ability to stand by itself separate from the society in which it had its origin and perhaps even its context, artists come close to and some actually slide over into a total and narrow commitment to the exclusiveness of art. Yet undeniably art finally exists as a social resource to the public. The art work seeks the public and finds its completion in public view, a point that Duchamp never tired of making. And, as Frederick Franck says, the sympathetic viewing of a work of art "becomes a celebration of the goodness of being alive." Indeed, frequently the end beyond the artist's end of painting is to mock complacency, to startle or to delight, to map out the condemnation under which we live in the manner, say of a Kienholz or a Segal, in other words to establish some relation because we live by relations. What results is not without its admixture of amusement and sardonic tolerance. Wayne Thiebaud's work looks as if everything had been put through a detergent wash, and provides an ironic view of the American fetish of cleanliness. The same elements of parody are found in Lichtenstein, Rosenquist, Oldenberg, and others. Accepting much in the American environment, these artists nevertheless respond to the imp of perversity, so that there is a basic ambiguity in their attitude, part irony and part endorsement. Certainly the work with which they deal is itself composed of ambiguous gestures, many of which undercut its seeming seriousness. Thus the photograph of the Robert C. Scull home, the New York taxicab and insurance magnate and angel to Pop artists, in which the family is being formally served by the maid as all sit in their Pop environment of Rosenquist and Lichtenstein paintings and on their own plastic-covered chairs—to protect the expensive fabric.

While there must always be some distinction between subject content and painting content, since the latter incorporates the artist's own moral response to what he is dealing with, the line of demarcation between the two has been increasingly narrowing. And where previously art served to give coherence to our lives, indeed trained us to see the world as art saw it, now the reverse seems to be coming true. Except for the occasional person like the Paris nightclub owner who goes to all the art happenings to get ideas for his striptease show, art is less apt to give us our cues than to take its own cues from its environment. Today we are all happening, artists included, as if some rich Emersonian reward attaches to one's experiences of the particular. The comparison is apt. Emerson lamented the particulars of social experience and constantly called men to higher forms, yet was fascinated by the intensity of isolated experience no matter how much it violated his sensibilities. The same is true for the avant-garde artist today.

Indeed, avant-garde statements today constitute a kind of latter-day transcendentalism. Most of the familiar attitudes are there: the easy polarization of individual and society, the reliance on an intuitive subjectivity, the stress on the individual as the repository of all that is good and noble, the distress over the collective nature of man, the belief that individuals must rise above their surroundings—

transcend them—to reach that pure authenticity where all is reconciled in the autonomous person, the tendency to emphasize the moral side of man rather than the social or the religious, the elitism, the faith in art as a means of striking the prophetic note and redeeming the great unwashed, even the naive belief that societies can be organized on the basis of love rather than of justice. On the side of their practice, however, artists are simpler and perhaps truer. They remain devoted to the intrinsic vitality of their medium, and, as George Rickey says, wish to communicate "deep values in human action, without being decorative, 'illustrative,' photographic, didactic, sentimental, or academic."

Philosophy and American Studies

by

John Lachs

It may be surprising to hear that philosophy keeps pace with the hemlines. But in fact there are as many changing philosophical fashions as there are styles of wearing skirts or, nowadays, hair. In the last thirty years alone a dozen waves of philosophical sentiment have washed over our universities. In this ebb and flow of opinion, movements disappear as quickly as they were created. The high tide sees a contagion of common belief; when the waters recede the heroes of the day are beached and left to fossilize.

But not only is the mind of philosophy inconstant. Her heart, like the hidden soul of a lady of fashion, is radically dialectical and innocently double. There is never just one fashion in philosophy or in love: those who know seem to find it particularly pleasurable to embrace one alternative in full view of the other. So in philosophy today we have two great but divergent bodies of opinion. The linguistic analysts maintain that the task of philosophers is to examine the way in which certain puzzling words are used in ordinary language. Phenomenologists, by contrast, assert that we must examine the quality and meaning of experience as it is ordinarily lived. The former feel that language somehow is the key to wisdom and sanity. The latter proclaim that in some way human experience provides a direct access to reality.

Please do not be alarmed. I shall not try your patience with an analysis of the ordinary use of the phrase "American Studies" or the words "popular" and "culture." And how I experience or what I feel about American Studies is not nearly as interesting as what it is. There are some philosophers, and I should like to be counted among them, who try to learn from the fashions of the day without being swayed by them. My interest is in beings or, in a wide sense of the word, things, and in the concepts by which we understand them. Experiences may illuminate these ideas about things, and words may ill-express them; if so, we ought to try to have illuminating experiences and we should in any case watch our words. But the test of it all is how well we can put our concepts together to grasp the hang of things, and even that may not be known until we have tried to act on it and seen what we can *do*. This may well be old fashioned talk. But if no one objects to the old fashioned in home cooking or in antique furniture, why should we protest it in philosophy?

My topic is the value of philosophy for American Studies. One way, of course, in which philosophy may be useful for American Studies is the manner in which poems are useful in the study of literature. Every discipline must have some subject-matter. Just as poems constitute a part of the subject-matter of literature, American philosophy properly constitutes a part of the material that scholars engaged in the pursuit of American Studies may examine. I should think that philosophical writings present a particularly rich field of study. If we take clear, well-developed and vigorously defended discursive positions as expressive of the commitments of the writer, they may well serve as our best clues to the recognition and understanding of some era, social movement or state of mind. But significant as this role of philosophy is, it is not the one with which I am concerned. I am less interested in what philosophy can reveal in a passive and symptomatic role than in what it can actively contribute to the scope and methods of American Studies.

This very scope of American Studies should have endeared it to the hearts of philosophers. A generous and productive multi-faceted approach combined with the generality of the task of understanding the American experience should serve to give rise to the sort of multiplicity-in-unity philosophers have always prized. There is virtually no end to the conceptual possibilities the field presents. There is room for minute analysis, for the interpretation of symbols, for the unification of diverse phenomena under laws—and all of this with a view to gaining a clear, judicious and synthetic vision of a total form of life. In its ultimate objectives American Studies is a philosophical enterprise of the oldest, most difficult and most rewarding sort: it is a search for essence. An American Aristotle or Plato would have been glad to join the search, had he not thought of starting it himself. Why, then, have contemporary philosophers by and large failed to respond to this challenge? Why are so relatively few philosophers making such relatively minor contributions to American Studies today?

I do not pretend to know the answers to these questions. It is possible that an exaggerated sense of professionalism has caused philosophers to believe that attention to minute technical problems is the only appropriate or rewarding activity. Another pertinent fact is that philosophers are perhaps the only mortals who take pride in their ignorance of empirical matters. Their willingness to endure considerable discomfort to remain in this state has certainly helped to make their contributions to American Studies minimal. But ultimately perhaps only those of us responsible for the education of graduate students are to blame. To chase the elusive essence of America requires a soaring and ambitious mind well fortified with the skills that yield comprehensive vision. This is difficult work and the students we turn out are ill equipped for it. Something surely is lost in our world of hurried research. We lack the skill of patient observation and sometimes even the patience for skilled observation. The days of the great forbearing, dispassionate observers of nature and society appear to be gone. Who would want to spend a lifetime in the careful study of some species of animals or of *Homo Americanus* in its native haven when he can gain fame by weighing the finely minced brains of mice or collect grant after grant to issue questionnaires and quantify the opinions of the nescient? One wonders what research projects such shrewd observers of the American scene as de Tocqueville and Santayana might have proposed to some rich committee for generous support and speedy execution.

What could philosophers contribute to American Studies, if they wholeheartedly embraced the enterprise of exploring and understanding the American experience? Ideally, their contribution could be staggering. The reason is obviously not that philosophers are somehow intrinsically wiser than other mortals. There is not the least reason for this view and if anyone claims there is, I shall be glad to introduce him to the hundreds I know who constitute the counter-evidence. The source of the potential contribution of philosophers is their special training and their bent of thought. Philosophy has at least two different but interrelated functions. The first is the critical one of striving for clarity, precision and the sensitivity to conceptual distinctions. The second is the constructive one of unifying, under concepts of uncommon generality, a wide variety of apparently unrelated theories and phenomena.

Let me first of all speak of the contribution that may come from the side of critical philosophy. In the strict sciences the experimental and manipulative aspects of research safeguard us against much conceptual vagary. But even there, of course, the more tenuous, the more mediate, our connection with fact, the more room there is for free conceptual construction. And the more general and more elaborate our conceptual structures, the more opportunity there is for our concepts to be fatally ambiguous or vague or simply vacuous. This represents a particular danger in such fields as history and literature where the test of hypotheses is difficult and always far from complete. And in American Studies, where frequently we do not even know what would constitute an empirical test—or even evidence—for certain views, the pitfalls of thought are almost impossible to avoid. A tempting shortcut here, a luscious generality there, and we find ourselves hopelessly entangled in a net of scrambled models and senseless explanations. Even a bit of carelessness can lead to talking nonsense, especially the sort of nonsense that continues to impress as profound beyond the grasp of ordinary mortals.

Here is where the critical thought of the philosopher might help. His sensitivity to distinctions, the care with which he has learned to form concepts and to construct hypotheses may be exactly what is required to rid us of some confusions and to eliminate those creampuff theories that are as lightweight as they are sweet to savor. Let me offer a concrete example.

In American Studies one may quite naturally speak of "the American mind" and "the American character." I myself have repeatedly referred to "the American experience." It is, of course, perfectly legitimate to speak in such generalities, so long as we keep clearly in mind that they are just that. If we can remember that these concepts are shorthand for a vast and virtually unstatable multitude of trends and phenomena, we shall run little risk of error. Candid and frequent reference to what William James fondly called "the cash value" of such ponderous conceptions is as salutary as it is difficult and unnatural for the soaring mind. Our natural inclination is to bring our thought in conformity with our language. Where our words suggest unity, we are insensibly led to think unity. At first we speak of "the American mind" as a matter of convenience and abbreviation. But soon we find that tacitly we begin to think of it as a unitary being that has a claim to existence on its own. We never have to reach the stage of personification: it is quite enough if, thinking of America as an individual existent though not necessarily as a conscious person, we assign to it properties and relations, and eventually rights and privileges, that are applicable and appropriate only to the individual beings that constitute it.

The errors that can flow from taking abstractions for actual and unitary entities are grave and far from just academic. The political, ideological and moral disasters that come of presenting the state or the community as somehow possessed of a life of its own and setting that life against the claims of its citizens are too obvious to all of us to need discussion. The danger for American Studies is that speaking loosely of such things as "the American national character" we may give aid and comfort to those who, high-minded about the good of the abstract whole, quickly forget the rights of real beings. If we succumb to the temptation to view trends, collections of individuals and relative uniformities as real beings with properties and powers, our theories will inevitably deteriorate to the level of mythology. We shall see history as the struggle of quasi-animate forces for the good. We shall view each nation as an organic Leviathan alive with need and perpetually in pursuit of its desires. And we may well think of each epoch or race or class or large-scale social event as endowed with its own soul or moving spirit.

The plain fact is that such mythology is both false and harmful. There is no such thing as America independent of its citizens and their interrelations. America is the totality of individual Americans past and present, along with the immensely complex ways in which they interact. The American character is not the unitary character of some superhuman being but simply an indefinitely large and relatively loose collection of habits and characteristics. The American experience is not that of a single conscious being subject to the laws of organism. I trust I do not even have to say that the American way of life is not a unified mode of being that can serve as the standard of anything. And when in the drift of human events it becomes possible for us to act in relative unison in exploiting some opportunity for growth and life, the mythologizing mind may well call this our "manifest destiny."

The mistake of which I speak is not confined to the work of sociologists, historians and literary critics. The temptation to think that states and societies are real existents has also led many a philosopher into error. But philosophers surely should know better. They need not be and they ought not to be deceived about such things. Their special education should have given them the onto-logical sensitivity requisite for distinguishing the abstract from the real. It is precisely this skill and others like it that may help those in American Studies to avoid some of the pitfalls of theorizing about matters that are so wide in scope, so interesting and so difficult. This could be the contribution of critical philosophy to American Studies.

The contribution of the constructive or synthetic aspect of

philosophy will also be conceptual. Here empirical research and the careful clarification of our ideas are presupposed and the philosopher sets himself the task of developing concepts and constructing theories of a very high level of generality. Some philosophers, such as Whitehead perhaps, engage in the enterprise of unifying the concepts or results of the special sciences in terms of a scheme of ideas that is as broad as it is rich in deductive consequences. Others put forward views that cut across the special arts and sciences and freely utilize them without reducing all their results to unity. Now it seems to me that American Studies consists primarily though not solely in just this latter sort of inventive interdisciplinary generalization. Once again, it would be absurd to suggest that only philosophers can or ought to engage in this activity. The flight of the productive imagination that is the heart of creative thought is not the exclusive property of anyone. And at any rate, genius is not a result of method. But short of genius, philosophers are especially likely candidates for success at generalization. On the whole, they stand a better chance of developing creative new formulations more often than others for at least three reasons. The first is their sensitivity, acquired through their special education, to the common features of apparently diverse phenomena. The second is their practice, roundly denounced by admirers of myopia, of taking a general view of things. The third is their habit, become almost uncontrollable by frequent repetition of considering each fact and idea in the context of its relations.

How much insight have we gained by the introduction of the concept of the genteel tradition in American life? The idea makes sense of a wealth of otherwise disconnected facts. It cuts across the conventional lines between the individual sciences and arts whose object or part of whose object is America, and illuminates not only their results but even their objectives and the manner in which they are conducted. And, perhaps most important of all, significant portions of our direct experience appear shot full of light when we view them through this conceptual apparatus. The idea of the genteel tradition, first developed by George Santayana in an address at the University of California in 1911, is a paradigm of the sort of contribution constructive philosophers may make to American Studies. If there were an appreciable number of able philosophers at work observing and reflecting on the qualities of the American experience, it is likely that before long we would understand ourselves a little better. At any rate, we might at least grow beyond the stage where some of our actions surprise us more than they surprise total strangers.

Where will these new insights come from? Having recently seen our first child born, sometimes I find myself asking where really anything comes from. There are many able scholars in American Studies and there are some good philosophers. But nothing organic can be *made* to grow. We can prepare the ground, then plant and water; from there the darkest forces of nature must do their work. Thoughts are no different from children or radish seeds in this regard. Labor is our homage to the generative order; growth is nature's gift to those who work. We must do our part and then perhaps we shall witness some insight flower in our minds and words.

Out of the Clouds and into The Earth: New Directions for American Studies

by

Wilcomb E. Washburn

The American Studies movement originated in the 1930's largely as a result of the dissatisfaction of some scholars in English literature departments with the non-recognition accorded American literature by their departments. In the following years American literature was put on the map and a great sea of ink spilled attempting to establish a theoretical foundation for the organizational form in which the largely successful revolt was institutionalized. That organization not only elevated American literature to an honored place but emphasized the need to approach American materials broadly, in a multi-disciplinary approach. The word "culture," in its anthropological sense, was occasionally used in describing the object of such study.

The battle to establish the theoretical validity of a cultural approach to American history was won, but the attempt to establish a permanent institutional framework was not, and the claim of a special intellectual theory to the body of work known as American studies has been called seriously into question. It has been impossible for American Studies departments to muscle their way into full acceptability in American universities. It is well, perhaps, to accept this as a fact of life. Not that an English Department, or an interdepartmental committee, are better "homes" for American Studies, but that it is probably impossible to prove that a separate department with status equal to that of any other department on campus would be any more valid.

More threatening has been the intellectual challenge to the attempt to establish a theory of American Studies. The emergence of a theoretical literature in the American Studies field was probably motivated more by an attempt to justify the shaky new institutional forms of American Studies than by a disinterested search for theoretical principles in the subject matter of the field. The result of the attacks on the theory (or theories) of American Studies has been to dim the lustre of the American Studies emblem, while the reams of paper expended in defense of the various theoretical formulations of American Studies have done little but inundate the defenders.

Is it not time, perhaps, to shift from the barren ground of theoretical controversy and to expand the practical boundaries of the "discipline"? That expansion can go in several directions. It can, as Jay Gurian has suggested in his article "American Studies and the Creative Present" (*Midcontinent American Studies Journal*, Vol. X, No. 1, Spring 1969), tap the creative individuality of students working with problems of current significance. But the expansion can also go further back into the past and away from the literary emphasis of most American Studies programs. Have we not gotten too far afield from the specific facts and processes of American culture in the pursuit of symbolic meaning in literature and in the quest for the essence of national character?

I would propose that the American Studies movement welcome and embrace the emerging discipline of historical archeology. Historical archeologists are presently without a real home. The discipline has emerged by dint of individual initiative and the support of institutions such as Plimoth Plantation, Inc., Colonial Williamsburg, Inc., and the National Park Service. Academic homes for historical archeologists are few and far between and when they exist, as at Harvard University, or at the University of Arizona, they exist in Departments of Anthropology as an adjunct to work with Indian cultures. At the University of Pennsylvania historical archeology, because of the initiative of Anthony Garvan, is included in the American Studies program but exists on a part-time basis and only because of Jack Cotter's willingness to teach on the side in addition to his Park Service duties.

Historical archeology is at the take-off phase. It can actually create, or rather uncover, new evidence to support descriptive and interpretive studies of American cultural history: The surface has only been scratched. What little has been done rests in the limited evidence of museums and historical restorations that are themselves the product of comparatively recent interest and effort. Contrast this picture with that of the traditional literary efforts in the field of American Studies. There the same ground is often reworked. Few new insights are being unearthed in this process, and the penalty of triviality is often being paid, not only by the individual researcher but by the discipline as a whole.

How can an American Studies department embrace historical archeology? Let me give you an example of what the Smithsonian is doing, and hoping to do, in this field. First of all, the American Studies Program of the Smithsonian is attempting to utilize existing expertise in historical archeology at the Smithsonian to support the training of graduate students in historical archeology. Secondly, the American Studies program is exerting its influence to push for the hiring of a full-time historical archeologist in order to be able to exploit the potential sites in the Washington area, both in terms of the advancement of knowledge, the training of graduate students, and incidentally the collection of specimens to add to the data bank of cultural objects already acquired by museums throughout the country. The Smithsonian is presently supporting a project undertaken by the State of Maryland to excavate St. Mary's City, the 17th century colonial capital of Maryland. (We already have students who have worked at archeological and restoration sites in Annapolis, which is our eighteenth-century "historical laboratory".)

The St. Mary's project is principally the work of the St. Mary's City Historical Commission, created by the State of Maryland, and of St. Mary's College, located in the town of St. Mary's. These groups are interested in Smithsonian participation because of the resources of specialized talent that the Institution can bring to bear. The Smithsonian is interested in the project because of the potential for advancing knowledge in colonial history both by research, excavation, and the training of future scholars through work in the area.

We find that some of our best graduate students are increasingly restless with the traditional curriculum of American Studies, not solely because it is book and library oriented, but because the sometimes sterile manipulation of the increasingly muscle-bound corpus of American Studies materials is becoming more difficult for the widely experienced youth of today to accept.

Work in historical archeology seems to many students to be on the frontiers of knowledge. They are literally the first to see what they are uncovering; they are not treading well-worn paths. Although a rigorous *method* must be followed, the work can be done by the student. He is not merely listening to the professor tell about the results of his own research. In an era of increasing student sophistication and discontent at the spoonfeeding and lecture course methods of the past, the freedom and responsibility associated with work in historical archeology is attractive.

I will not go into details of particular "digs" or of particular methods except to note that the number of potential sites is almost limitless, and to emphasize that the use of statistical techniques is making the total content of archeological excavations more significant to the scholar than the recovery of particular items of sufficient distinction to encourage display in a museum case. Nor will I talk about the disciplines which are the companions of historical archeology: industrial archeology and architectural history, which seek to record the information about the past while it is still above ground. All these approaches to the American past are comparatively lightly traveled. The superhighways of modern literary criticism are jammed with graduate students who seldom know of the existence of these archeological "shunpikes" to the past.

Perhaps my literary colleagues will express their disgust at my denigration of their concerns by ridiculing the results that can be expected from the pursuit of historical archeology. What, they may say, will be found in the earth but a mere miscellany of pottery pieces, rusted metal, and empty wine bottles? Although the conventional attitude to "pots and pans" history, as a subject inferior to the study of the great ideas and great events that sweep across the surface of everyday life, is understandable, it is not necessarily wise. Take any of the objects that may be found underground and consider what modern scholarship can tell us about it in comparison with what scholars a generation ago could make of it. In order not to seem to be stacking the deck, let me take what may perhaps be the least attractive artifact that could be found: excrement, to which, in its dried and hardened form, we may apply the word "coprolites" from the Greek *kopros*, meaning dung, and *lithos*, meaning stone. In a recent study in *Science* magazine (8 August 1969) of "Biological and Cultural Evidence from Prehistoric Human Coprolites" Robert F. Heizer and Lewis K. Napton have reconstructed the diet of prehistoric Great Basin Indians from the desiccated fecal material left in various caves in the State of Nevada. In their study Heizer and Napton published a list of over 50 constituents found in the coprolites of a particular cave. By an analysis of these constituents, which include plants, mollusks, insects, fish, birds, and mammals, and of the frequency with which they appear, archeologists can tell us more precisely than ever before about dietary patterns and food-preparation practices of the inhabitants of the sites.

The opportunities afforded by such material for the study of communicable or deficiency diseases, environmental sanitation, epidemiology, pathology, ethnobotany, and the like are immense. When one considers that the major element in determining the existence and status of races has more often been disease than war (the whole history of Indian-white relations in this country is an example) the importance of studies of such humble material is evident.

Let us honor the great literature that Americans have produced, but let us not inundate that literature with a flood of often repetitive interpretive and analytical glosses. Let us get out of the transcendental clouds of essences and ideas and into the earth: into the humus, through the sherds, and down to the coprolites, where the humble material clues to man's activities on earth still remain.

Public Support of United States Authors

by

John W. Nichol

Especially in the fall season, it seems, warm support for United States authors and artists exudes from the highest places in our government.

Item. **October 26, 1963—President John F. Kennedy** on dedicating the Robert Frost Library at Amherst:

> I see little of more importance to the future of our country and our civilization than full recognition of the place of the artist. If art is to nourish the roots of our culture, society must set the artist free to follow his vision wherever it takes him.

Item. **September 29, 1966—President Lyndon B. Johnson** on signing the bill creating the National Foundation for the Arts and Humanities:

> In the long history of man, countless empires and nations have come and gone. Those which created no lasting works of art are reduced today to short footnotes in history's catalogue. Art is a nation's most

precious heritage.

Item. **September 4, 1969—President Richard M. Nixon** on appointing Nancy Hanks as the new chairman of the National Council and Endowment for the Arts:

> One of the important goals of my administration is the further advance in the cultural development of our nation.

But when spring arrives and the time comes around for down-to-earth grappling with amounts of money for congressional appropriations, we get a different story.

Item. **February 27, 1968—The House of Representatives** debate on a bill to extend and increase the authorization for the National Foundation for the Arts and Humanities:[1]

> **Mr. Anderson, Illinois:** Even as we stand here this afternoon, and as the Communists are trying to tighten the noose around Khe Sanh, and as we see more than 18,000 of our countrymen dead in this most tragic of all conflicts, the time has come, ladies and gentlemen, to disenthrall ourselves of the notion that this war is just something of subsidiary importance. I do not care whether a person is a hawk or if he is a dove, until that war has been finished it ought to be the main business of this country.

> **Mr. Gross, Iowa:** Roger L. Stevens is apparently the big pooh-bah of the arts and humanities, or whatever *you* want to call it. *I* have a few other names for this expenditure. Now it is my understanding that this outfit has not been in operation very long but they have certainly learned a lot about the art of asking for a helluva lot . . . and settling for less. I have no doubt that there were some representatives of the University of California lurking in the shadows and corridors waiting to pick up another fast buck or two . . . .

These fellowships range from $8500 to $15,000 each year and would permit research into such vital areas as "Medieval Spanish Satire and Invective." . . . $15,000 went to Leroy Jones for his Black Arts Theatre who has produced such gems as "The Toilet." . . . I understand that some $70 million in grants were pumped out to foreign scientists to do research in such projects as smells of ocean fish and perspiration problems of the Australian aborigines. . . . Or to train eighteen Good Humor ice cream peddlers in Connecticut. . . . All I want to say in conclusion is I am sure the Marines over in Khe Sanh simply cannot wait to hear of this bill. I am sure they are waiting with abated breath over there in that besieged compound for passage of this bill.

Mr. Fino, New York: Now I want to make it very clear just what sort of boondoggles are to be financed under these schemes. . . . They want $22 million this year and $32 million next year—to subsidize any bearded agitator who can wield a paint brush, any screwball folksinger who can hum "We Shall Overcome," and any Vietnik who can strum a guitar. . . . Aid to individuals is liable to turn out to be nothing more than a subsidy for hippies, beatniks, junkies, and Vietniks. . . There is no doubt that this section could be used to subsidize Red Chinese and North Vietnamese documentaries designed to serve propaganda purposes. I would . . . prevent the endowment from giving money to Vietnik folksinging groups, anarchist theatre troups, Communist movies and Black Nationalists who put on plays describing white people as homosexuals. I want to be sure that this endowment does not become a gravy train for agitators and malcontents who pervert "art" into an attack on the foundations of the American way of life.

> **Mr. Ashbrook, Ohio:** I believe that there is a real threat that creative arts will be smothered by the bureaucratic hand which is so clear in this legislation . . . the hidden control which comes from holding the purse strings and rewarding those who conform . . . . Mr. Chairman, I offer a substitute amendment. . . . This would cut the authorization from $60 million for fiscal 1969 and $82 million for fiscal 1970 back to the level of spending for the fiscal year 1968 which was $11.2 million.

The substitute amendment passed 261 to 130.

I cite these selected, even exaggerated, statements on both sides of the exceptionally controversial question of government support for literature and the arts because they tend to highlight the complexity and difficulty of trying to translate an ideal into action. Very simply stated, the problem is this: Is the United States mature enough, confident enough, flexible and broadminded enough, humble enough, as a culture and as a civilization, to be able to step in to free the writer from the harsh demands and censorship of bureaucratic control and standards? Are we ready to support the writer who may disagree and criticize, who may tend to bite the hand that feeds him?

Many informed Americans still reject the idea that good art can come out of government control and official programs. Historically, Platonism, Puritanism, and Communism have all assigned an important role in society to the arts—but only if the arts were generally conservative and tended to support the ideals and faiths of the establishment.[2] Today many serious critics and writers alike have said that the best thing the American government could do for the artist would be to leave him alone. But such an attitude ignores the fact that no society leaves an artist alone, especially, perhaps, a democratic society. It may even be that the basic interests of art and democracy conflict, that they are, in essence, incompatible. Art left alone in a democratic society seems to become a commodity; large scale support and distribution tends to standardize the arts; they become the playthings of status seekers, social promoters, educational technicians. The democratic mystique operates against the essential detachment, separation, alienation, or independence necessary for creative vision. Thus what democratic government support should do—if anything—is to free the artist for this essential independence, to protect him from the necessity for "success," to help him avoid the entrapment which occurs when (as one writer put it) yesterday's avant-garde experiment becomes today's chic and tomorrow's cliche.[3] But the knotty question still remains whether a public which has been brought up on concepts of success, chic, cliche, and kitch can gird itself to the extremely painful task of providing the support and then "letting the chips fall where they may." Can the United States recognize and avoid the real risks of government control, political bias, the stifling of individual and independent activity, and the attempts to set standards for the use of its money? Arthur J. Goldberg, former Supreme Court Justice and Ambassador to the United Nations, is one who thinks it can. "I might say," he writes, "that this live sense of danger is in itself the best guarantee that we could have for artistic freedom. . . . We should be perfectly honest and open about the problem of interference with the freedom of the arts and attempts to compromise the integrity of the artist. . . . [but] We should acknowledge also that the marketplace exerts its own forms of censorship which can be as unyielding and rigid as any feared by opponents of subsidy. . . . Subsidy, in short, may be less a strait-jacket than the box office."[4]

However, too much of the argument pro and con on this question of government support has been based only on private opinions, wishes, political biases, or isolated examples which happened to turn out well or badly. If we can look at the whole pattern of the American government's experience from the beginning in subsidizing writers, we should be better able to make a balanced judgment both as to the basic value of government support and as to whether we have yet arrived at the necessary accompanying maturity as a nation.

A graph of the actual support the American government has provided for literary culture reveals some embarrassing but interesting things. Using the some forty-five authors of literary note (give or take a few depending on one's definition of "literary note") who have received some sort of government position, support, subsidy, or aid, we find in the first 35 years of our nation's life a rather minimal concern with the giving of specific government appointments to literary men. From 1789 to 1825, only Phillip Freneau (a translating clerk in the State Department), Joel Barlow (Consul to Algiers and Minister to France), and James K. Paulding (the Secretary of the Board of Navy Commissioners and Navy Agent for New York) received places in the Federal government structure. But beginning with the administration of John Quincy Adams, Jackson, and Van Buren—and with the institution of the spoils system—there is a gradual, steady build-up until during the Harrison-Tyler years alone, from 1841-1845, four separate appointments were made: Washington Irving (Minister to Spain), John Lathrop Motley (Secretary of the Legation at St. Petersburg), John Howard Payne (Consul to Tunis), and James McHenry (Consulate at Londonderry). Also in the years immediately preceding this period, public appointments were given to James Fenimore Cooper as Consul at Lyons (an appointment in name only), Paulding as Secretary of the Navy under Van Buren, Orestes Brownson as Marine Hospital steward at Chelsea, and Nathaniel Hawthorne as weigher and gager in the Boston Custom House.

But even this was only the beginning. From 1845 to 1881 literary men came increasingly to share the benefits of government patronage. Such diverse figures as John P. Kennedy, Samuel Goodrich, and Louisa May Alcott all worked for Federal salaries, and during the Lincoln-Johnson years (1861-1869), the high point of nineteenth-century patronage was reached. During this short period, eight literary men were given positions ranging from consul to clerk: William Dean Howells, the Consulate at Venice; Hinton Helper, the Consulship at Buenos Aires; R. H. Dana, the U. S. Attorney for the District of Massachusetts; Bret Harte, clerkships in the San Francisco surveyor-general's office and the San Francisco branch of the U. S. Mint; Walt Whitman, clerkships in the Army paymaster's office; Bayard Taylor, Secretary of the Legation in Russia; John Burroughs, clerk in the Treasury Department; and Herman Melville, inspector in the New York Customs House. Indeed, the experience of Melville, who finally obtained his meager appointment only after *five* serious and concentrated efforts during the twenty years from 1846 to 1866, constitutes one of the fascinating yet embarrassing chapters in the history of government literary patronage.

After the early part of the 1880's when President Garfield was assassinated by a disappointed spoils system office seeker and an effective Federal Civil Service was established under the Pendleton Act, there was a minimum of opportunity for an author to get any kind of government support. Scattered appointments like those of Lew Wallace as Minister to Turkey and Brazil; John Hay as Secretary of State under McKinley; or Thomas Nelson Page as Ambassador to Italy—along with Teddy Roosevelt's strange championship of the poet Edwin Arlington Robinson—were about the only breaks in the long dry spell from 1870 to 1933 and the advent of Franklin Roosevelt. The Roosevelt era marked a revitalization of the nation's official interest in its literary intellectuals. Aside from the many writers who benefited from the Federal Writer's Project (like Richard Wright, Conrad Aiken, John Steinbeck, etc.), five authors were recognized with Federal posts: Robert Herrick, Secretary of the Virgin Islands; Stephen Vincent Benet and Carl Sandburg, Office of War Information; and Robert Sherwood and Archibald MacLeish who between them held ten different jobs in the Roosevelt administration. Out of this renewed governmental concern for the welfare and the contribution of the literary man came the contemporary movement—under Truman, Eisenhower, Kennedy, Johnson, and Nixon—to recognize the place of literary culture in American life and to recognize that the government *has* a responsibility toward this aspect of culture as well as toward science.

Unfortunately, the lesson of all this past experience in government patronage is not immediately clear; much work remains to be done, work for which this paper is merely an outline. The specific circumstances surrounding each appointment, the attitudes of the officials responsible for the appointments and subsidies and the public pressures operating in each reflecting the public attitude in America toward the place of the writer in society must be all evaluated. The fascinating part is the realization that so many of our American writers have been involved in some way with Federal support: the embarrassing part is the realization that over all—and in comparison with most other countries of western civilization—the United States has given such miserly attention and largess to its literary sector.

NOTES

[1] *Congressional Record*, Feb. 27, 1968, pp. H 1400 - H 1438.

[2] Lyman Bryson, "Arts, the Professions, and the State," *Yale Review,* n. s. 36 (June 1947), 637.

[3] Gifford Phillips, *The Arts in a Democratic Society* (Santa Barbara, 1966), pp. 6-9.

[4] *New York Times Magazine* (11 March 1962), p. 26. Reprinted in Veneta Colby, ed., *American Culture in the Sixties* (New York, 1964), pp. 85-92.

The Artist and the Government: The P. W. A. P.

by

Joel H. Bernstein

With the Stock Market Crash of 1929 and the mass unemployment that hit the country, drastic changes took place in the relationship of the Government to the art community. By 1933, over 10,000,000 Americans were unemployed and the majority of the artists, who in good times were at best a marginally successful economic group, were exceptionally hard hit because of diminished private patronage. This was the more tragic because it was a period of exciting regional production and new interest in mural work that had been stimulated by the Mexican experiment that was started in 1926. At that time, Mexico, under the leadership of President Obregon, began to hire muralists at workmen's wages to decorate public buildings and the best murals of Jose Orozco and Diego Rivera resulted.

When the Depression hit America full force and the impetus toward relief for the artists got underway, Alfred Barr, Director of the Museum of Modern Art in New York, working through government officials, was a primary factor in bringing the idea that artists should have the same relief that other citizens were receiving and at every opportunity he promoted his plan. Finally Barr mentioned it to a young girl who was a member of the family of a cabinet member and she finally persuaded her parent to bring the matter to the attention of the President of the United States. At the same time, George Biddle, himself a prominent muralist and also a classmate of Roosevelt's at Groton and Harvard, wrote to the President in May, 1933,advocating murals as a means of communicating the ideals of American democracy and at the same time he championed government patronage of art.

Roosevelt generally endorsed the ideas expressed in Biddle's letter when he answered: "I am interested in your suggestion in regard to the expression of modern art through mural painting. I wish you would talk some day with Assistant Secretary of the Treasury Robert, who is in charge of the Public Buildings Work."

Conferences with Assistant Secretary L. W. Robert, Jr., artists and others concerned were arranged and by November 29, 1933 Secretary Robert released the following statement:

> Provisions for the encouragement of the fine arts has always been recognized as one of the functions of the Federal Government, and it is obvious that such provisions should be enlarged in times of depression. The work of artists and craftsmen greatly aids everyone by preserving and increasing our capacity for enjoyment, and is particularly valuable in times of stress. . . . We consider it a great pleasure to encourage the movement, and hope that it will promote the appreciation of art in our country. . . . We realize that the encouragement of art is a vital force in our civilization.

Robert's statement represented a sharp break with the past. The stage was set for the Government to join with the American artists, but it had taken a depression to bring the union about. A coordinating committee was organized to make Biddle's suggestion operative and in one fell swoop the United States Government had quickly taken an official position that attempted to wipe out the old stereotypes of the artist living in an attic, existing on inspiration and shunning society. The artist was now being brought into the mainstream of society with the administration in Washington lending a helping hand.

On December 8, 1933, a meeting was held at the home of Edward Bruce that added a new set of initials to the New Deal: P. W. A. P. (Public Works of Art Project). Attending the meeting, in addition to the committee, were Mrs. Franklin Delano Roosevelt, certain leaders in American art, particularly the leading museum directors, and Government officials.

George Biddle commented that until the time that the Government lent its support to art as it had just committed itself to do, neither "liberality nor intelligence had been shown by architects and governmental departments" when dealing with paintings and murals.

Before the December 8, 1933 meeting in Washington, Federal Emergency Relief Administration director Harry L. Hopkins had promised $1,039,000 of FERA money to get the Public Works of Art Project under way so that when the group met at Edward Bruce's home they had concrete material with which to begin their work and make plans.

The project was soon launched. It was decided to divide the nation into sixteen regional areas, each region with its own administrator. The object was to decentralize the program even though the co-ordinators and the main office were to be located in Washington, D. C. The local regional committees were to have sole voice in selecting the artists to be employed in their respective regions and Washington was to take no part in that aspect of the program. Conditions were to be set up so as not to "deflate their [the artist's] inspiration." The regional organizations were primarily concerned with embellishing Federal and other publically owned institutions and buildings such as Indian reservations, parks, public schools, hospitals, land-grant colleges, custom houses, municipal libraries, zoos, and other such public structures. The program was supposed to be temporary and it was essentially organized and initiated as a relief program. At the outset, for example, professional skills were secondary in importance to need, although a majority of the artists that were eventually employed had significant art experience. After the local committees were completed on December 12, 1933, Forbes Watson was appointed as technical director, which put him in charge of the esthetic details of the project, and Edward Bruce was selected as secretary of the Advisory Committee. He was responsible for the organization, distribution of funds, overall planning and could be considered P.W.A.P.'s chief executive. If one man can be singled out as the guiding spirit behind the seven month P.W.A.P., it was Edward Bruce.

In addition to his many accomplishments in government and business, Bruce was also widely known in art circles for his painting. Both as a business executive and eminent artist, Bruce was qualified for his role of leadership in the P.W.A.P. His understanding of art and artists enabled him to see clearly problems as they arose and solve them without being unsympathetic to either the administrative or creative elements of the Project.

In February, 1934, Edward Bruce was optimistic about the project and its ultimate success. He declared at that time that all of the regional chairmen and committees were unanimous in their enthusiasm for the project and they reported that excellent results were evident throughout the country. He added that no matter what the eventual outcome of the project would be, the P.W.A.P. would have a lasting effect on the cultural and artistic life of the United States. Even when Bruce made that statement, he already realized that the P.W.A.P. was instituted for a short duration to provide temporary relief to artists caught in the economic distress of the 1930's. In April, 1935, Congress, acting upon a suggestion from President Roosevelt, reorganized the entire works program and created the Works Progress Administration. The W.P.A. eliminated the Civil Works Administration and with the demise of C.W.A. went the P.W.A.P.

When the Public Works of Art Project was instituted, the organization was clear and precise. Forbes Watson, eminent writer and art critic, serving as technical chariman, together with Bruce, administered the grant from Harry Hopkins. The grant was free except for the following restrictions: all the money could only be spent for the purchase of art works and for salaries for the artists; and the work done by the artists on the federal payroll belonged to the Government and could be placed only in buildings supported by taxpayer's money.

The original grant was made on December 5, 1933 and with it went the proviso that it had to be spent by February, 1934, although a subsequent grant extended the deadline until April 28, 1934. The immediate goals of the program were to keep about 2,500 artists alive during the winter of 1933-1934 and at the same time to raise the morale of the art community. By December 20, 1933, 735 artists and three laborers had already been employed. These figures grew to 1,444 artists and 168 laborers. Every state in the Union was represented. Individual artists were paid within the range of $26.50 to $42.50 per week, depending on their skills, experience and particular project. From this salary they ordinarily paid for their own materials if these were relatively inexpensive but on occasion, when the cost of materials became so high that the artist was unable to purchase them and still take some money home, the individual community where the work was being done made the purchase. The pay scale was determined by the prevailing wage rate that was paid to skilled craftsmen who were employed by the Civil Works Administration.

By the end of December, 1933, over fifty mural projects were underway across the country in cities and towns including Dallas, San Antonio, Denver, Philadelphia, Pittsburgh, New Haven, Connecticut and Iowa City. By June, 1934, when the project finally was terminated, over 501 murals had been completed or were in their final state.

During the entire course of P.W.A.P., government control was kept at a minimum. At no time were artists coerced to do a particular type of work nor were they inhibited by rules or procedure which interfered with their artistic integrity. The general theme "The American Scene" was adopted to insure for the Government works of art that would "embellish" the public buildings and at the same time would give freedom to the artist to express himself as he wanted. The artist was permitted to work in the media of his choice. while the scope of the theme allowed the artist to "select from any phase of the life and setting of a vast country."

Once the subject was decided upon and submitted to the regional committee, the artist had complete technical freedom for the execution of the work. This was possible because the two criteria for the selection of a given artist to work in the Public Works of Art Project were first, his need for employment and second, his capabilities as an artist. While need was of primary importance, a particular artist of sculpture had to exhibit some advanced degree of skill in his chosen field of work. After the selection, the only technical control which the regional committee exerted was the approval or rejection of the artist's preliminary designs and sketches if the work under consideration was to be permanently affixed to a public building. This was of course a safeguard for the Government and at the same time it prevented the artists from embarrassing moments inasmuch as once the plans were approved, he then had the full support of his regional committee.

The project flourished from the beginning. It was greeted with enthusiasm from a great majority of people in the art world as well as from the public. A letter from Woodstock, Vermont arrived at the P.W.A.P. office in Washington that summarized much of the feeling:

> The spirit in which the artists in Woodstock are going at it, I am sure, pleases you very much, and makes you feel how worth while it is, as they are more than anxious to do their best and to produce things which will do them credit. We almost feel as if we had a new lease on life, as though suddenly we had a new incentive for existence.

Artists and communities all over the nation responded well. Because of the excellent co-operation, overhead expenses absorbed less than 5% of the funds and the money made available to P.W.A.P. by Hopkins and the C.W.A. went almost entirely to the payment of artists employed on the various projects.

The P.W.A.P. was not, however, without its critics. Controversial from the first, there were various points on which it was attacked. The main difference of opinion centered around what should be created and more specifically, in what style. At the very outset of the

Project, an editorial in *Commonweal* appeared hoping that "modern" art would not characterize the work done in the course of the P.W.A.P. Speaking of the artists, the editorial continued: "Perhaps artists with a few regular meals in prospect will see something in the American scene other than 'jazzmania,' unflattering likenesses of subway crowds already bad enough, barren-looking forms and distorted women."

As early as the first month of the program conservative artists and art groups involved in P.W.A.P. work protested that the Federal Government accorded an undo advantage to so-called "modern" artists." They complained that the long established art organizations had been severely slighted because they had not been consulted when the Public Works of Art Project was in its infant stages. Harry W. Watrous, president of the National Academy of Design, acting as an unofficial spokesman for the group of conservatives summed up the feeling. He stated that "such government action as placing the administration of an important appropriation into the hands of one specific art group lends an atmosphere of exploitation of so-called 'modern' art to the project."

Mrs. Juliana R. Force, director of the Whitney Museum of American Art and the chairman of the regional committee for P.W.A.P. in the New York area answered Watrous' charge. She stated that her instructions from the government were to "relieve artists in distress, not to promote any particular kind of art." The controversy became heated and widespread. Cartoons appeared in leading magazines but little if any change was made in selection of artists and no controls were added to accommodate the more conservative groups.

In retrospect there seems little or no evidence to support the contention that "modern artists" were favored in any way although a great deal of the work that resulted from the commissions issued by the Public Works of Art Project would have to be classified as modern or at least contemporary. This seems more the result of young artists searching for new directions than it does favoritism on the part of the regional selection committees of directives from Edward Bruce and Forbes Watson in Washington, D. C. Bruce himself entered into the debate as he summed up quite clearly the approach of his department when he addressed himself to the new work produced in the P.W.A.P. He concluded:

> While of course, it shows the signs of a definite art tradition and an art background, it is amazingly free from isms and fads and so-called modern influences. Ninety per cent of it is modern in the best senses. Any expression by an artist of the reaction on him of the world around him as it exists today is bound to be essentially modern. The word "modern" in connection with art has been badly misused. It conveys to the minds of most people merely invention which has been instituted for art in so many art centers.

It seems that the salient point to make concerning the debate between modern artists and the more conservative or traditional is that this was a feud that existed not only in America but throughout the world of art on an international level. The P.W.A.P., with its use of public funds, forced the controversy into the open for the public to witness.

There were other criticisms leveled at the new attempt to help distressed artists. When the Public Works of Art Project was first inaugurated in the New England area, there was a general hesitancy to participate because the policy at the very beginning was to accept artists more on the basis of need than on artistic ability. It started as "first come—first served" situation that caused many of the better artists to balk. After the program ran for a few weeks and the difficulties were smoothed out, quality became increasingly important in the selection of the recipients of the work commissions. With this change, New Englanders changed their attitude and the area became an active center for P.W.A.P. work.

From an entirely different point of view, young unrecognized artists in New York and Chicago accused the program of favoritism to "name" or well-known artists. C. J. Bulliet, art critic of the

Chicago *Daily News,* suggested that many of the best artists in the area were unknown and that they had become so disgusted at the "cynical, unconcealed favoritism shown to a particular group," that many of this group just refused to even apply for jobs in the Project. The implication here is that many of the unknown artists were superior to those more famous and that the Public Works of Art Project should have afforded them the opportunity to have their work seen and criticized. According to Bulliet and others, the Project was not doing this since they were sticking to the names that were safe and established.

One of the central issues in criticism of the Public Works of Art Project centered around the Government's role in art and what controls it would exhibit. An old issue in American history, it appeared again during the New Deal, not only in the field of art but in all areas of the new Roosevelt programs. The Baltimore *Sun,* in an article said: "These artists are natural Bolsheviki, and some morning the collectors of customs at Galveston, Texas will wake up to find, sown in the lower left-hand corner of a grand panorama, described as 'Roosevelt Leading the Rugged Individualists Out of the Wilderness,' a diminutive figure of a fat man named Hoover, fishing with one hand, and, with the other, thumbing his nose at the whole thing."

This article seemed to suggest that there should be control since the artists themselves could not be trusted. Their political views were attacked from what seems to have been a standpoint that was somewhat dated. The idea that all artists are radicals and revolutionists has virtually no substance in fact. The mention of Bosheviki and Communist propaganda is a theme that was expressed often during the Public Works of Art Project. It was, however, a constant club being wielded by some—those groups that actually feared the infiltration of American ideals by revolutionaries and also by those who constantly used it as an excuse to deride a program which they opposed for reasons other than political.

In actuality, the artists that were employed in the P.W.A.P. are hard to classify and certainly no generalizations can be made that would be valid for a majority except that they all had some serious art training.

The backgrounds were varied, the ages ranged from youth to maturity, and the skills covered a wide scope. Prominent names in the art world (Chaim Gross, Peter Blume, Grant Wood and Edward Bruce for example) participated in the same program with such unknown artists as Charles Campbell, Rinaldo Cuneo and Allen True.

There were many artists and critics who were skeptical that a program such as the Public Works of Art Project could be effective enough from a purely esthetic point of view to make it worthwhile. Vladimir Mostli, a leading artist from the Pittsburgh area, questioned the wisdom of the program:

> Suppose that among the boys and girls who go to work painting murals in public buildings, there are pre-Raphaelites and painters of nudes. What would it be like to have said painters of nudes putting a lot of the same on the walls of a school? Or the preRapahelites doing Diogenes in a barrel to remind the taxpayers that they are in the same?

Others criticized the program strictly from an esthetic point of view. This group was not particularly concerned with censorship or favoritism and while its members admitted that the P.W.A.P. helped to feed the hungry artists, they still felt that it did very little to help the development of art in the United States. Gilbert White, a prominent American painter who had taken up permanent residence in Paris, in an article appearing in the New York *Times,* was one of the very severe critics.

It is interesting to note the divergent views held by Mr. White and the art critic C. J. Bulliet. White claimed that the renowned artists were slighted in favor of young, inexperienced painters while Bulliet argued that the famous were shown favoritism at the expense of the young and talented. The evidence seems to indicate that both men were incorrect or correct to some degree because the Public Works of Art Project employed artists from both categories.

Nevertheless, there was a great deal of support from prominent to neophyte artists, critics, and art administrators for the type of patronage that P.W.A.P. supplied. The noted American sculptor, Jo

Davidson, had no fears that the artists would be hampered or controlled because they were employed by the Government. " 'Official art.' What was Greece, what was Egypt, what was India? Wasn't that official art?", Davidson asked. "Did it matter to the artist of India that Buddha had to be pictured with definite, immutable gestures? Does it make any difference that Venus de Medici had always to be portrayed the same way? That doesn't make all the Venuses alike. The greatness of some exists anyway."

To many, probably the majority of people involved in the art world, Davidson's analysis made good sense. The Government seemed to lean over backward in its efforts not to interfere in the selection of artists or in the work that they did, once they were selected to take part in the program. The P.W.A.P. had been created on the most decentralized lines possible to eliminate bureaucratic controls from Washington. The test of the project, of course, rested with time and the results could be gauged only after the P.W.A.P. had been under way, the products of the artists were examined, the artists themselves were questioned and the public's response was evaluated and clarified.

Several questions present themselves as one studies the history of the P.W.A.P. What changes did the Public Works of Art Project provoke in the art world? Of almost more importance, what response did it elicit from the American Public?

Always a difficult area to analyze because of its subjectivity, there are nevertheless several generalizations that can be made that are valid in a vast majority of cases. It is evident from even a casual perusal of the works produced that the American artists began to stay clear of "Greek ladies, with cheese cloth bound about their nipples, cluttered with scales, lambs, sheaves of wheat." No longer did the young artists of America draw Hellenic nudes representing the Spirit of American Motherhood, Purity and Democracy. The new subjects were vital parts of Americana: modern treatments of the stage, primitive art as it contrasted with the new contemporary work, the Uncle Remus cycle, recreational life, the C.C.C. camps, and areas that played a role in America's life. American industrial development provided subject matter as well as the cultural and physical environment. The industries of New Haven; Charles Goodyear and rubber; Brewster and carriages, Thomas Sanford and the match; industrial production, food production and agriculture; this was the new American art.

Forbes Watson commented that more than at any time during the Twentieth Century, as the Government embarked on the P.W.A.P., the American artists were contemplating the American scene. He felt that more than ever before they were looking at life around them so that the Government's project would ultimately result in a five native record.

Possibly the greatest and most enduring contribution of the Public Works of Art Project was that it made the public art-minded. The wall between the artist and the layman crumbled. No longer did art belong to the upper classes; there was a definite democratization. Since the previous patronage had come almost entirely from the American "aristocratic" section of the population that had a hold on the nation's "culture," P.W.A.P. tended to change this as the Government began to actively participate. A writer in the New York *Times* commented: "If the Public Works of Art Project accomplished nothing else, its permanent value would have been established by the fact that with one powerful blow it has undermined the altar of snobbishness and artificiality that had been erected to art." The public support for the program was evidenced by the fact that many local communities supplied all the materials so that the artist could receive maximum take home pay without a major layout for supplies. When the American public had the chance to meet and work with the American painters, muralists, sculptors, etchers and the others involved, new ideas and new understandings grew. Old stereotypes, false impressions and ignorance began to disappear. Artists proved eager and willing to cooperate in producing works for their neighbors; and the members of the communities were willing to work along with and encourage the artists. The wholesome relationships was solidified when the public learned that the creative artist, regardless of his stature or lack of it, was willing to receive honest wages instead of rewards for his talent. Productive achievements were possible because "the machinery existed, the talent existed, and the demand existed."

Mrs. Julian Force, in acknowledging that there was a great stimulus given to intelligent interest in art by the P.W.A.P., also managed to keep the scales balanced and her own enthusiasm in check when she admitted that there were some artists who stretched out their commissions beyond the period set for their completion in order to gain additional wages. However, she contended, and my research has concurred with earlier findings of April, 1934, that the vast majority of those employed by the Government during P.W.A.P., performed their tasks conscientiously.

In evaluating the Project in terms of its success or failure to the art community of the nation or the degrees somewhere between these polarized positions, one seeks the answers to two major questions: What benefits did the Public Works of Art Project give to the participating artists during the Depression and what aesthetically did the artists contribute to the public from their work under Government patronage?

The answer to the first question is readily apparent as one studies the statements by the artists themselves. Letters on file in the central office of P.W.A.P. from participating artists speak of the "restoration of morale, of renewed self-confidence, of the sense of being at last acknowledged as an important member of the social family, with a place in the economic system." Artists did not complain about their wages or the fact that they were dependent on the Government for their economic survival but rather they expressed gratitude for the employment. A great many artists actually considered it an honor to have been put on the Government payroll.

As the regional committees continued to do their excellent job of increasing the idea of public service, public works, and the obligations and duties of the Government to the public, artists and sculptors continued to submit overwhelmingly encouraging reports to Washington. Chaim Gross stated that until 1933 he had had a very difficult time surviving because of economic problems. But, "fortunately the Public Works of Art Project was organized at that time by Edward Bruce and this was a great material aid to me, as well as many of my friends."

The second question presents a somewhat more difficult

problem. Obviously any aesthetic evaluation is partially subjective and when this is introduced as evidence it lends itself to a solid barrage of criticism. Nonetheless, I believe that it is germane to go ahead and present the critical reviews of the P.W.A.P. work.

To think that the art produced during the period from December, 1933, to June, 1934 under the sponsorship of the United States Government was either all good or all bad would be naive and would indicate simple ignorance of the creative process. Besides the good, and there was much in that category, there was also an enormous amount of rubbish.

George Biddle, after viewing about two or three hundred examples of Project work that were in Washington, D. C., commented that he considered it "on a par with much of the French and American art exhibited at the very best New York dealers." He added that, "it must be remembered that much of the work is by young and unknown artists.

Quantitively a vast number of works were completed during the period of December, 1933 to June, 1934. The number of bas reliefs, drawings, oil paintings, tapestries, mosaics, batiks, frescoes and pieces of sculpture totaled 15,663. The final tabulation of cost for these works of art was $1,408,381 distributed among a total of 3,521 artists during the seven month period that the Public Works of Art Project was in existence.

Perhaps the climax for the P.W.A.P. was the show that was held at the Corcoran Galleries in Washington, D. C. in the spring of 1934. The show consisted only of works done by artists employed by the Project and it was very favorably received. Some of the most eminent critics in the nation not only praised the works and the artists, but they also mention with admiration and enthusiasm the program that enabled the Government to actively become a patron of the arts. Helen A. Read, art critic of the Brooklyn *Daily Eagle,* termed the show a "concrete and effective vindication of an idealistic experiment as the most sanguine promulgator of the project could have wished for." Albert Franz Cochrane of the Boston *Transcript* added that, "Given a reason for working, the artists of P.W.A.P. have produced creditably." The most glowing review, however, was one written by Edwin Alden Jewell, one of the most respected art critics in the nation, which appeared in the New York *Times*. He felt that the exhibition was impressive on several counts. It offered the spectator, he wrote, "a panorama that is nationwide in scope. Thus the fact that the P.W.A.P. is a national project attains appropriate dramatization. You feel the sweep and the breadth of the creative impetus the government has by this means provided. Another very gratifying aspect is its inclusion of so much conspicuously good work by artists as yet unknown. . . . Thirty-three states are represented, and the good things produced are well distributed."

The show itself was conspicuous for its lack of Goddesses, and the new emphasis on the subway, a beauty shop, show ladies fallen from Parnassus, industrial scenes, and the Western landscape. The old idealized visions of particular subjects was washed away by the new flow of vigor and youth.

There was some minor criticism of the Corcoran show in terms of money expended for the quality of the art produced but by and large this particular criticism was insignificant in terms of the general praise.

By June 30, 1934, the P.W.A.P. had run its course. Although it had been extended beyond its original deadline, the concept of work relief was destined to be absorbed by other organizations and thus funds were no longer allocated to that fairly isolated agency.

Even when the P.W.A.P. was officially ended some scattered censures from several parts of the country cropped up. In San Antonio, Texas, two P.W.A.P. murals in the city auditorium came under heavy fire from the American Legion because the Legion felt that the works included symbols of communism. The two murals to be painted at the Riker's Island Penitentiary was rejected by the Municipal Art Commission of New York City because it felt that the designs were "psychologically unfit" to be seen by the prisoners although the designs had been prepared in collaboration with trained penologists and members of the New York Commission of Correction together with Mayor La Guardia.

The P.W.A.P. received much criticism during its short life span, but it should always be remembered that it aided, for the first time in America's history, the Government's recognition of the social necessity of art. Not only did the Government recognize the same responsibility that it had formerly reserved for indigent plumbers and bricklayers, but it accepted a further responsibility to foster art and keep it alive during the period of economic distress in the 1930's.

In a more practical vein, the P.W.A.P. illustrated to the nation a lesson that the C. W. A. had also learned during its short existence. The idea that work relief was utilized in many other New Deal organizations. Also, the work relief, to be effective, had to be diversified in such a manner as to provide the various occupational groups jobs which were fitted to their particular training and experience.

After P.W.A.P. was terminated, the value of art to the community found new expression in the organization of the Section of Painting and Sculpture which was a part of the Treasury Department. The idea of the need for employing artists for work utilizing their individual professional skills was fostered and found expression in the Federal Art Project of the W. P. A.

In 1943, at the time of Edward Bruce's death, the New York *Times* summarized the view of many when it said the following about the P. W. A. P.

> Now and then the results were not altogether happy, but in the main competition kept the standard surprisingly high. It was a democratic process which unearthed much new talent.

Art For Whose Sake:
The Federal Music Project of the WPA

by

Neal Canon

In 1817 when Congress was considering the purchase of art to decorate the capitol, several representatives argued that "it is neither just nor proper for the government to become the patron of the fine arts; that no such expense ought to be authorized until the faith of the government was redeemed by the fulfillment of all its pecuniary obligations; nor, indeed until every debt was paid rising out of the War of the Revolution."[1] Resistance to government support of the arts has been as persistent as the national debt. In 1961 when a bill to establish a Fine Arts Council was presented, Representative Gross could not conceive of spending $100,000 for the arts when the nation already had a debt of $290 billion. Enough Congressmen agreed to kill the bill. That same year a $4 billion increase in the $40 billion defense budget sailed through Congress without a hitch. Government support of the arts is not in the American tradition.

Any politician can make political hay with a rollicking jibe at art—like Harry Truman's criticism of a painting included in the 1945 State Department overseas exhibit: "If that's art, I'm a Hottentot!"

But politicians are not just courting public favor. Their views concerning art are genuine and surely closer to popular taste than are the views of the art world. "I don't know much about art, but I know what I like" is the classic statement of American popular criticism. President Eisenhower gave his version of this adage when commenting on the inclusion of Jack Levine's irreligious painting of an overstuffed general in the Moscow Art Exhibit of 1959. He stated that the next selection committee for such an international show should have "one or two people that, like most of us here, are not too certain exactly what art is, but know what we like and what America likes."[2] Eisenhower's statement may not have had the charm of Mark Twain's: "It is a gratification to me to know that I am ignorant of art," but it does express a grass roots attitude that has to be reckoned with in the relationship between government and the arts. When a democratic government gets involved in the arts, the result will reflect popular tastes and attitudes.

What is revealed in any contact between government and the arts is the tremendous gulf which separates the world of the fine arts from the masses. Many observers of the American cultural scene see the split between the "high, private arts" for the few and the "popular arts" for the masses as the most important topic for concern in the arts today. This problem is neither distinctively American nor contemporary, and indeed it is doubtful that even those civilizations most admired for cultural or aesthetic unity, Greek civilization, for example, ever achieved an ideal integration of art and society. But attitudes toward the place of the arts in contemporary American culture are at a point of crisis. The term "cultural pluralism," often used to describe the complexity of the American scene, may well be only a euphemism for a culture in chaos. Attitudes of the artist toward society range in endless variation from hostility—"The masses be damned"; condescension—"perhaps a limited audience can be educated to appreciate my work"; arrogance—"if its popular it must be bad"; indifference—"like man, I'm just doing my thing"; to vague social awareness—"of course all art depends upon an audience." Aesthetics and criticism today are doing little to clarify the relationship between the artist and society.

Missing from the current diversity of attitude is any strong feeling for the social significance and grounding of art. It is doubtful that any serious evaluation of the American scene could even consider the possibility of cultural unity—a climate in which the creativity of artists, writers, and musicians both flows from and contributes to the society as a whole. In fact few American artists or critics would find this an important field of concern. Looking at this in historical perspective, one can see that a significant transformation has taken place in the last thirty years. In the 1930's, artists and critics were vitally concerned with cultural unity and the social nature of art—a climate directly linked to the liberal philosophy and spirit of the New Deal.

In the New Deal period, government's interposition as a third element in the relationship between art and society revealed basic conflicts in aesthetic theory which are unresolved today. Both *l'art pour l'art* and the Genteel Tradition were seriously challenged in the wave of cultural nationalism and social significance which characterized the New Deal era. In the Federal Arts Projects philosophies and attitudes had to be matched with political, economic, and social realities. And attitudes toward the relationship between art and society, carried out in practice in the Arts Projects, had to face the scrutiny of the government and the public.

The Federal Arts Projects were established in 1935 as a part of President Roosevelt's new relief program to be administered under the Works Progress Administration. They were not seen as programs of federal support for the arts, but rather as an integral part of the relief program. There were, after all, musicians, artists, writers, and actors on the breadlines as well as bricklayers and office workers. Six months after the inception of the program, more than 40,000 unemployed artists, writers, musicians, and theater workers were at work.

The roots of a problem which was to plague the projects throughout their history can be seen in the Administrative Order establishing the program. It states that the two-fold purpose for the Projects was "(1) to provide proper employment for unemployed eligible artists, musicians, theater workers and writers, and (2) to provide valuable service to the community." The latter could be accomplished in two ways:" (a) by producing works or presenting performances which meet professional standards for the benefit of the community, and (b) by promoting and conducting among residents of the community such leisure-time activities as will increase their participation in music, art, literature, and drama." This is further qualified: "In-so-far as possible, priority should be given to work in professional pursuits, especially where such is the desire of the eligible workers. However, workers in this program may engage as leaders in their respective fields in recreation and leisure time program . . . ."[3]

There are a number of problems apparent in this statement. It infers that a musician or artist working in a recreation or leisure-time education program is *not* engaged in a professional pursuit, and that he *is* being a professional artist or musician when he is "producing works or presenting performances which meet professional standards." Professionalism requires a certain distance between artist and audience. "Producing works and presenting performances" provides this distance; "increasing participation" through leisure-time activities does not. The phrase "where such is the desire of the eligible worker" acknowledges that artists and musicians do not traditionally think in terms of serving the community.

A Federal Music Project manual[4] prepared by Dr. Nicolai Sokoloff, Director of the Project, further emphasizes professionalism: "The general purpose of the Music Project will be to establish high standards of musicianship, to rehabilitate musicians, and to educate the public in an appreciation of musical opportunities." This last phrase says more than its author intended. It provides the key to understanding a prevalent idea concerning the relationship between art and society.

A situation in the Massachusetts Project illustrates how the conflict between professionalism and community service made itself felt. When quota reductions were ordered in September of 1936, Louis Cornell, State Director, objected to Sokoloff's demanded cuts in the "outstate" units rather than in Boston. Re-auditions had been ordered and several outstate small orchestras and choruses were completely disbanded. Cornell objected to this policy on the basis of service to the community. He pointed out that the FMP organizations in cities such as Springfield in western Massachusetts were providing the only music in the entire area, while Boston already had many music opportunities. Sokoloff defended his position strictly on the basis of professionalism: the Boston units were the most competent musically and should be retained for that reason. A check of the national performance statistics for any given month will show that professional competence and size of the musical organization could not be equated with service to the community. For example, in January of 1938, the Omaha Symphony Orchestra, a modest unit of 38 musicians, presented 75 concerts during the month to a combined audience of 27,000; in New York City two federal orchestras, each with approximately 100 musicians, gave only 5 concerts to a total of 8,158.

But the Massachusetts incident did not end with Sokoloff's decision to cut the western Massachusetts units. In the months that followed the cuts and Cornell's dismissal, the Washington office was flooded with letters of protest. Some were addressed to the Director, others came through the WPA Administrators, others were channeled through Massachusetts' Senators and Representatives, and others came directly to the White House. The letters were unanimous in protesting the unfairness of the cuts in outstate Massachusetts. By March, 1937, pressures had been brought to bear from the right places—though it is impossible to tell just where—re-auditions were ordered, and approximately 250 musicians were reinstated.[5]

At a regional convention of the FMP in Boston, June, 1938, Sokoloff gave a speech which further reveals the conflict between professionalism and community service.

> There is a very strong criticism toward our particular project. The government has felt that we have done many splendid things but we have somehow failed to make it more of a community participation. They feel we have not stressed enough what is known as "social music." By social music they may mean one thing,

> thinking another. I believe social music in the true sense, is when qualified able musicians perform the works of art in such a way that it is made indispensable to every man, woman, and child. . . .I do not think it is our business to participate with every Tom, Dick, or Harry who has no musical ability. It is our duty to clarify in our own mind and to classify our communities and the efforts of the communities by the professional and the non-professional.[6]

It is extremely important to note that Sokoloff indicates that the pressure for more "social music" came from the government. The earlier "case study" of the Massachusetts incident shows how public opinion and government influence can be related.

Sokoloff reacted to government pressure toward social music by redefining social music in terms of his concept of professionalism. In doing this he affirms a traditional attitude which holds that only "works of art" have real significance. There is only one music, fine art music, and that "our duty" is to see that community participation (in which someone might actually find enjoyment and fulfillment in learning to play the banjo) is kept in its place—the "non-professional." This, as well as his earlier statement "to educate the public in an appreciation of musical opportunities," links Sokoloff directly with the Genteel Tradition. It would be impossible to fully explore this tradition here, but two statements by Daniel Gregory Mason, of the Boston Masons, composer and critic, will show its significance for this situation.

In an article, "Democracy and Music,"[7] Mason deplores the French Revolution's producing a mass "primitive" audience which through its demands for sensation fostered the trends of program music and impressionism—trends which debase true music. "How could it be otherwise," he concludes. "Enlightened minds and hearts, we must remember, are the finest and rarest fruits of civilization, to be cultivated only under conditions of decent leisure, fair physical and mental health, and free association with 'the best that has been done and thought in the world.' " In another article Mason quotes Emerson: "The masses are rude, lame, unmade, pernicious in their demands and influence and need not to be flattered but to be schooled. . . Masses—the calamity is the masses." Mason then comments: "We need to revise some of our ideas about popular education, especially about the relation of the masses to the arts. . . . Why not stop leading unthirsty horses to the water? They only muddy it."[8] Two aspects of the Genteel Tradition as reflected in Mason's attitude are important for understanding Sokoloff's position: a narrow definition of what qualifies as music (Mason couldn't even accept Debussy, to say nothing of a banjo tune) and no coddling of the masses.

In the same speech in Boston, Sokoloff announced that the government was appointing a new assistant for the FMP for the development of folk music and recreation aspects of the program—the government's solution for creating more community participation. The man chosen, Charles Louis Seeger, had been music director of the Resettlement Administration and vice-chairman of the Joint Committee on Folk Art. Seeger, who was firmly grounded in Marxist aesthetics, had taught at the New School for Social Research and had written the music articles for the *Encyclopedia of the Social Sciences.* He was one of America's most highly regarded musicologists. One of his first projects with the FMP was the preparation of a manual, *Music as Recreation,*[9] which attempted to reconcile some of the differences between professionalism and community service.

It goes without saying that Seeger's views differed sharply from those of Sokoloff. In the recreation manual Seeger comments that "the professional musician had rather rejoiced in the removal of his own experiences from the reach of the average man and has considered a moderate amount of frightening of unskilled beginners as in the long run a good thing." He also suggests that professional cant had nearly persuaded America that music (meaning fine art music) was an esoteric mystery, but he sees some hope with the "reassertion of the manly arts of banjo, guitar, and harmonica playing, and of ballad singing."

Seeger directly refuted the ideas that fine art music represents the ultimate value in music and that music is the universal language. He holds that music is subdivided into many musics and that "when it comes to the sub-divisions (of idiom), it is a question whether the musical 'dialect' of various localities and of various income levels are not more unintelligible to other than their possessors than are the various dialects of speech." He would not accept the traditional concept which would call only one dialect good music. He rather asks: "Good for whom? Good for what?"

Seeger believed that some degree of accord could be reached between social music and fine art music, and challenges musicians to show that "the broadening of interests and of social and cultural contacts can grow out of the intensive cultivation (professionalism) of music skills." The substance of Seeger's philosophy is contained in his belief that there must be "less regard for music as an end in itself and more as a social function."[10]

The conflict in the Federal Music Project between professionalism and community service is a somewhat veiled manifestation of the larger issue of "art for art's sake" versus the social or non-autonomous theory of art. "Veiled" because "art for art's sake" was passé in the 1930's; liberalism and social consciousness had taken over. No one in the 1930's said "the masses be damned." But in musical thought, the substance of the art for art's sake philosophy lingered. Elie Seigmeister noted in 1938 that "while in literature the Ivory tower, art for art's sake theory is no longer accepted, this concept still prevails with regard to music, which is still considered as largely a vague intangible experience unrelated to all other experience."[11] As the most abstract of the arts, music is least susceptible to non-aesthetic evaluation. Poetry and painting are traditionally bound to meaningful content, but music by its very nature tends toward autonomy. While there seemed to be no serious alternative to "social theater" in the Federal Theater Project, the Federal Music Project had difficulty in meeting the thrust of social consciousness which characterized the New Deal era.

Criticisms of the various Art Projects seem inconsistent, but they merely illustrate the differences which exist in the arts. Because music is abstract and not tied to meaningful content, the Music Project avoided most of the charges of Communist and New Deal propaganda brought against the Theater and Art Projects. It would seem that the art and theater projects were being criticized for *too much* social consciousness. Federal Theater productions such as *The Living Newspaper, Power, The Revolt of the Beavers,* and *One Third of a Nation* were scorching in their social commentary. *Injunction Granted,* a play depicting labor's disputes with the courts, drew huge crowds, partly because labor union locals bought large blocks of tickets for their members.[12] Marc Blitzstein's *The Cradle Will Rock,* a work of vigorous social criticism cast and rehearsed by Federal Theater, is recognized as the most important work in the American musical theater before 1945–comparable in importance to Kurt Weill's *Dreigroschenoper.* The productions at Federal Theater were constantly criticized by the conservative press and the New Deal opposition.

Even the WPA leadership had difficulty in defining proper community participation and social concern. At the very time that Sokoloff and the Federal Music Project were being criticized for lack of community participation and social music, Hallie Flanagan, director of the Theater Project was called on the carpet by WPA officials concerning the newspaper published by the project. "Wasn't there too much emphasis on the poverty of the Federal Theater audiences, too many pictures of shirt-sleeved crowds in the city parks? Wasn't the Federal Theater magazine being sold at worker's newsstands?"[13] Later, the Dies Committee's charges of Communist domination of Federal Theater led to the closing of that Project. The Federal Theater was being *too* effective in its social concern, in bringing relevant, vital theater to a mass audience.

Undoubtedly the difference between the Music Project and the other arts projects can be traced, at least partially, to the relative lack of creative activity in the Music Project. The Federal Theater Project, although also a performing art project, produced chiefly original plays rather than standard repertory. The Art Project was, of course, basically a project for creative artists–muralists, easel painters, and sculptors. The first objective of the Music Project was to provide employment for *performing* musicians. This in itself chiefly precluded creative activity. The conservative nature of orchestral musicians and of concert hall tradition is well known and is certainly inimical to innovation.

The Music Project did get involved indirectly with composers and creative activity through the Composers' Forum-Laboratories. Although the forums employed performing musicians, they were organized primarily for the purpose of bringing out new works by contemporary American composers. It is significant that in this one aspect of the Federal Music Project which did involve the composer, nationalism and the social significance of art became prominent issues just as they were in the other projects. The activity of these forums indicates that social significance and the social nature of art pervaded the entire cultural scene.

A unique characteristic of the Composers' Forum-Laboratory was the confrontation which occurred between composer and audience in the open forums which followed the musical performance. The New School for Social Research in New York City had instituted composers' forums before the opening of the Federal Music Project, but the FMP took over the New York Forum and started new forums in more than a dozen cities across the nation. A lively audience was assured for the New York Forum with the New School background and with the director of the Forum, Ashley Pettis, fresh from a position as music editor of *The New Masses.*

Topics which continually recur in the transcripts of the forums are "social significance" and nationalism. When Marion Bauer was asked, "Do you approve of nationalism in music?", she replied that it seemed a forum evening would not be complete without that question. She continued: "I do not believe that we can say music is not American because it does not reflect the Negro, Cowboy, Indian, or our Plains. What do people expect? What do they want? What is 'American'?" Miss Bauer's somewhat defensive "What do people expect?" indicates a relationship with her audience and the public which is somewhat threatening to her. The questions and comments from the audience were penetrating and insightful.

In another session Werner Josten was criticized for his Neo-Classicism: "Do you feel that your compositions would be more significant if their inspiration came from events of our times? How do you reconcile your mode of expression with contemporary life?"

Following the performances of Ruth Crawford's difficult experimental works for string quartet, a member of the audience asked, "Why is your music so difficult to grasp? Do you really believe that your music is the future music of America?" Another asked, "Won't you please write some music that a greater number of people can listen to? This seems like music for the very few." To the latter question Miss Crawford replied, "I will, I have become convinced during the past two years that my next music will be simpler to play and to understand. But at the same time we should not forget that it is also important to write for the very few."[14] There was undoubtedly a profound influence upon the composers in the discovery that an audience had some interest in what they were doing and was looking for vital, meaningful music.

At times composers were the object of bitter attack from the audience; conservatives fared little better than experimentalists. At a Boston Forum, one composer who had reached his prime before the turn of the century was taking a lot of heckling from the audience. As was often the case, the criticism concerned relevance, social significance, and an outdated idiom. Finally he could take no more and exclaimed: "I would like you to know that I believe in God, I believe in the sanctity of the home, I believe in the Constitution of the United States, and by thunder, I believe in the C Major triad."

The interest of the audience was noted by the composers, and many of them commented on the musical atmosphere of the concerts. Virgil Thomson's comments to Ashley Pettis, New York Forum director, are not untypical:

> The concert of my works at the Composers' Forum-Laboratory was a great pleasure to me. An enthusiastic audience is always a pleasure to a performer. In this case, the enthusiasm was of a particular lively kind. Not the mass-reaction (commonly known as an ovation) that simply means the audience has been wowed. But a more vivacious participation that means a communication has taken place. . . .
>
> I fancy, also, that the mixture of music with informal

> talk about it has a good deal to do with the liveliness of your audience. Speech relieves the tension of musical listening. It is like cleaning out the mouth with a cracker in wine-tasting.[15]

There is abundant evidence that the issues which were prominent in the Federal Music Project were significant in the whole musical scene. Aaron Copland, writing in *Our New Music,* explains how social consciousness was translated into a stylistic movement:

> The only new tendency discernible in the music of the past ten years can be traced to this feeling of dissatisfaction on the part of composers at the lack of any healthy relationship with their potential public. As a result, two steps were taken: First, many composers tried to simplify their musical language as much as possible, and second, they attempted not only to make contact with audiences in the concert hall, but to seek out music listeners, and performers wherever they are to be found.[16]

Copland describes his composition from 1935 through World War II as in a style of "imposed simplicity," meaning "self-imposed." With a majority of major American composers in the 1930's (Copland, Harris, Thomson, Blitzstein, Cowell) developing toward simplicity, nationalism, and social consciousness, a purely stylistic trend was established which was then picked up by dozens of young composers in the late '30's and the war years, many of them quite unaware of the social, economic, and political origins of the movement.

In aesthetic theory, "art for art's sake" versus the social nature of art has been a central conflict for more than a century. Arnold Hauser states:

> *L'art pour l'art* indubitably represents the most involved problem in the whole field of aesthetics. Nothing expresses so acutely the dualistic, spiritually divided nature of the artistic outlook. Is art its own end or only a means to an end?. . . The purpose of

> the work of art constantly wavers between these two points of view, between an imminent being, detached from all reality beyond itself, and a function determined by life, society, and practical necessity. [17]

American culture had never been dominated by the extremes of this duality—the aestheticism of Walter Pater and Oscar Wilde, or modern Marxist aesthetics. It may seem incongruous to attempt to draw any significant conclusion in regard to this duality from the mundane circumstances of the Federal Music Project, but the professionalism-community service conflict reveals this problem in a concrete situation.

One of the objectives of the Federal Arts Projects was to provide "service to the community" through "creating works or presenting performances which meet professional standards." A professional musician, like Nicolai Sokoloff, is faced with a dilemma when he is confronted with the possibility that the community is not being served even when the musician is presenting the highest professional standards. But if the aesthetic tendency is toward art for art's sake, professional standards must come first. Professionalism implies that the ultimate value in art is in the work of art itself. In the final analysis, whether or not the community is served, whether or not there is an audience or public is unimportant—even when the political circumstances dictate that one must say that it is.

When Sokoloff gave his definition that "social music in the true sense is when works of art are performed in such a way that they are made indispensable to every man, woman, and child," he is merely stating his faith that true art conquers all. And it is obviously a blind faith, completely out of touch with reality. Each year thousands or hundreds of thousands of people hear great works of musical art performed by the greatest orchestras, opera companies, and soloists, to little or no effect. The attitude could be compared to the medieval doctrine, *ex opere operato,* concerning the efficacy of the Sacrament—one merely needs to be in the presence of the Sacrament for it to work its grace. When the artist or professional musician perceives that his "great art" does not always work its effect, he faces a crisis. Art for art's sake at the full (aestheticism) is one answer. In 1939 when the lofty ideals of the Music Project were brought into question and political pressures began to build up, Dr. Sokoloff felt he must resign as director of the project. If standards of professionalism could not be maintained, there was no hope for any real value in the Music Project.

The cultural climate of the New Deal did not support art for art's sake. Professionalism, as Sokoloff interpreted it, could not meet the social thrust of the era. When Copland stated that the only new trend of significance in American Music in the 1930's was the composer's concern for his audience he was voicing the central concern of all of the arts in that period—a concern for social significance. Interestingly, this was the *avant garde* movement of the decade. One writer comments that the "intellectual and spiritual climate (of the New Deal) was Roosevelt's general attitude that the *people mattered*."[18] This translated into aesthetic theory would give "art for life's sake" or "art for the people's sake," not "art for art's sake." A chorus from Marc Blitzstein's *The Cradle Will Rock* sets the proper tone:

> And we love Art for Art's sake,
> It's smart for Art's sake
> To part for Art's sake
> With your heart for Art's sake
> And your mind for Art's sake
> Be blind for Art's sake
> And deaf for Art's sake
> and dumb for Art's sake
>
> Until for Art's sake
> They kill for Art's sake
> All the Art for Art's sake.[19]

NOTES

[1]Ralph Purcell, *Government and Art* (Washington, D. C., 1956), p. 15.

[2]Frank Getlein, "Politicians as Art Critics," *New Republic* (July 27, 1959), p. 11.

[3]*WPA Bulletin 29, Supplement No. 1* (September 30, 1935).

[4]*Federal Music Project Manual: Preliminary Statement of Information* (October, 1935).

[5]Record Group 69, FMP Files, WPA State Series, Massachusetts, 651.311. Record Group 69, in the National Archives, Washington, D. C., contains the voluminous documentary material on all the Federal Arts Projects.

[6]"Report of Regional Conference" found in George Foster's unpublished collection of materials on the Federal Music Project held in the Music Division of the Library of Congress.

[7]*Musical Quarterly,* III (October, 1917), p. 649.

[8]"The Depreciation of Music," *Musical Quarterly,* XV (January, 1929), p. 13. These statements both come from the decade prior to the depression; not even D. G. Mason was to express this view so blatantly in the 1930's.

[9](May 1940) Published as Community Service Circular #1, WPA Technical Series.

[10]The quotes by Seeger in the preceding paragraphs are from his "Music as Recreation."

[11]*Music and Society* (New York, 1939), p. 9.

[12]Jane de Hart Mathews, *The Federal Theater 1935-1939* (Princeton, 1967), p. 112.

[13]Mathews, p. 127.

[14]It is an interesting sidelight to note that Miss Crawford's String Quartet was written in 1931, but had not been performed because of its extreme difficulty. The hours and days of rehearsal put in by the Forum Quartet can seldom be available to the composer.

[15]The above quotes are all from transcripts of the Composers' Forums Transcripts." Found in Record Group 69; WPA, FMP Files, *Miscellaneous, "Composers' Forum Transcripts."*

[16](New York, 1941), p. 118.

[17]*The Social History of Art* (New York, 1951), p. 732.

[18]Frances Perkins, in Schlesinger, *The Politics of Upheaval* (Boston, 1960), p. 652.

[19]In Wilfred Meller's *Music and Society*, (London, 1950), p. 218.

The FWP and the Popular Press*

by

Esther K. Birdsall

When a writer in the *Washington Post,* (October 26, 1969) stated that the National Council of the Arts represents the first Federal financial involvement in the arts, he was either betraying his youth or lack of homework or both. Had he never heard, for example, that the Federal Writers' Project (FWP) spent 27,189,370 dollars to fill seven twelve feet shelves in the library of the Department of the Interior[1] with publications ranging from the state guides to pamphlets of regional interest? Or was he reflecting the idea expressed by Ralph M. Easley, Chairman of the Executive Council of the National Civic Federation that the FWP was riddled with inefficiency, controlled by the Communists and that its ranks were swelled with persons who had never published and who contributed to the general unproductiveness of the project?[2]

The FWP was in many respects a complex organization charged with providing relief to unemployed writers, researchers, newspaper reporters, and white collar workers.[3] Under the original direction of Henry G. Alsberg, this army of workers was to collect information for the projected five volume American Guide. State and city guides were to be by-products of this collecting effort begun in 1935. Interestingly enough, the five volume work never materialized but before Lyle Saxon presided over the funeral of the FWP, which had undergone a change of name by then, in 1943 (*Time,* February 15, 1943), each state had had a guide. In addition to the state and many city guides, the FWP was responsible for such best sellers as *A New England Hurricane,* books on Negroes, and excellent off-beat works like *Who's Who in the Zoo.*

An organization charged with the dual task of providing relief and producing copy which commercial publishers would print naturally provoked much controversy. This controversy is reflected in the many reviews and articles that appeared during the turbulent existence of the FWP. Press problems appeared early, for collecting the information needed for the guide books took time and unlike a mural of the Federal Arts Project could not be produced overnight. It was therefore necessary to release bits and pieces of this collecting activity before the first FWP publications appeared. Most of these press releases were innocuous enough, but the story that Captain John Smith was the first American slave trader by having sold an English boy to the Indians in 1609 aroused the nation's ire and particularly that of the state of Virginia. The popular press lost no time in reporting the reaction to this debunking of a popular hero.

According to the *Washington Post* (February 21, 1936), "The City of Norfolk, Va., is regarded as good New Deal territory. But when WPA boondogglers begin debunking Captain John Smith, a Virginia hero, that is something else." According to the news item, the Norfolk Advertising Board asked Senator Harry F. Byrd and Repr. Colgate W. Darden, Jr.,"to protest to WPA about the story, charging that it libeled a romantic figure and was not warranted by the facts." Darden agreed that there was no factual evidence of the slave trading. *The Washington Herald's* account of the Smith release on the same date added another unfavorable image to the FWP thus: "The 1,500,000 WPA writers' project entrusted with the job of compiling an 'American Baedecker' was under fire on two fronts yesterday. Closely following a protest to President Roosevelt on the appointment of Katherine Kellick, wife of the Soviet Embassy's publicity director, to the post of field supervisor, patriotic societies in Virginia were up in arms, charging the 'debunking' of Captain John Smith."

Finance and Commerce of Minneapolis (January 20, 1936) changed the suggested release headline "Sold Down the River" to "John Smith Deglamorized" and printed the release with no editorial comment other than "It could be true." *The Ogden Standard Examiner* (February 21, 1936) ran the release as a three paragraph story that focused on Smith's relationship with Pocahontas as indicated by the headline "Pocahontas Thought Smith Wasn't So Hot." On the other hand, the *Worcester Evening Gazette* as late as May 19 ran an editorial asking the FWP to take it easy on debunking national figures. It concluded, "Many people may be found to say that a good legend is worth more even than a guide book."

From these few examples, it can be seen that even before the first state guide appeared, the FWP made good copy. Charges of boondoggling and Communist infiltration, along with inefficiency and wastefulness, would be leveled again and again.

However, thanks to the energy and talent of Vardis Fisher, the first state guide, *Idaho: A Guide in Word and Picture* appeared early in 1937. All the reviews preserved in the National Archives and in the manuscript division of the library of Congress[4] praised the work highly, and gave the FWP some favorable publicity.

Shortly after the Idaho guide, *Washington: City and Capital* appeared. As the guide to the nation's capital, it was widely reviewed. According to the *New York Times Book Review* (April 25, 1937), it was an excellent guide except for its weight, "so heavy, in sheer bulk, that it would be a considerable load to carry even as far as the train. It weighs nearly 5½ pounds. Samson himself would hesitate to go sight-seeing with such a burden as that." (The Samson reference found its way into a number of subsequent reviews.) However, the *Times* reviewer also noted that "The chapter on the Negro Quarter of the city and Negro life in Washington shows, close to the beginning of the book, that the authors are not afraid to look at some of the less cheerful aspects of the national capital."

When compared with the Idaho guide, however, the Washington

guide did not fare too well. According to the literary editor of the *Cleveland Press* (May 15, 1937), there was grave danger that the inferior Washington guide rather than the superior Idaho volume would become the model for future guides. Besides being too heavy "even for reading in an easy chair," the volume did not contain illustrative photography. Also, "the . . . text of the Washington book [compared with that of *Idaho*] is stylistic hodge-podge. Some of the writing is pretty good. Some—like the chapter on 'Literature in Washington'—is as bad as such gets." He concluded his review with "The WPA Washington book should make a pretty good door-stopper."

Jay Lewis in *The Norfolk Ledger-Dispatch* (June 14, 1937) also deplored the weight of the Washington Guide when he wrote, "it . . . is about as inviting as an official report and so heavy as to be utterly unfit for warm weather reading." More important is his observation "If anything, it proves that nobody in the Government Printing Office, not yet the W.P.A. knows much about the book publishing business . . . ." Lewis was echoing the suspicions of many reviewers and readers who did not realize that the bulk of the guide was due to its having been printed on glossy paper, a process that resulted from some misunderstanding of directions on the part of the government printing press personnel. Nor did Lewis and others point out to their readers that future guides would be published commercially.

Another achievement of the FWP in 1937 was the appearance of several New England guides published by Houghton, Mifflin. These publications gave pause to some of the detractors of the program. As early as September 1, 1937, *The New Republic* had reminded the reactionaries that publishers simply do not buy manuscripts for books which do not sell. The fact that publishers were publishing work of the FWP refuted "their [the reactionaries'] charges of boondoggling, hurled at the project." How many reactionaries read *The New Republic* is difficult to ascertain, but it should be pointed out that this publication, though not exactly a popular one in any sense of the work, was the most consistent champion of the FWP during its controversial existence.

However, the appearance of the commercially published New England guides was not an unmixed blessing. Governor Charles F. Hurley of Massachusetts who had written a glowing introduction to the Massachusetts guide became incensed when he learned that the compilers had indicated a miscarriage of justice in the Sacco-Vanzetti case. Furthermore, he was not too happy with the section devoted to labor conditions in his state. His outrage precipitated an act that would limit the freedom of subsequent FWP publications. According to this act, a special policy editor was to be placed in the Washington office whose task it was to review "all copy and remove all material deemed impolitic and offensive," (*The Nation*, December 24, 1938). Another hampering effect of Hurley's reaction was the need for "state clearance, often political and obtainable at considerable sacrifice." Jarel Putnam, the author of the article in *The Nation,* also foresaw that the policies would initiate a drop in the quality of the guides. There would be a tendency "to conform to a stereotype, to freeze into a hard-and-fast form, all material clipped and fitted by formula." Unfortunately, Putnam's last prediction was in many respects fulfilled. One need consult only the folklore sections of some of the guides to see some of the local legends emerge as a homogeonized mess.

Although the four New England guides were generally favorably reviewed, and without too much comment on the Sacco-Vanzetti treatment, they precipitated two discussions in *The Saturday Review of Literature* which raised some provocative questions about the objectives of the state guides. The first review (September 25, 1937) began with a number of states' objections against some of the guides, such as the chapter on labor conditions in Massachusetts. However, the reviewer continued . . . "we have never felt a pressing need for a chapter on labor relations in a tourist guide." He felt that readers consulted the guides to find out where things, like the House of Seven Gables are. He deplored the fact that the guides "are all too cluttered up with our cultural heritage." In fact, he went so far as to say that the WPA had published no guide books in the real sense of the word and concluded, "It isn't a guidebook if you have to leave it in the car." Similar sentiments appeared in a review of the New

England guides, May 14, 1938. The reviewer began with some questions about the FWP in general and concluded that Washington never really understood what it wanted. In his opinion, guidebooks and "a summons to a finer way of life" were incompatible. It is regrettable that these two reviews did not generate some additional examinations of the aims of the guides which included the dissemination of culture, stimulating the economy by encouraging travel, and keeping thousands of white collar workers off the dole. However, it is obvious that the FWP's role as a purveyor of culture was most open to debate.

But the New England guides, especially on the regional level, were attacked for their inaccuracies. A typical regional attack appeared in *The Concord Daily Monitor* and *New Hampshire Patriot* (March 25, 1938). "It is pitiful," the review began, "that substantial expenditures of taxpayers' money should be spent in publication of a collection of inaccuracies in the name of 'New Hampshire–A guide to the Granite State.' " After several critical comments on the introductions, the reviewer gleefully cited such inaccuracies as the incorrect address of the museum of the New Hampshire Historical Society.

City guides also received mixed reviews. *The New Orleans City Guide,* one of the pioneers in the city series, was very favorably reviewed, even when the reviewer had some reservations about the FWP (*Baltimore Sun,* April 3, 1938). Interestingly enough, the New Orleans guide like the earlier Idaho guide was produced under the firm editorial guidance of a popular writer, Lyle Saxon. The guide's remarkable accuracy is attested to by the fact that most reviewers could find only one omission: the birthplace of Brander Matthews, whose home bore the plaque of his birthday, 1852. By and large, reviewers dwelled on the exotic portions of the work, such as Mother Catherine's "anointin uv de innards" cult.

New York Panorama, another city guide published in 1938, had many unfavorable reviews. A critical notice entitled "Made Literatûre" in the *Herald Tribune* (September 14, 1938) assailed not only the cost (45,000 dollars a month) of *New York Panorama* but also the expenditure of a vast sum of money, 160,000 dollars in

Maryland, for a guide which had not yet appeared. Stanley Walker's review (*Herald Tribune,* September 18, 1938) also deplored the cost of *New York Panorama,* which was so great that no ordinary book publisher could have met it. The liberal press, on the other hand, felt that one of the justifications for the FWP was the fact that research for the guides and other publications could be done at a low cost. Without a subsidy, the material for the guides, which were after all commercially published, could not have been collected. Walker and others would have countered with the generalization that FWP involved too much waste.

Even FWP's publications like *American Stuff* that did not involve collecting material were scrutinized for wastefulness. Whereas the guides were in a sense non-creative because of such editorial policies as uniformity of format and communal authorship, with a few exceptions to the latter, *American Stuff* was creative. It was work done after hours on the FWP staff. The reviews raised such questions as to whether the FWP was needed and whether an organization consisting mostly of hacks could be effective in compiling information and manuscripts for the guides. According to the *Washington Post* (September 15, 1937), *American Stuff* appeared primarily because writers could not "wax poetic over Trenton's cheese factory." However, when they dreamed and put their dreams into *American Stuff,* "the very best thing in the book is still the cheese factory." Like a number of reviewers, the *Washington Post* reviewer was distressed by the writers' pre-occupation with reality or with "viewing life from the roadside ditch," as Henry G. Alsberg wrote in the introduction.

Oddly enough, the poems, short stories, and essays in *American Stuff* received little attention; most of the reviewers singled out the collections of folklore entitled *Americana* interspersed between the literary works. An anonymous reviewer in the *Detroit News* (September 5, 1937) typified this practice when he wrote: "It is probable that the various items listed under the head of 'Americana' will be the most interesting to many readers—and without much doubt most instructive and valuable. These provide keys to the American scene from writers with first-hand knowledge." The last sentence shows that he did not know exactly what he was talking about, for his so-called knowledgeable writers were after all folklore collectors. Hershel Brickell in the *New York Post* (August 23, 1937) was especially fond of the Negro sayings; however, he continued, "Some of the Americana is pretty thin, too. Folk-stuff can be merely repetitious and tiresome." Eugene Armfield was more selective in his evaluation of "Americana" in *The Saturday Review of Literature* (September 4, 1937). He liked such items as "Preacher's Song" but found "Phrases of the People" pointless in "a volume of creative work." Like other reviewers, he obviously did not understand folk creativity, of which "Phrases of the People" is an excellent example.

One of the FWP, re-named the Writers' Program in 1939, publications that stood the test of time is *These Are Our Lives.* Perhaps one of the best descriptions of this publication appeared in *Time* (May 1, 1939). According to this review, W. T. Couch, the regional director, "sent his best writers out to get the life stories of a typical cross section of Southern sharecroppers." No editorial comment was allowed; the stories were to be told in the first person. The results of the interviews, were to be judged on the basis of " 'accuracy, human interest, social importance, literary excellence.' " *Time's* quote of Charles Beard's pre-publication comment, " 'As literature more powerful than anything I have ever read in fiction' " is still valid.

These Are Our Lives, which has recently been reprinted by Arno and the *New York Times* in the American Negro: His History and Literature series, in 35 stories tells it like it was for the Southern poor, black and white. Although the available reviews indicate that the merits of the work were recognized during the '30's, they also suggest that most of the reviewers were either ignorant of the criteria established by Couch or they chose to ignore them. Stanley Walker's review in the *New York Times* (May 25, 1939) consisted of summaries of some of the stories and concluded with "The effect of the whole is that of history of a new and peculiarly honest kind." Virginius Dabney was most impressed by the fact that the collection did not parade a group of Southern degenerates before the readers (*Saturday Review of Literature,* May 27, 1939). Although some passages in his review show some awareness of the greatness of the work, his pre-occupation with "Caldwellian or Faulknerian excursions into the cesspools of Southern crime, degeneracy, and lust" detract from the positive evaluations of the work. However, an editorial in the same issue of the *Saturday Review of Literature* called *These Are Our Lives* "one of the most distinguished of the books prepared by the Federal Writers' Project."

Another non-guide book, *Drums and Shadows,* produced by the Savannah unit of the Georgia project, also baffled the reviewers. Although it had excellent advance publicity in Georgia papers, the regional popular press did not review this collection of Gullah folkways much. Most regional reviewers like the one on the *Atlanta Constitution* (January 12, 1941) simply quoted long passages from the collection and concluded rather lamely, "All of the character sketches are highly informative." Those who reviewed the book unfavorably, usually did so for the wrong reason. For example, Roi Ottley of the *Herald Tribune* listed a number of limitations and concluded "Because of the limitations of the WPA staff, largely untrained, the volume does not emerge as a definitive work." Whatever the shortcomings of the Savannah staff, Ottley should have realized from the introduction that *Drums and Shadows* was not intended as a definitive work on the Gullahs.

As already noted, FWP also received attention on the editorial pages of the popular press. A particularly vitriolic editorial appeared in the Charleston *News and Currier* (May 9, 1938). The writer was typical of the many FWP detractors with his insistence that carpenters and ploughboys were worthy of relief but writers *never.* Furthermore, he deplored the fact that the taxpayer was forced to subsidize the writer who wrote what no publisher would buy. The last charge was particularly unfair because the materials of the FWP, with a few exceptions, were published by commercial publishers. But he had little use for printing presses either as his impassioned "Let's have a moratorium on writing and printing presses" indicated.[5]

However, the acrimony generated by the FWP during the '30's was forgotten in the fall of 1941 after President Franklin D. Roosevelt in a letter to Florence Kerr, Assistant Commissioner of the

Work Projects Administration, proclaimed November 10-16 American Guide Week. Perhaps the anonymous writer in the *Washington Daily News* (Oct. 30, 1941) summed up the reaction most succintly and accurately in the following statement: "WPA has never had time to take many bows. It has been too busy dodging brickbats, but on November 10 WPA will stand up and ask for applause and chances are it will get it. Occasion will be the start of National Guide Week, celebrating the completion of WPA's Guide Book Series. The books have won universal praise and paradoxically, they were the product of WPA's most criticized activity—its writers project."

NOTES

*Research for this study was made possible through a summer research grant from the General Research Board of the Graduate School of the University of Maryland.

[1]*Time,* February 15, 1943, pp. 95-96.

[2]Cited by Charles I. Glicksberg in "The Federal Writers' Project," *The South Atlantic Quarterly,* XXXVII (April 1938), 163.

[3]An excellent objective contemporary account of the beginning and problems of the FWP is that of Blair Bolles, "The Federal Writers' Project," *The Saturday Review of Literature,* XVIII (July 9, 1938), 3-4; 18-19.

[4]Although according to Merle Colby's *Final Report on Disposition of Unpublished Materials of WPA Writers' Program, April 8, 1943* (no pagination), "a list of references to articles published in periodicals about the Writers' Program and similar material" was carefully deposited in the Federal Works Agency Library, no such list has been located even with the assistance of the Library of Congress reference personnel.

[5]An unsigned editorial in the Raleigh, N. C. *The News and Observer* (May 11, 1938) answered most of this vituperative editorial's objections to the FWP.

The Social Meaning of Television Censorship

by

Eckard V. Toy, Jr.

Mark Twain once observed that Americans had three precious things: freedom of speech, freedom of conscience, and the prudence never to practice either.[1] Commercial television appears to confirm this observation. It is commonly acknowledged that government agencies, networks, sponsors, and local stations all regulate the content of television, but the daily routine of this editorial hierarchy is usually not visible. The University of Wyoming has several hundred scripts and production schedules of *General Hospital, Gidget, The Flying Nun,* and *Peyton Place* in its archival collections. These source materials lack the significance of the controversies stirred by the firing of the Smothers Brothers, the silencing of opponents of the ABM, or the resignation of the head writer on *Laugh-In,* but they are probably more representative of day-to-day censorship practices.

These television programs, which were all products of the American Broadcasting Company, appeared between late 1963 and early 1968 and paralleled in time the presidency of Lyndon Baines Johnson. But these series projected an image of society that betrayed class biases and institutional conservatism and seemed far removed from the Great Society. Debates about good taste have sometimes obscured the essentially conservative social content of programs whose entertainment role was also a means of social education—establishment theatre as opposed to guerrilla theatre.[2]

General Hospital and *Peyton Place* were rooted in proven styles; nevertheless, television, like the stage, was on the threshold of experimentation, limited though it has been. When "you bet your sweet bippy," "ring your chimes," and "Wrinkle your prune" have become as common as "sock it to me" and "let it all hang out," the entertainment and social revolutions have come together. Of course this observation is somewhat diluted by the memory of a recent presidential candidate and his chaplain playing unaccustomed roles on that very program.[3] Perhaps to make fun in the *Laugh-In* way, as Dan Rowan explained in the October, 1969, *Playboy,* is not really revolutionary.[4] Yet it did seem strange to see our champions of morality and law and order against a background of candid one-liners, double entendre, bikini-clad girls with active graffiti, and the park bench marauder. This participation made the politician and the preacher almost too human. Perhaps, though, this entertainment role was less obscene than the evening last August 14, when an entire nation had to play "guess who's coming to dinner." It makes much more sense to have presidential candidates on *Laugh-In* than it does to have a prayer-supper with the astronauts.

Nearly everyone is familiar with racy dialogue and humorous incidents that editors have overlooked. *Laugh-In* strikes so quickly that much of the content is lost. This is unlike the satirical stumbles of the Smothers Brothers. And on the *Tonight Show* there was the artful scene when Ed Ames accidentally clobbered an outline figure of a cowboy right in the crotch with a trusty tomahawk. Although this episode was on videotape, it had a spontaneity that made it acceptable (in much the way that instant replays take on more meaning than the original). An example of planned deviation, with subliminal overtones, was in an episode of *Get Smart,* when the camera focused over the Chief's shoulder to reveal five telephones to foreign countries hanging from the wall. Those phones to Berlin, Paris, London, and Tel Aviv were hanging vertically, while the center phone to China was conspicuously cross-ways. Or there was the time when Johnny Carson told about giving the peace sign to a striking cab driver and getting only half of it returned.

Too often, perhaps, we think of censors protecting us from naughty things like those, but Mason Williams has described it better in his poem that explains the censor as cutting holes in the mind. There was the incident when the sponsor's representative objected to a scene where Petula Clark touched Harry Belafonte on the arm. And there was Bill Cosby's routine about religion on the *Tonight Show* when word after word was silenced. This merely made the context seem worse. What or who determines good taste? Commercials are among the worst offenders. Can TV successfully adopt a movie rating system: A for *Lassie;* B for *Gunsmoke;* or X for Buddy Hackett? (Alan King recently commented that of a 48 minute segment taped by Hackett and himself, fully 28 minutes were impossible to use). Commercial TV stations have sometimes presented movies with brief warnings that they were for mature audiences. Two years ago, a Milwaukee, Wisconsin, television station owned by the liberal Milwaukee *Journal,* refused to show a cleansed version of *Never on Sunday.* The same evening, a much less politically liberal station in Madison, Wisconsin, showed the movie. Why? Audience rating, organized opposition, or station censorship? Where was the controversy when the movies *Georgy Girl, Fail Safe,* and *Tom Jones* were shown in the fall of 1969? Again, on news programs, signs in student demonstrations have sometimes been shown with their four-letter words emblazoned for all the world to see. Yet it is virtually impossible to present the words audibly, as an ETV production about the Chicago demonstrations recently proved. Provocations and epithets were mouthed like so many silent brickbats. The producer complained to no avail that the psychological impact of the confrontations was missing. Of course, we can always refer to the enlightened policies of NASA and the astronauts when it comes to cursing. Lenny Bruce could be an astronaut but not a TV performer. Yet we idolize the urbanized rural innocence of Johnny Carson. And where have you seen Dick Gregory recently? He is either on educational TV or sharing Hugh Hefner with Mort Sahl, another occasional visitor to commercial television.

Time magazine has defined "Pastore's Complaint" as "A phobia against violence and sex on television, exacerbated by recent disturbances in American society and by the Noxzema 'take-it-all-off' commercial."[5] Unlike *Portnoy's Complaint,* the Pastore ailment hinges on the belief that there has been too little motherly (translate government) concern for the welfare of the child. But is Senator John O. Pastore's carrot and stick procedure with the television industry and with the Federal Communications Commission sufficient to reconcile the problems facing the viewer? These arguments about violence and sex on television have been with us for nearly two decades.[6] On the one hand, some persons who reject the nude theatre, the sexual revolution, and sex education in the schools demand a reduction in sexuality on television. And there are many other persons, who do not fear sex, demanding that more be done to regulate violence on TV. In 1954, Walter Lippmann wrote: "believing as I do in freedom of speech and thought, I see no objections in principle to censorship of the mass entertainment of the young. . .the risks to our liberty are. . .less than the risks of unmanageable violence."[7] Now the National Commission on the Causes and Prevention of Violence has criticized the television industry: "Television entertainment based on violence may be effective merchandising, but it is an appalling way to serve a civilization—an appalling way to fulfill the requirements of the law that broadcasting serve the 'public interest, convenience and necessity'."[8] This concern about violence and sex brings into focus question about what extent television should reflect society as it is, as it ought to be, or as it is thought to be.

During the administration of President John F. Kennedy, this nation was on a narcissistic binge, and criticism—preferably self-criticism—was acceptable. In some ways, there was an easing of the internal control mechanism in the TV industry, and it appeared as if there might be improvement. Educational television failed to challenge commercial TV, but there was hope. It is common in our pluralistic society to have tension between the ideal and the real, between conformity and pluralism. It seemed for a while that the Kennedy style might reconcile rather than polarize. In McLuhanese, President Kennedy's cool image was made to order for a cool medium in a potentially hot time. But he also failed. The pseudoenvironment of Camelot was as false as Dwight D. Eisenhower's small town or the electronic pseudo-environment of television. Today, President Nixon serves as our link between the artistically bland and the socially blind. Too often the television images created by and about white middle-class America have neglected this conflict of values. To what extent does the image of this homogenized middle-class society carry over into the ghetto? To what extent should the ghetto sub-culture be packaged for middle-class consumption? Which is the more misleading, *Julia* or the *Tonight Show?*

Money is the source of television creativity and also its goal. In August, 1969, the FCC disclosed that the television industry grossed $2.5 billion in 1968, nearly 11 per cent more than in 1967. Television is a thriving business and entertainment is marketed. When FCC Commissioner Nicholas Johnson visited Hollywood this past summer, he offered a forum for criticism of the business-oriented industry.[9] But even the creative people had little concrete to offer as alternatives. Tom Smothers suggested that something like the Westinghouse plan would be preferable to network programming. This, again, assumes that local stations would be more interested in quality, possibly more competitive, and less interested in neutralizing the content of programs.

E. B. White wrote in *Harper's* magazine in 1938: "I believe TV is going to be the test of the modern world, and that in this new opportunity to see beyond the range of our vision we shall discover either a new and unbearable disturbance of the general peace or a saving radiance in the sky. We shall stand or fall by TV—of that I am quite sure."[10] As a mass medium, television tends to be conservative in its political and social content, partly because of the fear of offending any large portion of the audience and also because it is a business and its goals often clash with the role of the intellectual as a critic of society. In 1936, William S. Paley complained about radio: "Too often the machine runs away with itself . . .instead of keeping pace with the social needs it was created to serve."[11] Television faces a similar dilemma.

Even if we shy away from the semantic gamesmanship of Marshall McLuhan, we find common problems. Once condemned as "The Timid Giant" by Edith Efron, television was described by McLuhan as a process that "involves us in moving depth, but it does not excite, agitate or arouse."[12] But now we have an article by this same Edith Efron in *TV Guide* for September, 1969, decrying "hot" subjects. In her article, "The 'Silent Majority' Comes into Focus: Television News Departments Are Now Swinging Their Cameras to the Right," she sees the cause of this reversal as "too much attacking of the United States, its institutions and its citizens, on the airwaves."[13] She cites a survey conducted by *Television Age* magazine suggesting "that the public has been satiated with studies of . . .urban crises. . .racial tensions. . .dope addiction and poverty." One TVnewsman described this new mood as "the Nixonization of the airwaves."[14] This particular poll indicated that local broadcasting stations were becoming more openly hostile to network news and documentary programs. This is something for Tommy Smothers to consider.

Television is a Gulliver-like product of the technological revolution and social and economic centralization. Unlike radio, television began full-size as a child of the networks. Its growth coincided with the maturing of the associational impulse in American life that contributed to the development of organized ethnic groups, church associations, and patriotic societies. These organized external influences combined with governmental, network, and commercial bureaucracies to give television a supervision that radio had lacked when independent stations and untried performers created auditory chaos. The solution lay in organization and centralization. The network system imposed new rules.

Ad-lib talk was virtually banished, professionalism developed and controls were imposed as most programs were written and rehearsed. Prior censorship or prior restraint became common. Room for error was eliminated and opportunities for experimentation were reduced. As corporate controls were reinforced, public demands for censorship diminished. Erik Barnouw suggests that the link between civil-rights and censorship struggles in the 1920's helped thaw controls over the media and "brought a change of environment."[15] But there was another factor also. By the 1930's, "more than half [of radio's] revenue came from ten advertising agencies." This situation has not changed appreciably.[16]

The Federal Communications Commission licenses individual television stations, but it does not license the networks. The National Association of Broadcasters, which represents only about two-thirds of the television stations in the country, adopted a television code in 1952. Each network has between thirty and fifty editors and assistants who attempt to enforce that code. In addition, they are also guided by network regulations, sponsors' restrictions, and the characteristics of the audience.

In 1965 a Gallup Poll reported that 58 percent of Americans thought that censorship laws were not stringent enough because communications could contribute to immorality, irreligion, subversion, or error. Most television writers would probably agree with Gordon Shelby that editorial "censorship usually is not necessary."[17] Jack Gould wrote in 1959 that an advertising agency representative claimed that most writers, producers, and directors were aware of problems and that "script conflicts have become fewer and fewer."[18] The former head of NBC's broadcast standards department, Ernest Lee Jahncke, Jr., summed up the network viewpoint in an article in 1969.

> We believe that TV is and should be a mirror of society, but that it should only reflect society up to a certain point. TV will always be the most conservative of the performing arts—not only because of the

> kids in the audience, but also because people over 30 have sensibilities and moral standards that must be recognized.
> You could say we try to stay just a step or two behind the times.[19]

Frank and Doris Hursley, the creators of *General Hospital* and a new series, *Bright Promise*, soon to be produced by Bing Crosby Productions, state that they have never had trouble with censorship. Possibly, as they admit, this is because they are familiar with "network objections to controversial subjects, violence and such topics as suicide, [and] overt sexual material." Yet the Hursleys have written about "artificial insemination, birth control, drug abuse, and the common types of social injustice,"[20] and their experience seems to confirm the observation that daytime serials often are regulated less than evening programs.

General Hospital evolved from an outline called "Pulse of Life" written in October 1962. When the Hursleys first proposed the series, they cited an analysis of daytime audiences indicating that the most effective plots concerned love triangles of married people in their thirties. In addition, the authors planned "young love, occasional melodrama and other identifiable problems, emotionally treated."[21] In this first phase of creativity, a kind of reverse censorship took place. Editors suggested: all of the characters were too nice, so make one "bitchy," make another character "quite unsympathetic" because "We're not going to make villains of doctors, so a single civilian is a god send." One editor added: "I'm a pushover for the story of someone doomed to die—the Dark Victory Syndrome—but in the serial with its accumulating suspense the outcome of Leukemia is all too predictable. What if Eddie were to be paralyzed in an accident and need long-range therapy, occupational or otherwise. (The Men Syndrome) Or another less predictable disease—old fashioned TB would once have done it."[22]

The Hursleys have demonstrated that writers who know their audience and their editors can work virtually unchallenged.

General Hospital is essentially *Peyton Place* in a hospital. With well established precedents and rather confining plots, the series maintains the facade of middle-class respectability and professional competence amidst considerable sexuality and emotional distress. The Hursleys confidently expect the series to continue for another two or three years.

When we shift from the daytime serials and game shows to evening entertainment, we note a distinct difference in the variety and composition of programs. *Peyton Place* succeeded in establishing itself in the evening hours, but similar efforts have generally failed. The variety hour or the situation comedy has been more common in prime time, and *Gidget* and the *Flying Nun,* both produced by Screen Gems for ABC, fit this latter category. *Gidget* was based upon Frederick Kohner's short novel of the same name, which had already been successfully exploited by Hollywood in three movies, *Gidget, Gidget Goes Hawaiian,* and *Gidget Goes to Rome.* In a kind of critical obituary notice, James and Renee Munoz analyzed the viewer response for *TV Review.*[23] The Munoz's gave the program a high rating based upon the transformation of the father into a positive character from the negative role in the movies. The television series focused on the relationship between Gidget and her father, and the generation gap idea was implicit in the production. The ratings tended to confirm that the network got the audience for which it aimed. *Variety* described *Gidget* as a "middle-class fantasy,"[24] and the network editors, an advertising agency, and Frederick Kohner, the original author, sought to keep it that way.

Ironically, the same editor who had responsibility for *Peyton Place* [it was on the air a year earlier] was assigned to this production, but the executive producer balked after she mutilated the pilot film: "I happen to know that both the ABC program department and [her] superiors in New York have found no fault with the areas mentioned. . ."[25] The network assigned new editors, but the results were about the same. The basic problems were dress, language, and innuendo. Attempting to avoid the beach bum image, the producer reminded the casting director:

"It is vital that those episodes of Gidget involving school sequences be peopled by clean-cut, attractive-looking youngsters." [26] Throughout the series this was the theme.

One female editor ordered deletion of a beach scene showing "voluptuous" girls and she also objected to a "close-up of Gidget on her knees on the bed facing her father where her night clothes reveal her well-rounded bosom." [27] It was not clear whether the editor feared incest or believed that a sixteen year-old girl should not be so equipped. Three other censors took turns editing the scripts and rushes, but the result was similar. Whether male or female, they generally reacted against vigorous dancing, tight sweaters, and skimpy bathing suits. Ideas were seldom a factor. In one notable case, a male editor who was perplexed by the bust exercises called for in the script pleaded: "Whatever they are be very sure they are acceptable for viewing." [28]

These examples of editorial actions are common to most programs, although perhaps more stringent with those intended juveniles. But there are other censorship activities that extend beyond the NAB Code and simple editorial questions. At one point an editor reminded the director to "be sure this allergy bit in these scenes will be acceptable to your sponsor." [29] The script described a character as allergic to soup, and the sponsor was Campbell's Soups. Another example was a reference to aspirin, and the editor noted: "the 'aspirin' mention is contrary to your sponsor's interests. Please check with your ABC Co-ordinator for possible conflict." [30]

Like many productions, *Gidget's* sponsors worked through an advertising agency, in this case, Batten, Barton, Durstine & Osborn, Inc. The agency, representing Armstrong Cork Company, reserved its approval of certain episodes until they were completed. The "Great Kahoona" segment caused considerable apprehension for the agency when Gidget was found in a compromising situation. The scene had passed the editor, but the agency representative called it "very, very suggestive" and commented: "Believe me, neither Ed nor I are overly sensitive to these things but we were both unpleasantly startled, especially since Gidget is a teenager." [31]

Although eventually approving this episode in modified form, the agency notified ABC that a script, called "Gidget's Foreign Policy," was objectionable, and the agency "reserve[s] the right on this program to withdraw our sponsorship without payment in the event the finished product is unacceptable to us."[32]

Each episode was also reviewed by Frederick Kohner, the original author. In one segment, entitled "All the Best Diseases Are Taken," the script called for Gidget to engage in social protest and demonstration. Kohner condemned this script as "a very disturbing entry and one that could do harm to the series." He explained:

> Gidget is made the speaker of a fringe movement. . .De facto Gidget is here the exponent of a minority group. References to "demonstration," "Berkeley," "bomb," "hammer and sicle!" [this was 1965] have too serious connotations today to be treated lightly. . . . Obviously this is not the stuff Gidget pictures are made of. I for one couldn't find anything to laugh about here. The father being warned and almost threatened by University functionaries seems to be as unreal as his subsequent wishy-washingness. [sic]
> The first 8 segments were so delightful and so engaging that I feel new writers coming into the series should made it a point to read and *study* these excellent scripts in order to adapt themselves to the happy and healthy climate in which our girl thrives.[33]

The ABC editor had nothing to add. Perhaps, though, there was one redeeming feature of this series. Several times the Casting Department had been reminded; "In accordance with studio policy to employ minority groups, please consider casting such persons for the following roles:"[34] Sergeant Kulpepper, Officer Joe Hanley, a waiter, Miss O. Stoddard, a janitor, and another officer. Toward the end of the series a memo requested up-grading minorities to minor character roles.

Television executive William Sackheim and actress Sally Field, who had worked together in *Gidget,* were united again in the *Flying Nun.* Based on the novel, *The Fifteenth Pelican,* by Tere Rios, this production began ambitiously. The image of the father had changed slightly, and there was also a mother in the new series, Mother Superior. The geographical location in Puerto Rico created a slightly different setting, but this sociological factor was secondary to the institutional setting. One element was added to this production–close ties with the National Catholic Office for Motion Pictures and Television which gave promotional and technical assistance.

During the spring and summer of 1967, Jackie Cooper and Screen Gems pushed a thorough promotion with screenings for church officials and favorable reviews in church newspapers. In addition, there was an abortive effort, without his knowledge, to use the Vice President of the United States, Hubert H. Humphrey, in a promotional scheme. In the spring of 1967, a private screening for members of the Los Angeles Archdiocese, including Cardinal McIntyre and Assistant Sheriff James Downey, a prominent Catholic layman, met with a positive response and offers of technical assistance and contacts with influential Catholics in other cities.[35] By the end of July, the National Catholic Office for Motion Pictures and Television was active in an advisory capacity, the first time the National Office had served as adviser to a program shown in prime time. With its cooperation, private screenings for church officials were held in New Orleans, Baltimore, Atlanta, and Denver. With minor exceptions–there was criticism by some Catholics that the program was silly and even anti-Catholic–the response from most church members was favorable.

The principal concern of the church advisers was with technical questions about religious practices, but, on occasion, the National Catholic Office and a nun assigned by the Los Angeles

Archdiocese suggested changes that went beyond technical matters. In this series, the ABC editors played a secondary role to the outside advisers and to the producers as well. In fact, the network seemed to have accepted a secondary role in many ways. William Sackheim commented about one script: "I think [it] is awfully schmaltzy and rather flat. The ABC guys will probably love it."[36] In general, the nun assigned by the Los Angeles Archdiocese was more protective of the church's image and more concerned about sexual connotations than was the National Catholic Office. She was also more likely to reject slang expressions, and on one technical matter, the Sister corrected the implications of the script by stating: "the business about 'questioning an order' is rather *un*-realistic." Generally, the National Office merely described lines as "double entendre," "banal," and "close-to-sacreligious." But in one script where Sister Jacqueline expressed anger at the Mother Superior by saying, "I just wonder which member of the Trinity you've replaced,"[37] the National Catholic Office indicated that this

> remark would be *most* offensive to Catholics. No nun would ever speak to anyone in such a fashion, let alone to the Mother Superior. This line *must* be taken out from this office's point of view.

A somewhat different line, "The rack went out with the inquisition," was described as in "bad taste."[38]

A public relations executive of Screen Gems met with the head of the National Office on August 14,1967, and reported that he was very cooperative. She was positive that "our relationship can be a useful one for the show," and she confirmed that "on the matter of good taste. . .the script changes that might be suggested are only 'suggestions,'" and the National Office trusted the production people to act accordingly.[39] Most suggestions were accepted.

This relationship between the producer and the National Office helped the series. When the *Catholic Register* of Denver,

Colorado, published a letter criticizing the series as harmful to Catholicism, the National Office used its influence to plant reviews favorable to the series. A Screen Gems executive noted, hopefully, "This should increase receptivity to the show and get across the 'endorsement' angle."[40]

At the end of August, only shortly before the network premiere, Screen Gems shifted its publicity campaign to the theme of general entertainment and away from Church connections. The Executive Producer declared: "I do not think that it is wise for us to actively pursue public tie-ups for the show and Sally with Catholic organizations and events."[41] Screen Gems dropped its special promotions among Catholics a few days before the series went on the air.[42] Nevertheless, the National Catholic Office continued in its role as technical adviser.

In mid-September, the line between technical advice and taste was breached. There were several scripts in which the National Office made suggestions about scenes involving Sister Bertrille with Carlos, the male lead. Referring to a scene where Carlos put his arm around the Sister, the head wrote:

> This Office definitely wants the scene dropped. In addition to the fact that a layman would never do such a thing, no nun would tolerate such action. The second telecast had him kissing Sr. Bertrille and this Office cannot approve any romantic tie-up between the two characters.[43]

In another script, institutional conservatism was involved when a Brother Paul referred to an "Ecclesiastical Encyclopedia"that was 60 years old as "a menace to education." The memo from the National Office merely called the sentence "silly."[44] Again, in December, when a character suggested that her sister not date Carlos because "He's not a Catholic," the National Office objected:

> This response is offensive to Catholics be-

> cause it is one of the false statements made about the Church that Catholics can only marry Catholics. It is a terribly unecumenical line in this day and age and is offensive.

The head of the National Office often reiterated that he was not an arbiter of "essential matters of taste," but he cautioned that the author of "My Sister, the Sister," failed to write family entertainment. "You cannot get much lower in a swill barrel than to use double entendre material on a show geared for youngsters. I simply cannot fathom why 'The Flying Nun' has to become crude."[45]

The first Nielsen analysis of the *Flying Nun* confirmed that the program appealed primarily to young children and female teenagers and adults. A service called TVQ ranked *Flying Nun* first among children, ninth among teenagers, and about nineteenth among all adult female viewers. Children were intriqued by the gimmick of flight. One studio executive tested children and found "that heavy integration of flying into the series is essential to their future involvement in the show." He considered this factor "overwhelming."[46] Yet, the head of the National Catholic Office was convinced that the series had "a spiritual message of some dimension," and that some scripts effectively "imparted the Judeo-Christian structure of ethical conduct."[47]

Again, William Sackheim expressed concern for minorities. In a memo to Jackie Cooper, Sackheim wrote that several Black performers had been employed, but (to the best of his knowledge) no scripts had been received from Black writers and no Black technicians were on the production crew.[48]

The differences between the *Flying Nun* and *Peyton Place* were more than geographical. *Peyton Place* was based on the well-known novel by Grace Metalius about life in a small New England town. Some ABC executives worried about adapting this novel to television, but the ABC Director of Broadcast Standards reported that after a few letters opposing the effort, mail was generally favorable and many viewers identified closely with the characters.[49]

The chief editor for the series, a lady in the Hollywood office of ABC, was sometimes supplemented by two men and another woman, but there were seldom any distinguishable differences in their treatment of the material. *Peyton Place* had a freedom of characterization not permitted many other evening programs, and the editors faced a dilemma in attempting to reconcile the conflict between soap opera subjects and prime time viewing. Although not considered a family program, *Peyton Place* attracted a composite audience and the editors were especially concerned with physical actions, teenage mannerisms, word substitutions, and violence. There was a constant effort to portray teenagers as only slightly more worldly than those shown on *Gidget*. Yet, the general story lines were seldom challenged. Superficial changes in characterization were more common. Despite the relative freedom of subject matter, the editorial guidance seemed aimed at eliminating innuendo rather than directness. Explicit relationships were less vulnerable than implied ones. In a scene where a sexually frustrated father attempted to stroke his daughter's hair, the editor ordered: "Please substitute something with less incestuous overtones."[50]

Although the number of incidents depicting physical violence was not great, an automobile accident scene was softened, a bloody fight was made less bloody, and an editor requested that an episode about an autopsy not be shown on Thanksgiving Day. The director was also reminded not to let a gun "fire into the camera–i.e., living rooms of America."[51]

The evidence of editorial involvement was constant, but the level of concern varied. Fully one-third of the changes involved word substitutions, primarily in the area of sexual relationships. While word substitutions were quite common, other violations of the NAB Code were not as apparent. In fact, there were more recommended changes because of real or potential conflicts with sponsors than with the Code. Tobacco companies were among the most important sponsors of *Peyton Place*, and this caused numerous problems. When *Peyton Place* was scheduled to have two cigarette sponsors in the fall of 1967, the director was told to eliminate as much smoking as possible because of their competitive situation.[52] Cigarettes were not to be used or abused in certain ways: "do not grind cigarettes out on the floor in deference to. . . sponsors:" they were not to be "stubbed out in cold cream jars. . . in deference to cig sponsor;" ashtrays were to be clean; use of pipes and cigars was to be cleared with sponsors; chain-smoking was to be modified; and cigarettes were not to be ground out under foot, thrown to the ground, or dangled from mouths. And one scene was changed after the warning that "smoking and narcotics often arouse cigarette sponsors."[53] Even potential sponsors were not neglected, and one editor cautioned: "a possible coffee or food sponsor won't like the line about Allison not liking coffee."[54]

Sometimes it was difficult to distinguish between an editor's concern for observing the NAB Code or the network's rules and his personal opinions. One editor removed the sentence, "I think death is right for some people," and suggested that the mention of suicide be deleted, since "too many young people are thinking about it."[55] The social roles of professional men and law officials were protected by the Code and by editors who strictly enforced positive attitudes toward certain ideas. In *Peyton Place* doctors and lawyers were prominent among the characters and their professional images were protected: "eliminate the idea that country doctors are inferior;" "caution [not] to destroy the public's confidence in women doctors;" patients and nurses were not to abuse or challenge the doctor's roles as father figure and humanitarian; and doctors were not to cause undue pain to their patients. "Insistent" was substituted for "bullying" in reference to a lawyer, and there was to be no implication that the police were "heavy-handed" or brutal. Even the success ratio of the police was to be improved: "all this talk about the inadequate police work doesn't build up respect for law and order."[56]

Religion was to be defended, the marriage ceremony was to be revered, and affairs and adultry were to be condemned:

> Sharon can be in love with a married man–
> but this cannot be an affair–and since crime

> cannot be rewarded—somewhere ahead *she* must learn the sorry lesson of fooling around with a married man. Betty must also rebel —so our viewers will learn the error of this way of life. Caution—caution. [57]

A reference to one character intending to do humanitarian work in Peru was questioned because the statement implied Peruvian inferiority. The editor asked that the speech be modified "so we won't seem to downgrade our South American friends."[58] One of the most extreme examples concerned a scene that was deleted from an episode in 1966: "we must be certain Webber's dislike is against Rod's nonchalant attitude toward money rather than any slur on the credit card practise [sic]."[59]

The sheer bulk of this series made it inevitable that more editors' reports were available than with the other programs. Yet, there were qualitative measurements that indicated that this program was less censored in basic ways than *Gidget* and the *Flying Nun.* Substantive editorial comments and criticisms seemed to decrease gradually, and the primary concern after the first few months was to correct technical matters, substitute words, and protect sponsors. Throughout the series the editors consistently softened speeches and imposed correct social relationships and positive values. Walter Doniger, the director, suggested to the producer that *Peyton Place* adopt as its motto, "The Sins of Non-Commission are Greater Than the Sins of Emission."[60]

Obviously, the problems considered in this paper are not as serious as some of the more recent manifestations of censorship. Irving Wallace, whose movie the *Chapman Report,* was virtually unrecognizable after editing for television, was active on a committee opposing the ABM. On the committee's behalf, Arthur Goldberg asked the networks to sell them air time. NBC and CBS refused because they claimed this position had received adequate news coverage and because they were reluctant to get involved with the equal-time provisions. ABC did not respond at all, and several independent stations turned the committee down.[61]

In October, 1969, it was reported that Paul W. Keyes, the producer and head writer of *Laugh-In* had resigned. After vigorously defending the program last summer, he has now been quoted as saying that *Laugh-In* is "slanted, vulgar and dirty."[62] He implied that the trend had accelerated during the past few months. If this is true, why should *Laugh-In* be protected and the Smothers Brothers fired? Is content less important than ratings? Is it merely the approach? An examination of censored scripts of the Smothers Brothers confirms that the controversy was not simply a question of good taste. Richard W. Jencks, an executive of CBS, countered arguments against the network: "If [critics] mean that we should not reject

> entertainment material because it has topical comment of a controversial nature, then we agree wholeheartedly. If, on the other hand, they mean that we should allow any performer who by his talent has earned exposure to a microphone or camera to voice his own personal political views at any opportunity he chooses, then we disagree.
>
> Someone has to be the judge of the difference between entertainment and propaganda.[63]

The Smothers Brothers engaged in political and social satire, and they lost ground in the ratings.[64] Either situation was sufficient to cause trouble for them. Perhaps we might borrow a few words from the David Steinberg sermonette about Jonah that was cut from one program and suggest that the Smothers Brothers in their *New Testament* way literally grabbed the establishment by the *Old Testament.*

NOTES

[1]Paraphrased in Morris L. Ernst and Alexander Lindey, *The Censor Marches On: Recent Milestones in the Administration of the Obscenity Law*

in the United States (New York, 1940), 269-70. See Ralph E. McCoy *Freedom of the Press: An Annotated Bibliography* (Carbondale, Ill., 1968), for an extensive survey of literature about censorship. McCoy includes many titles that deal with television.

[2]See, for example: Bob Tweedell, "CBS' Jencks, TV Writer Barrett Raise Questions on Taste," Roundup Section, Sunday Denver *Post,* November 2, 1969, 21, 27; Charles Winick, *Taste and the Censor in Television* (New York, 1959) [An Occasional Paper for the Fund for the Republic on the Role of the Mass Media in The Free Society]; Harold C. Gardiner, S. J., *Catholic Viewpoint on Censorship* (Garden City, New York, 1958); and Edith Efron, "You Can Take Your Choice," *TV Guide* (November 1, 1969), 12-16.

[3]They were, of course, presidential candidate Richard M. Nixon and the Reverend Billy Graham. The following incidents were viewed by the author.

[4]"Playboy Interview: Rowan and Martin," *Playboy,* XVI (October, 1969), 83-100; 199-205.

[5]"Premieres: The 'New' Season," *Time,* XCIV (September 26, 1969) 80.

[6]Bob Tweedell, "Networks, NAB Claim Violence Data Is Old; Progress Cited," Roundup Section, Sunday Denver *Post*, October 19, 1969, 25, 31; "What Is TV Doing to Them," series in *TV Guide,* October to November, 1969; Robert D. Kasmire, Vice President, National Broadcasting Company, Inc., October 17, 1968, before the National Commission on the Causes and Prevention of Violence"; Richard W. Jencks, President of CBS/ Broadcast Group of the Columbia Broadcasting System, Inc., "The Problem of Violence in Television Entertainment," a talk before the Radio and Television Society of Hollywood, June 17, 1969; Statement by Frank Stanton, President, Columbia Broadcasting System, Inc., before the Subcommittee on Communications, Senate Commerce Committee, March 12, 1969; and "Remarks" of U.S. Senator John O. Pastore at the National Association of Broadcasters Luncheon, March 24, 1969.

[7]Walter Lippmann, "The Young Criminals," New York *Herald-Tribune,* September 7, 1954.

[8]Robert Gruenberg, "U. S. Commission Deplores TV Violence," Denver *Post,* September 24, 1969, 6. Also see "How Much Violence Is There on Television?" *TV Guide,* July 12, 1969, 26-30.

[9]Phil Kerby, "Nick Johnson in Hollywood," Denver *Post,* September 16, 1969, 18. See, especially, the criticism of censorship by FCC Commissioner Nicholas Johnson, "The Silent Screen," *TV Guide,* July 5, 1969, 6-13; and

a rebuttal by Richard S. Salant, President of CBS News, "He Has Exercised His Right--To Be Wrong," *TV Guide,* September 20, 1969, 10-19.

[10]Quoted in Gary A. Steiner, *The People Look at Television: A Study of Audience Attitudes* (New York, 1963), 3.

[11]Quoted in Fred W. Friendly, *Due to Circumstances Beyond Our Control. . .* (New York, 1967), xi.

[12]Marshall McLuhan, *Understanding Media: The Extensions of Man* (New York, 1964), 337.

[13]Edith Efron, "The 'Silent Majority' Comes into Focus: Television News Departments Are Now Swinging Their Cameras to the right," *TV Guide,* September 27, 1969, 6. Vice President Spiro T. Agnew's attack on television news commentators must be viewed from this perspective. The full text of his Des Moines, Iowa, speech can be found in the Denver *Post,* November 14, 1969, 45.

[14]Efron, "The 'Silent Majority' Comes Into Focus," 9.

[15]Erik Barnouw, *A History of Broadcasting in the United States: A Tower of Babel* (New York, 1966), 197.

[16]Barnouw, *A History of Broadcasting in the United States: The Golden Web, 1933-1953* (New York, 1968), 17.

[17]Gordon Shelby, "Traitor to My Class," in Harry J. Skornia and Jack W. Kitson, *Problems and Controversies in Television and Radio: Basic Readings* (Palo Alto, Calif., 1968), 106.

[18]Jack Gould, New York *Times,* July 12, 1959, in Skornia and Kitson, *Problems and Controversies,* 419.

[19]Quoted in Bob Tweedell, "Interesting Aspects to Smothers Poll," Denver *Post,* June 2, 1969, 24.

[20]Frank and Doris Hursley to Author, June 26, 1969.

[21]"Notes on a Medical Daytime Serial," October, 1962, Frank and Doris Hursley Collection (University of Wyoming Archives, Laramie, Wyoming).

[22]Richard Dunn to Armand Grant, February 5, 1963, Hursley Collection.

[23]James Munoz and Renee Munoz, "Gidget: A Viewer Analysis," *TV Review* in William Sackheim Collection (University of Wyoming Archives, Laramie, Wyoming).

[24]Quoted in Munoz, "Gidget: A Viewer Analysis," 67.

[25]Memo, Harry Ackerman to Sonny Chalif, April 26, 1965, Sackheim Collection.

[26]William Sackheim to Bob Ellsworth, June 9, 1965, Sackheim Collection.

[27]Editorial report, April 20, 1965, Sackheim Collection.

[28]Editorial report, February 3, 1966, Sackheim Collection.

[29]Editorial report, December 10, 1965, Sackheim Collection.

[30]Editorial report, February 3, 1966, Sackheim Collection.

[31]Memo, Adrian Samish to Harry Ackerman, July 26, 1965, Sackheim Collection.

[32]Edmund Souhami to Screen Gems, October 22, 1965, Sackheim Collection.

[33]Frederick Kohner to Sackheim, July 31, 1965, Sackheim Collection.

[34]Memo, Legal Department to Sackheim, May 11, 17; August 19, 1965; February 9, 1966, Sackheim Collection.

[35]Memo, Roz Wyman to Jackie Cooper, March 17, 1967, Sackheim Collection.

[36]Note by Sackheim, April 17, 1967, Sackheim Collection.

[37]Memo, July 13, 1967, Sackheim Collection.

[38]National Catholic Office for Radio and Television to Mrs. Rosalind Wyman, August 14, 1967, Sackheim Collection.

[39]Memo to Jackie Cooper, August 18, 1967, Sackheim Collection.

[40]Memo, Johanna Grant to Marvin Korman, August 23, 1967, Sackheim Collection.

[41]Memo, Marvin Korman to Harry Ackerman, August 30, 1967, Sackheim Collection.

[42]Memo, Roz Wyman to Jackie Cooper, September 5, 1967, Sackheim Collection.

[43]National Catholic Office to Screen Gems, September 15, 19, 20, 1967, Sackheim Collection.

[44]National Catholic Office to Screen Gems, October 23, 1967, Sackheim Collection.

[45]National Catholic Office to Screen Gems, December 5, 1967, Sackheim Collection.

[46]Memo, Bill Grant to Jackie Cooper, November 7, 1967, Sackheim Collection.

[47]National Catholic Office to Mrs. Rosalind Wyman, November 8, 1967, Sackheim Collection.

[48]Memo, Sackheim to Cooper, February 27, 1968, Sackheim Collection.

[49]Grace M. Johnsen to Author, September 24, 1969.

[50]Editorial report, June 4, 1964, Paul Monash Collection (University of Wyoming Archives, Laramie, Wyoming).

[51]Editorial report, October 31, 1966, Monash Collection

[52]Editorial report, May 15, 1967, Walter Doniger Collection (University of Wyoming Archives, Laramie, Wyoming).

[53]Editorial reports, October 7, 12, 1964; January 6, 1966, Monash Collection.

[54]Editorial report, June 30, 1965, Monash Collection.

[55]Editorial report, November 19, 1965, Monash Collection.

American Catholic Popular Fiction

by

Paul R. Messbarger

The recorded experience of American Catholics provides the historian with a superficial narrative in two parts: first, violent struggle, radical experimentation and improvization, and sectarian fervor; followed by regularization of belief and behavior, organization of ecclesiastical machinery, and a vast and durable spirit of complacency. The water-shed period for American Catholics occurred during the years following the Civil War, up to about 1900, and it offers a convenient mirror image of what was taking place in the larger society. During that period Catholics settled some of the more urgent questions of their institutional existence: whether in fact they would continue to be a small and fragile community on the periphery of American society, or whether they would become an integral part of that society. The issue was decided by the sheer bulk of Catholic immigration following the Civil War. The Catholic population grew from three million in 1866 to over twelve million in 1900.

A more complicated question, however, concerned the terms of accommodation to the larger society. For twenty years this issue was debated at every level of ecclesiastical life. Not until the birth control issue of the last twenty years has Catholicism faced a more compelling or more divisive problem. The partisan positions that emerged were loosely analogous to the divisions in the Black Community today. One group of purists, largely German in national origin, argued for a nearly complete separatism. American society, they said, was not only politically hostile to Catholic interests, it was culturally opposed to Catholic values. Cooperation of any kind between Catholics and Protestant or secular forces would confuse the faithful and likely contaminate belief. They campaigned for the establishment of separate ethnic Catholic communities to await that moment when the inherent superiority of Catholic belief and culture would work a kind of triumph over all other competing systems.

This program, ironically a kind of Catholic sectarianism, was opposed by another group, largely Irish, who saw in the institutions of the Republic and the moral climate of American society fit instruments for the revivification of Catholicism. Loosely labeled "Americanists," they argued for more open contact between Catholics and Protestants, for an updating and liberalizing of Church structures, for the gradual adoption of the idiom and style of contemporary America.

These two parties battled for the control of the American Church through the 1880's and 1890's, and the public contest ended only when the Pope (Leo XIII) intervened with a letter to the American hierarchy, defining certain nationalist tendencies (called "Americanism") as heretical. This encyclical, *Testem Benevolentiae,* effectively silenced partisans of both kinds and drove the combatants—such as they were—underground.

This debate is the celebrated Americanist controversy of Catholic history, a story that has been told innumerable times, and told well, but only at the level of Church politics. There is, of course, a social history of American Catholics for this period, a history not so well known and rarely well told. It's this history that I'm most concerned with—the record of social belief and behavior of American Catholics rather than the political configuration of bishops and priests—and it's this history that I want to write about.

For the sake of brevity, let me pass over a great deal of

evidence and argumentation to make one rather elaborate claim. Apart from this partisan politics, and virtually oblivious to it, Catholics worked out a mode of accommodation to American life that might serve as the very model of successful social integration. What makes it difficult to analyze is that the categories of political behavior described earlier (Americanism and separatism) seem strangely mixed if not working reverse effects. American Catholics developed and practiced a program of activities that by the end of the century provided at least a nominally religious designation for nearly every activity and association they might need. The Catholic education system is the most notable of this vast array of duplications. In addition there were Catholic professional unions, Catholic fraternal organizations, Catholic Boy Scouts, Catholic art, Catholic philosophy, Catholic applesauce.

With such an elaborate network of organizations and with a well disciplined laity, one would suppose that Catholics were effectively isolating themselves from the larger society, were placing themselves in a position that made especially difficult any movement to enter the mainstream of American life. In fact the result was just the opposite. Catholics assimilated with a speed and facility as great as any important immigrant group in America, and for the very reasons we would expect to result in a prolongation of the process. Two factors explain the results, at least in my judgement. One is that the total culture of the Church organization supplied the immigrant Catholic with powerful psychological supports that readied him to eventually move into the larger arena. He had, that is, the strength of a cultural identity in addition to his ethnic supports to draw on as he faced life in secular America. Secondly, except for certain exotic forms of worship and a clerical mystique, these church organizations were nearly always duplicative of secular organizations. Thus as Catholics drew more and more toward a totally distinct sub-culture, they simultaneously became more like their non-elect brethren. The American Catholic of the twentieth century became then a veritable stereotype of loyal, patriotic, stridently vocal Americanism.

The function of literature in this process of acculturation was extremely important if not central. In particular, Catholic fiction shows itself as both an instrument of cultural adjustment and an indirect record of the process itself and the tensions it engendered.

I should mention that what I mean by Catholic fiction is a species of imaginative literature that is institutional in a remarkable way—fiction by, about, and for Catholics. That such a mode of writing should have emerged is in itself significant; that nearly all fiction written by Catholics during this period should eventually come to bear the full marks of Church sanction is even more remarkable.

I wish to trace the origins of this literature and the official rationale that established and enlarged its importance. Then I want to classify the literature itself as to dominant motifs, themselves suggestive of a division and tension within the faithful that helps to clarify the process that I described earlier.

By the 1860's the novel was established as a sufficiently popular and engaging literary form in America that Catholic spokesmen were forced to deal seriously with it. By that time there was already, it should be pointed out, a small body of novels written by Catholics and published by Catholic firms. But official acknowledgement was withheld until after the Civil War. Isaac Hecker, a convert to Catholicism, once facetiously confessed that he was aware of the richness, variety and moral force of this ever so popular art, having spent the better part of one afternoon studying the genre. While this attitude was typical of Catholic apologists, Hecker also directed his fellow Catholics to give serious thought to the didactic possibilities of fiction, noting that Protestants had already seized on the novel to entertain and instruct their members as well as to attract converts to their ranks.

Hecker's attitude quickly came to dominate the leadership of the Church. This change in attitudes follows a rather familiar sequence that runs as follows: 1) Open hostility to fiction as a dangerous beguiler of the unsophisticated reader, undermining his morals, corrupting his faith; 2) If the appetite for novels is so firmly established among the masses, a wise Church can only labor to employ this form for the good of its members—thus baptizing the novel. 3) The third step starts with the claim that the truth and exclusiveness of the Catholic religion reveals itself in the superiority of Catholic culture. Therefore Catholic art must be superior to non-Catholic art—all other things being equal. Demonstrating this superiority becomes an important part of the battle for souls, in holding the loyalty of existing church members.

Given the existence of strong theoretical supports for a Catholic literature, the institution was not long in developing the means for large scale and controlled production. Although the literary industry never came under the direct control of the Catholic hierarchy, despite numerous attempts to place it there, and even though the agents of literary productivity remained independent and largely commercial—the entire process took on the appearance of a carefully coordinated venture. The writer marketed his works in Catholic magazines and through Catholic publishers, and he took his notions of professionalism from his membership in a guild of Catholic writers. Catholic publishers confined their lists to works by Catholic writers and promoted sales through Catholic periodicals and organizations. Catholic reviewers enforced a very narrow and parochial set of literary norms, celebrating the safe writer and ignoring works that failed to follow the exact rubrics laid down by the religious community. Most critically, a special readership was fashioned from a wide variety of Catholic organizations and educational programs. The Catholic school, Sunday schools, Chautauqua-like summer camps, local reading circles—all combined to create and shape literary taste among Catholics which was consistent with the aims of the institution on the one hand, the publishing industry on the other. Thus by the early 1880's literature had become an important part of the Church's effort to create a distinct and total culture for the membership. The enormity of this enterprise can be partially assessed by the following figures:

In 1860 there was a bare handful of Catholic novelists; by 1880 over forty novelists were writing regularly for Catholic publishers. By 1900 over one hundred American Catholics had written and published at least one novel. In 1891, Benziger Brothers of New York, the largest publisher of Catholic novels, advertised a list of 116 novels, of which three-fourths were written by Americans. Before

1900 the enterprise had become so ambitious that one firm issued dime paper editions of Catholic novels; others found justification for anthologies of "the best of American Catholic fiction."

The result of this burgeoning apparatus linking writer, publisher, critic and reader was, from the artistic point of view, a harvest of mediocrity. The writer who challenged these rigid confinements on his art suffered a kind of literary excommunication. Those who acquiesced, frequently suffered a loss of their art. The great majority of Catholic writers, however, having been raised up and nurtured within this closed system, seemed by their extra-literary testimonies not to have suffered at all.

From the point of view of social adjustment, however, Catholic fiction can be judged less severely. The hypothetical reader of Catholic novels learned more than the major tenets of his faith and how to effectively defend that faith against Protestant assaults; he also learned a code of behavior that was a nice blend of secular and religious parts. Beyond the obvious didactic functions, the fiction implanted in the reader a sense of his special cultural heritage as a Catholic, his dignity as a person, his rightful claims on American society.

Cautionary tales that demonstrate the perils of drink or mixed marriage abound. So do stories that dramatize the theological superiority of Catholic doctrine by pitting a brave, brilliant Catholic apologist against a cowardly and dim if not vicious non-Catholic. Equally numerous are stories that merge a success theme with religious fidelity: the young man who practices his faith is more likely to achieve status and wealth in the community than the apostate or non-Catholic. The fashioning of Catholic lieutenants to George Washington, Catholic heroes of American conflicts, Catholic Horatio Algers, became a commonplace of certain kinds of Catholic novels.

The most important division of narrative motifs that emerges from the bulk of the novels is one based on class assumptions and geography. One group I call "cosmopolitan," the other "parochial." The cosmopolitan Catholic novel is most often located in a European setting and frequently in the past. The dominant themes of such fiction celebrate the golden age of Church-state confederation, elitist political theory, and genteel behavior. More contemporary versions of the cosmopolitan novel indulge a nostalgia for the good old days while arguing the necessity of the one remaining conservative and civilizing institution left to modern man—the Catholic Church. Where such fiction did locate in an American setting, almost inevitably it argued for the Europeanization of native culture. As one might expect, the most congenial American environment for this presentation was the semi-feudal South.

Parochial fiction, in contrast, worked its effects in a context of contemporary American society, sometimes employing for thematic purposes genuine social issues of the day. Slum life, financial disaster, machine politics, and ethnic alienation are some of the problems described if not faced in these novels. More often than not the dilemmas shaped by the author are resolved by a miraculous moral transformation—at the tearful urgings of a pure maiden. This is not to say that the depictions of American life are not honestly rendered and at times with considerable force; but like their non-Catholic counterparts, the Catholic writers regularly invoked a species of *deus ex machina* to bail themselves out of a logically impossible situation.

What comes through from the parochial novels, more clearly than descriptions of social conflicts, is the fashioning of a new breed of culture hero, a Catholic Jack Armstrong—decent, fair-minded, egalitarian, intelligent, able to work and work effectively in middle class America, and more often than not headed for the Catholic priesthood. It's this invention, a character at home in his church and his American society, whose function in one realm is strengthened and reinforced by his life in the other, that is perhaps the most important result of all this literary thrashing about.

This division bespeaks a reproduction at the metaphoric level of the political battle being waged among Church leaders. The difference is that these competing motifs occasioned no hostilities between writers, publishers or audience. It appears that both versions of Catholicism were accepted and approved by nearly all the principals of the industry; they appeared side by side in periodicals, publisher's lists, and review columns. The spirit of equanimity that prevailed over this phenomenon is, I take it, a clear indication of the ultimate compatibility of the two in a process of cultural adjustment. The cosmopolitan fiction instructed the American Catholic in the richness, antiquity and grandeur of European Catholic culture, a legacy to which he could lay a special claim. Parochial fiction defined his role in American society, reinforced his fragile and tenuous foothold in that society by furnishing models of success and fulfillment. Both were necessary emotional supports, I think, and both from a sociological point of view were enormously successful.

The student of modern American society may find in the historical design I have drawn authentic instruments of cultural assimilation, a means of an effective preparation for life in a pluralistic society. However, from the point of view of the total record of Catholicism in America, he may be forced to draw less sanguine inferences.

Except for the last fifteen years, Catholic life in twentieth century America yields a record of static immobility. Those literary inventions of the nineteenth century, intuitive fabrications born of the desperation of intense need, became the rigid and undeviating formulas of the twentieth century. The myth that was shaped (puny and graceless as it was) to provide the means of cultural liberation for the American Catholic in one era became the instrument of entrapment and constraint for his descendents.

That, however, is another story altogether.

Popular Fiction (1870-1900) Looks at Darwin and the Nature of God

by

Elmer F. Suderman

"The most striking fact in the intellectual history of the last third of the nineteenth century," says Merle Curti, "was the blow to the historic Doctrine of Supernaturalism by new developments in the biological and physical sciences."[1] The greatest threat from the sciences came with the publication of Darwin's *Origin of Species* (1859), which, to use Andrew D. White's phrase, "had come into the theological world like a plough into an anthill."[2] Darwin's theory called into question the existence of God,[3] but, just as important and more difficult for traditional Christianity to absorb was its challenge to supernaturalism with its assumption of an order of existence beyond nature and of a divine creator who stands outside of and above these laws.

The response of the popular novelists writing from 1870-1900 reveal the threat of Darwin's theory as it affected their belief in the nature of God. There were other issues but the question focuses on whether God was spirit or person, whether God transcended the universe or was imminent in it.

Not all of the novelists who interested themselves in God's imminence or transcendence were affected by the theory of evolution. Elizabeth Stuart Phelps and most of the others who wrote about the nature of the afterlife,[4] biblical novelists, and writers of novels which are religious tracts like John Bamford's *Elias Power of Ease-in-Zion* think of God's nature in strongly personal, sometimes naively anthropomorphic, terms. This view is summed up by George Hepworth, pastor of the Liberal Unitarian Church of the Messiah in New York City, who has one of his characters say: " 'If one begins with a personal and paternal God, . . he begins well; if he has doubts on that point, he ends before he begins.' "[5]

Other novels echo the statement, Charles Wall, Jr., the young preacher in W. M. Baker's *The New Timothy,* affirms to his skeptical young lawyer friend that God is a real individual, " 'as real as you and I.' "[6] Rose Terry Cooke in *Happy Dodd* comments, as Happy lies on her death bed, that the God who is with her and who will receive her is "no impersonal affection, no blind machinery, no great 'creative principle';.. it is the heart of a loving father, an almighty redeemer, that comforts human fear and weakness with this wonderful assurance of love and help."[7]

E.P. Roe in *Opening a Chestnut Burr* recognizes that questions about God's transcendence have been raised though he does not attribute them to evolutionary theory, and has his skeptical hero, Walter Gregory, ask Annie Walton if she believes what she has just sung in a hymn, that prayer is heard and answered by a personal God. She does, of course, believe, and he answers her:

> "I envy you, Miss Walton. I wish I could believe in a personal God who thought about us and cared for us–...Of course I believe in a supreme being...;but he hides himself behind the stars–He is lost to me in his vast universe."[8]

Annie wants to help Gregory overcome this deistic attitude; and Gregory, like so many free thinkers of this period, would like to be helped, especially by an attractive girl like Annie. If he could only feel, he says,that God cared for him in the way Annie cares for him, he would be satisfied. Like many of his skeptical friends in sentimental fiction, Gregory seems to trust a pretty girl more than God. But he dreads God's terrible and inexorable laws. Annie with the customary tears in her eyes confesses that she is not wise enough to argue such matters; she depends more upon feeling than upon ratiocination. And Gregory, either not seeing her tears or completely nonplussed by them, replies: " 'That is better argument—that is what I would like. You are not a weak, sentimental woman [ready tears, evidently, are no longer considered an indication of sentimentality], full of mysticism and fancies, and I would have much confidence in what you know and feel.' "[9]

Sarah B. Elliott in *John Paget* (1893) attempts to develop God's transcendence more logically, but is just as ineffective aesthetically. John Paget argues with his brother Claude that since he believes in "Good" as he sees it in people, so the greatest good then must reside in the highest personality: " 'Call this 'The Unknowable,' ...for me there is but one name, God the father. For that which satisfies the insatiable craving for a final cause—that which is the sum of all good, therefore of all that is true and beautiful—that is my God.' "[10] And John argues again that good cannot be thought of apart from some form, and that form must be personal.[11]

Expressing a firm belief in God as a supernatural personal being who loves and cares for his world and especially for his children, Baker, Cooke, Roe and Elliot discovered a God not in or equal to the universe, but transcending it, though not indifferent to, or even completely separate from it, indeed constantly present in it. In these respects the God of these novelists is the God of Orthodox Evangelical American Protestantism and was not affected by evolutionary theory.

But for other popular novelists this traditional view of God was substantially modified by the theory of evolution. As American theologians and preachers came to adapt evolutionary principles to religion, they argued that God was not, as the sentimentalists maintained, a personal being, nor, as deism maintained, the creator of a universe ordered by laws and sustained by its own inherent properties, nor yet the inscrutable Calvinistic deity beyond man's reach and understanding, but that he was imminent in the universe working out by the evolutionary process his divine plan as a benign force in the natural order. For evolutionary theism God was a great power "to which no limit in time or space is conceivable, of which all phenomena, as presented in consciousness, are manifestations, but which we can know only through these manifestations."[12] John Fiske, a leader in the attempt to show that evolution was an aid rather than a hindrance to religion, defined God as "the infinite and eternal energy from which all things proceed, and which is the same power that in ourselves wells up under the form of consciousness."[13]

Henry Ward Beecher's influence after 1883–when he wrote in the *Christian Union,* "I am a cordial Christian evolutionist"[14]–was of great significance in the acceptance of evolution by Christian writers and thinkers. Beecher's book of sermons "discussing the bearings of evolutionary philosophy on the fundamental doctrines of Evangelical Christianity" and "the application of evolutionary principles and theories to the practical aspects of religious life" had a wide influence in ameliorating the heated controversy caused by Darwin's Theory.[15] It is interesting to note that this controversy, one of the most vitriolic in American church history, is muted in the American novel. Indeed, one would have to conclude on the basis of the evidence in the novels that the evolutionary hypothesis was accepted without any great debate. As early as 1883 E. S. Phelps has Darwin in heaven. Since most of the novelists were romantic intuitionists who believed that God revealed himself intuitively to man rather than through the Bible they were not as perturbed as the supernaturalists at the effect of the theory of evolution.[16]

By 1898 an anonymous writer in *Current Literature* could report that Darwinism "which a few years ago was assailed as a denial of the Bible and Christianity by the whole Christian world," is today "quietly accepted by some of the most devoted and loyal clergymen of all the churches."[17] The novelists do not depict the assault of the churches against evolution but they do reveal its acceptance and rejoice with Aubrey Moore that science which at first appeared to have pushed the deists' God farther and farther away had appeared just when it seemed as if God would be thrust out altogether, under the guise of a foe to do the work of a friend. Darwinism had made it possible to " 'return to the Christian view of direct divine agency, the imminence of divine power in nature from end to end, the belief in God in whom not only we but all things have their being.' "[18]

The novelists writing in the latter 1880's and in the 1890's saw God as imminent in the world and thought of him as inseparable from and working within the natural order through evolutionary methods. Although there was still an inclination to retain the personality of God, increasingly he is seen as an ever-present, all-pervading spirit, as the source of all being, as the continuous unfolding of divine energy, or even as eternal and immutable law.

As early as 1884 Henry Adams in *Esther* presented Stephen Hazard, a liberal Episcopal clergyman, who saw evolution not as a threat but an ally of religion. Hazard may have been modeled after Adams' cousin, Phillips Brooks, who was from 1869 to 1891 the immensely popular and influential rector of Trinity Church in Boston and who accepted evolution as not inimical to religion. [19] In his first sermon Hazard preached an evolutionary theism arguing that "all being and all thought rose by slow gradations to God–ended in him, for him–existed only through him and because of being him.'[20] All life is an emanation of divine thought, and it is the function of the church to find enthroned behind all thought and matter " 'only one central idea–that idea which the church has never ceased to embody–I am!' "[21]

The Reverend Arthur Forbes in Celia Woolley's *Love and Theology* (1897), not as certain as Stephen Hazard that God is an impersonal principle, sympathizes with his wife and friends who object to his view of God as " 'something far off and unnecessary, except to man's thinking: an essential element in our poor human reasoning: a necessary datum of consciousness.' "[22] " 'How can such a God feel the woes of his creatures, or desire to reconcile himself with them?' " his friends ask (p. 288). Such a view rests on a few, thin intellectual speculations, which, compared with the message of Christianity, are nothing but dry husks for the really sinful and suffering (p. 106). But Arthur never changes his mind in spite of his and his friends' doubts and holds to his belief that God is "the continuous unfolding of the divine energy" (p. 391).

Minot Judson Savage, a prominent Unitarian clergyman, avowed disciple of Herbert Spencer, and one of the earliest American evolutionary theists,[23] writing in the same year as Woolley, has the Reverend Mark Forrest in the novel *Bluffton* express without any doubts his view that God is not personal and transcendent, but a spirit and imminent. After assuming a pastorate Mark reads widely and gives up his Calvinism, his faith in the Trinity and accepts God as universal and omnipresent spirit.[24] He believes in Christ as the manifestation of the unseen spirit which is God, but in the Father as a separate personality he cannot believe. It is possible, however, to have a close communion with God the Spirit, for this spirit is kind and loving, not cold and forbidding, and can respond to man. Convinced that such a belief is all that he needs to preach for a while, Mark busies himself trying to make his people better, rather than in solving abstruse theological questions (p. 82).

It is apparent, then, that American novelists represented the theological shift in the view of the nature of God which occurred as a result of the theory of evolution. Many of the characters are concerned with the issue: they represent various facets of the question. And with some cogency and clarity, they argue the problem so that it has been possible to trace it through the last thirty years of the century. But in no instance are the theological questions treated with any intellectual depth or profundity. But this superficiality was evident in American theological works as well. Indeed, it was an age suspicious of theology. Distinguishing between theology, defined as concern for the existence and the nature of God and his relations to man, and religion, defined as concern for the feeling and conduct of man toward God and toward his fellow men, the age thought of theology as narrow, inflated, intolerant, and cruel, and of religion as enlightened, tranquil, sympathetic and benevolent. George H. Hepworth expresses this view when one of his characters argues: " 'I have a notion that we've got too much theology in the world, and too little religion...man is bein' ruined by theology, and there ain't religion enough to go around. What we want is to seal off all our spekerlations about God and start in to do God's will.' "[25] Both novelists and theologians agreed that religion was more important than theology.

One aspect of the problem hardly touched by the novelists is the fervor of the opposition to evolution of the group which was to develop into American Fundamentalism. The intense and complex feelings which the theory of evolution aroused in Americans is no where caught in any viable form. While the novelists do give us valuable footnotes to the social and intellectual history of God, they do not give us what is more important for the artist: the feel and tone of the controversy arising from the change of opinion.

NOTES

[1]Merle Curti, *The Growth of American Thought* (New York, 1943), p. 531.

[2]Andrew Dickenson White, *A History of the Warfare of Science with Theology in Christendom* (New York, 1897), II, 70.

[3]For a discussion of the response of popular fiction to the erosion of faith in the late nineteenth century see my "Skepticism and Doubt in Late Nineteenth-Century American Novels," *Ball State University Forum,* VIII (Winter, 1967), pp. 63-72.

[4]I have discussed "Elizabeth Stuart Phelps and the Gates-Ajar Novelists" in *The Journal of Popular Culture,* III (Summer, 1969), 91-106.

[5]George H. Hepworth, *They Met in Heaven* (New York, 1895), p. 49.

[6]William Mumford Baker, *The New Timothy* (New York, 1870), pp. 334.

[7]Rose Terry Cooke, *Happy Dodd* (Boston, 1878), p. 408.

[8]E.P. Roe, *Opening a Chestnut Burr* (New York, 1874), p. 201.

[9]*Ibid.,* p. 201.

[10]Sarah B. Elliott, *John Paget* (New York, 1893), p. 163.

[11]*Ibid.*, p. 163.

[12]John Fiske, quoted in Richard D. Mosier, *The American Temper* (Berkeley, 1952), p. 243.

[13]The effect of evolution on American theology is discussed in Stow Person's *Evolutionary Thought in America* (New Haven, 1950), pp. 422-455; in Richard Hofstadter, *Social Darwinism in American Thought 1860-1915* (Boston, 1955); in Richard D. Mosier, *The American Temper* (Berkeley, 1952), pp. 233-257; in Arthur C. McGiffert, *The Rise of Modern Religious Ideas* (New York, 1915), pp. 166-186; and Frank Hugh Foster, *The Modern Movement in American Theology* (New York, 1939), pp. 38-58.

[14]Quoted in Winfred Ernest Garrison, *The March of Faith in America: The Story of Religion in America Since 1865* (New York, 1933), p. 92.

[15]Henry Ward Beecher, *Evolution and Religion* (New York, 1886). The quotations appear on the title page.

[16]Persons, pp. 439-450, shows how easily romantic intuitionism absorbed evolutionary doctrine.

[17]"The Drift of Religious Belief," *Current Literature*, XXIII (January, 1898), p. 57.

[18]Aburey Moore quoted in McGiffert, p. 181.

[19]Wallace Evan Davies, "Religious Issues in Late Nineteenth Century American Novels," *Bulletin of the John Rylands Library*, XLI, (March, 1949), p. 331.

[20]Henry Adams, *Esther* (New York, 1938), p. 7.

[21]*Ibid.*, p. 8.

[22]Celia Parker Woolley, *Love and Theology* (Boston, 1887), p. 288.

[23]Persons, p. 433. Savage had published as early as 1876, *The Religion of Evolution* (Boston, 1876) in which he articulated his views of evolution.

[24]Minot Judson Savage, *Bluffton A Story of Today* (Boston, 1887), p. 116.

[25]George H. Hepworth, *They Met in Heaven* (New York, 1894), p. 105.

Martians and Mythmakers: 1877-1938

by

Mark R. Hillegas

I

As Mary Barnard has recently reminded us, all the writing about myth by anthropologists, folklorists, psychologists, literary critics, and philosophers add up to a maze of contradictions and confusions. Out of this welter it is difficult to arrive at any very clear idea of exactly what a myth is. About the best one can say is that myth is originally non-literary (i.e. oral); a story about divinities, perhaps believed and perhaps not by the first creator of the story; often it seems to symbolize aspects of man's relationship to nature and the universe. One thing, though, seems clearer: myth is usually considered as something whose origins are lost in the mists of a distant past. As Miss Barnard puts it, we can, according to our definition of myth, never see a mythmaker in action: "If we do, he is not making a myth, but a song, a story, a dance, a dramatic production, perhaps a ritual."[1]

It seems to me that this concept of myth as something which

must have become traditional by the time we first catch sight of it neglects the very obvious fact that myths are being created all the time and that there exist important myths which in the last hundred years have sprouted from the soil of our scientifically and technologically sophisticated civilization. One of these myths is that of the superior aliens and their invasion of earth, a myth which begins with late nineteenth-century theories about the advanced Martians and the stories subsequently written about them and their conquest of earth. The myth is naturally not oral in origin since it appeared in an age of mass literacy and the high-speed printing press, and instead of supernatural beings it substitutes living creatures of enormous superiority; but otherwise it fits the loose definition of myth given above.

II

Before tracing the evolution of the myth of the superior Martians and their invasion of earth, I should point out that there is no single-factor explanation of the meaning of the myth; instead there are at least four interpretations, one or more of which are usually applicable. The first explanation has been compassionately and intelligently made in Robert Plank's *The Emotional Significance of Imaginary Beings* (1968). In a universe of matter and eternal space we are afraid of being alone. At times we are also fascinated by the idea of superior alien life because we are looking for a father who will take care of us—perhaps rescue us in the nick of time. On the other hand, when the aliens are hostile, they are a projection—and exorcism—of our human guilt.

The second explanation applies to the invasion stories and has an origin in historical events. As I. F. Clark demonstrates in *Voices Prophesying War* (1966), H. G. Wells's *The War of the Worlds* belongs in part to the tradition of stories describing imaginary future wars that received tremendous impetus with Sir George Chesney's *The Battle of Dorking* in 1872. It was written just after the efficient and mechanically advanced Prussian army quickly overran the supposedly greatest military power in the world in the Franco-Prussian War; and other stories of future wars from other countries and other times are similarly an expression of anxieties about what an enemy might do. Hadley Cantril's study of the panic following Orson Welles's radio dramatization of *The War of the Worlds* in 1938 shows that worry over the German threat was a major cause of the public hysteria.

The third explanation, and one which applies both to the superior Martians as well as their invasion, has to do with human reaction in the nineteenth century to the advance of science and technology, which had become spectacularly rapid. The attitude of general public and elite alike was ambivalent: on one side hostility and even fear, on the other admiration.[2] In the late nineteenth century, the first stories of invasions from Mars provided a perfect symbol for this ambivalent attitude: fear, when the Martians overwhelm and crush the earth in a few days; and admiration for their technology and science which could create a utopian future on earth. The same ambivalent attitude should still be present in our reaction to stories about superior but hostile aliens.

The fourth explanation is related to the first. The most viable treatments of the myth are the expression of the scientific sensibility, which finds beauty and order in the laws of nature. At the core of this sensibility there exists, I think, a religious impulse, which, with the pioneers of the first scientific revolution, was clearly conscious. Sir Butterfield explains it this way:

> ...not only was there in some of the intellectual leaders a great aspiration to demonstrate that the universe ran like a piece of clockwork, but this was itself initially a religious aspiration. It was felt that there would be something defective in Creation itself—something not quite worthy of God—unless the whole system of the universe could be shown to be interlocking, so that it carried the pattern of reasonableness and orderliness.[3]

I believe that this attitude lives on in many adventures in pure science, even if only unconsciously. At any rate it is not hard to conceive that pushing on to the ultimate meaning of the cosmos is a religious act. And I think that this sensibility, with its quest for meaning, informs the myth of the superior aliens. Not only are the characteristic ways in which the scientific sensibility views reality given direct expression, but the religious impulse embedded in that sensibility is symbolized by the aliens themselves, who, of course, have replaced the divinities of older myth. After all, in a scientific, post-Christian age, the only gods we can easily imagine are living creatures of a higher order of mind.

III

Everyone is aware, I'm sure, that the myth of the advanced Martians was most immediately inspired by Schiaparelli's discovery in 1877 of the so-called canals, but it would be helpful, even at the risk of repeating what some may know already, if I fill in briefly but more completely the details of the origin of the myth. It is important to emphasize from the beginning that it was seriously advanced as a scientific hypothesis.

To begin with, the interest in Mars which subsequently followed Schiaparelli's discovery of the canals is part of a long and rich tradition of speculation about other inhabited worlds and fictional journeys to these worlds. It is a tradition, as Professor Nicolson makes clear in her *Voyages to the Moon,* which began with the new astronomy of the seventeenth century and not earlier, since there could be no stirring of the imagination on this subject until the idea that there were other worlds was widely accepted. It took the work of Galileo, Kepler, and Newton in establishing the validity of the heliocentric view plus the discovery with the newly invented telescope of a seemingly analogous world in the moon and planets to suggest that the universe was enormously vast—perhaps infinite—and filled with a plurality of inhabited worlds.

Under the impact of the accelerating advance of science and technology in the nineteenth century, the tradition of speculation about life on other worlds took a new form with Schiaparelli's discovery of the "canals" in 1877. Observing Mars from the clear atmosphere of Milan, the Italian astronomer found that what had been taken for Martian continents were actually islands separated by a network of straight lines, running sometimes to a length of three or four thousand miles. He called them "canali" because he thought that they were "grooves" in the planet's surface, and the Italian word was mistranslated as "canals"—as Dr. Plank points out, a classic example of parapraxis. Although professional astronomers were generally skeptical about the existence of the markings, the public eagerly responded to the implication that intelligent life had produced artificial waterways on Mars, and the oppositions of Mars in 1882, 1884, 1886, and 1892 were newsworthy events. The 1890's were the peak of what the *Edinburgh Review* called the "great Mars boom, when public imbecility and journalistic enterprise combined to flood the papers and society with 'news from Mars.' "

While the detection of the canals was the chief cause for the excitement over Mars as a habitable world, Schiaparelli's discovery only furnished the capstone to a theory that Mars was a planet much older than the earth with inhabitants superior to man. The major source for this idea was the nebular hypothesis, according to which the outermost planets were the oldest because they were formed first and the innermost planets were the youngest because the most recently created. Thus Saturn, Uranus, and Neptune had to be cold and dead while Mercury, the planet closest to the sun, was still extremely hot. Only Venus, the earth, Mars, and perhaps Jupiter would be at stages in their development when life was possible. A second important source for the idea of the superiority of the Martians was the theory of evolution. It suggested that, if life began on another world, intelligent forms would eventually be produced, and on the aging Mars, where life started much earlier than on earth, creatures wiser than man would have to exist. The discovery of the great system of canals seemed to offer proof that Mars was inhabited by just such beings.

Discussion of the idea of an advanced Mars reached its climax in the books written by the American astronomer Percival Lowell, the first being *Mars* (1895). Lowell finds that the general physical conditions of Mars are hospitable to our form of life. While its atmosphere is only one-seventh as dense as the earth's, Mars's gravitational attraction, though less than the earth's, is sufficient to retain oxygen, nitrogen, and water vapor—in other words, an atmosphere chemically like our own. The dark blue band that forms along the polar caps indicates water, and Lowell relates the gradual shrinkage of the polar caps to the economy of the planet. As spring advances in one of the Martian hemispheres, the white polar cap shrinks, and the dark markings associated with the canals in that hemisphere become more conspicuous and greener as the water flows towards the equator. Then as summer progresses, the markings fade and turn brown. The scarcity of water on Mars, Lowell notes, "is just what theory would lead us to expect. Mars... is relatively more advanced in his evolutionary career."[4]

Because of this scarcity, Lowell reasons that there is but one course open to the inhabitants of Mars in order to support life: "Irrigation, and upon as vast a scale as possible, must be the all-engrossing Martian pursuit."[5] The Martians must have united into a supra-national community to perform the tremendous engineering feat of constructing the planet-wide canal system. They are evidently intellectually, socially, and technologically far ahead of us:

> A mind of no mean order would seem to have presided over the system we see....Party politics, at all events, had no part in them; for the system is planet-wide. Quite possibly, such Martian folk are possessed of inventions of which we have not dreamed, and with them electrophones [telephones] and kinetoscopes [motion pictures] are things of a bygone past, preserved with veneration in museums as relics of the clumsy contrivances of the simple childhood of the race. Certainly what we see hints at the existence of beings who are in advance of, not behind us, in the journey of life.[6]

Writers of novels and stories had no difficulty with the details of this advanced Martian civilization—late nineteenth-century technology promised a new age of electricity filled with marvelous devices and machines to make life easier and more pleasant for man.

The real turning point in the development of the Martian myth is Lowell's *Mars* in 1895; it is the work which most influences and shapes the imagination of writers. Significantly, the first major treatments of the myth in fiction appear just two years later: Kurd Lasswitz's *Auf Zwei Planeten* (1897) and H. G. Wells' *The War of the Worlds* (1898 in book form, 1897 in serial publication).

Further evidence that it took Lowell's book to launch the Martian myth can be found in the fact that all the Martian romances written between Schiaparelli's discovery of the canals and Lowell's book—that is, in the 1880's and the first half of the 1890's—are almost totally lacking in vitality, and the Martian myth is hardly developed in them.[7] In fact, as I recall, the canals turn up only in one or two. Some are inept satires, some crude romances, others dull utopias. Only Percy Greg's *Across the Zodiac* (1880), the most substantial of the lot, deserves brief description here before turning to Lasswitz and Wells.

In *Across the Zodiac* the unknown narrator discovers an antigravity force, Apergy, builds a spaceship propelled by this force, and travels to Mars at 40,000 miles an hour, where he lives for a time in the scientifically and technologically advanced Martian world. The world of Mars is pretty much that pictured by contemporary astronomy, though Schiaparelli's canals are not specifically mentioned. Martian civilization is what ours will be when science and technology are victorious. Greg provides the Martians with most of the inventions of his time and those which were to come in the foreseeable future: submarines, telephones, concrete houses, automobiles, the widespread use of aluminum, automatic factories, water purification, and many others. But Martian society is not utopian, for, although the material side of life has long been perfected, the people are not happy. Nor is Martian society democratic or socialistic in organization, these forms of government having disastrously failed. Except for a secret society, religion and belief in God are dead, and the only heresies are the anti-scientific. A good case could be made for considering *Across the Zodiac* as a precursor of twentieth-century anti-utopias—an extrapolation of our own world to a nightmare future.

IV

Kurd Lasswitz's *Auf Zwei Planeten* (begun in 1895 and published in 1897) was widely read around the turn of the century, going through several editions in German and selling thousands of copies. Within ten years, according to Willy Ley, it had been translated into Swedish, Norwegian, Danish, Dutch, Spanish, Italian, Czech, Polish, and Hungarian.[8] Lasswitz himself (1849-1910) was a writer, professor of mathematics, and a philosopher.

Auf Zwei Planeten is the first treatment of the Martian myth significant as literature, but interestingly enough it does not represent the form of the invasion story dominant in the twentieth century, which pictures the invaders as a cruel, superhuman menace. Instead, Lasswitz's Martians, though superior to men, are essentially human and come to earth as culture-bearers, hoping to lift mankind to their level. Their own world (where they live in continuous strip cities along the canals) is openly and unashamedly presented as a technological utopia, in which peace, freedom, dignity, and the perfection of intelligence have ultimately been made possible by the conquest of nature.

In a beginning slightly reminiscent of the opening of Jules Verne's *The Mysterious Island,* a German balloon expedition to the North Pole is wrecked just at the time it discovers a strange installation on an island exactly at the Pole. Drawn by the antigravity force which the Martians use to move flight vehicles between the polar island and a space station exactly one earth radius above the Pole, the members of the expedition lose consciousness as the balloon ascends into the thin upper atmosphere. When they recover, they find themselves guests of the Martians on the island.

And so begins a long but eminently readable story of the Martian conquest of earth. They come, as we have noted, not to enslave but to educate mankind—they are ethically, morally, intellectually, scientifically, technologically, and politically far advanced, and all they want from earth is air and energy to supplement the diminished supplies of their own, older world. But the stubbornness and pride of the English provokes a one-sided war with the Martians, in which the English navy is no match for the Martian airships and which lasts only a few days *(Auf Zwei Planeten* thus also belongs to the genre of future war stories). The Martians then establish a Protectorate over the earth; but, disintegrating under the effects of the earth's heavier gravity and moister atmosphere, they are unable to resist the corrupting effect of power; and in time their rule becomes despotic. Eventually a group of engineers in America, mastering the advanced Martian technology, secretly builds airships and in a surprise attack throws off the Martian yoke. Peace between the two planets is concluded, and earth is on its way to a utopian world state.

The meaning of *Auf Zwei Planeten* is made clear in a long essay, "Zukunfsträume,"[9] which Lasswitz published at about the same time as the novel. Lasswitz sees men as living within space and time, subject to nature's unbreakable laws, a product of the evolutionary process. And as mind and organs have evolved to adapt man to his environment, so scientific and technological progress are extensions of this process. The key to further progress is greater and greater understanding and mastery of nature, and with further understanding and knowledge man will develop a higher level of morality. "Goodwill," he notes, "is nothing without intelligence, and much more dangerous than malice is stupidity."

His Martians are culturally, of course, what men will be in the future—further along in the evolutionary process, the conditions of their planet have accelerated their mastery of nature.

> Mathematics and natural science had reached a climax in their development which looms before us humans as a distant ideal. The more difficult the aging Mars made the conditions of existence for the Martians because of the comparatively low supply of water, the more magnificent had been their efforts to develop a technology to dominate nature. They learned how to produce from their planet all these new powers and resources. The conditions of Mars favored the development of culture and civilization to

a much higher degree than the conditions of earth.[10]

The Martians have, of course, marvelous machines and instruments—spaceships which operate on an antigravity principle; the "Retrospectiv," which, capturing departing light waves can reveal the past; an instrument to send messages between the planets by means of light waves, and numerous others. But the real physical basis of the utopia lies in two discoveries. First, the Martians have enormous energy available through the direct conversion of sunlight into electricity. Second, they have an almost unlimited food supply because they can turn stones into bread: protein and carbohydrates from rocks, soil, air, and water without the photosynthesis of plant cells. On a planet with a surface one fourth that of earth, they maintain a population twice that of earth at an extraordinarily high level of average personal income. Such security of means has taken the edge off competition among the Martians, though it is not a communist world and there is no leveling of possessions. With the tremendous resources made available by the mastery of nature they have created a democratic world state, with all the guarantees of the maintenance of human life and dignity we associate with the welfare state.

The scientific sensibility is obviously at work in this vision of a technological utopia, and the search for the meaning of the universe as a religious act is strongly present throughout the book. Nowhere is this spirit more explicit than in the incident of the visit to the Martian station above the earth, when men for the first time see the earth as a world in space. Standing in a mysterious twilight, illuminated only by the reflection of moonlight on the rim of the gallery and earthlight on the ceiling above them, they look into a pitch black sky studded with a thousand brilliant diamonds. And in the middle at their feet hovers the earth in the form of the waxing moon shortly after first quarter:

> How great was the temptation to pride and triumph—how humble and awestricken they felt! The Martians respected their thoughtfulness. They, too, to whom the wonders of space were familiar, became silent in the presence of the infinite.[11]

Men and Martians bow their heads in reverence.

V

There are several striking parallels between *Auf Zwei Planeten* and Wells' *The War of the Worlds,* of which the basic idea of the invasion of earth by the superior Martians and the disastrous effect of terrestrial conditions of life on the invaders (Lasswitz's Martians get "earth fever" and Wells' die from bacteria) are immediately obvious. But as far as I have ever been able to determine, there was no influence, direct or otherwise, of one story upon the other. Indeed, it is impossible to see how there could have been as the two stories appeared almost simultaneously—*Auf Zwei Planeten* in October, 1897, and *The War of the Worlds* serially April-December, 1897. One might suspect that Lasswitz was inspired by the early installments of *The War of the Worlds,* but we know that Lasswitz had long been at work on his novel. More likely, both men were responding to the myth and particularly to its rich development in Lowell's *Mars* in 1895. Any influence, I think would be *Auf Zwei Planeten* on Wells' later writings, notably *A Modern Utopia* (1905).

The War of the Worlds is the most brilliant, most effective, and most influential of all treatments of the Martian myth. It is the myth in almost archetypal form, and its impact has been enormous. While it was being serialized in its authorized form by *Cosmopolitan* in America and *Pearsons* in England, it was being outrageously adapted to the purpose of yellow journalism by the New York *Evening Journal* and the *Boston Post.*[12] Immediately after publication, sequels appeared, such as Garrett Putnam Serviss' *Mr. Edison's Conquest of Mars,* which the New York *Evening Journal,* anxious to continue to exploit the great public interest in Wells' story, published serially beginning on January 12, 1898. Then it has been three times adapted to radio broadcasts that were so successful as to cause panics: Orson Welles' Mercury Theatre production in 1938, another in Chile in 1944, and still another in Ecuador in 1949. Finally, and most important as a measure of its impact, *The War of the Worlds* is the direct ancestor of hundreds of later stories about alien invasions from space.

Before analyzing the Martian myth as it appears in *The War of the Worlds,* we should note that the success of the story is not due exclusively to the fascination of the myth it presents. It is successful also because it is an extraordinarily well written, skilfully crafted work. Rich in circumstantial and topographical detail and working from the ordinary, everyday world of late nineteenth-century England, it is a classic first person narrative account in the manner of Defoe's *Journal of the Plague Year* of the enormous disaster which overcomes mankind when the incredibly advanced Martians hurtle through space to take our world from us. The climactic description of the panicked exodus from London has never been surpassed in any imaginary account of world catastrophe or future war.

But the ultimate explanation of the success of *The War of the Worlds* must be found in Welles' brilliantly imaginative use of the conventions of the Martian myth. Thus, instead of describing the physical conditions on the planet from which the invaders come, he makes their actions on earth and the objects brought by them reveal the nature of their world. The thin atmosphere on Mars is indicated by the "pulmonary distress" of the Martians in our own air; the lesser gravitational attraction on Mars is shown when the Martians, whose weight is three times greater here, vainly strain to raise themselves up on their delicate, tentacle-hands. The short-lived yet prolific red weed which comes with them explains the red color of Mars.[13] Details are filled in by a few, brief passages such as the following:

> The secular cooling that must some day overtake our planet has already gone far indeed with our neighbor. Its physical condition is still largely a mystery, but we know that even in its equatorial region the mid-day temperature barely approaches that of our coldest winter. Its air is much more attenuated than ours, its oceans have shrunk until they cover but a third of its surface, and as its slow seasons change huge snow-caps gather and melt about either pole and periodically inundate its temperate zone.[14]

Welles' narrator explains that Mars, older, further from the sun, and smaller than the earth, is "not only more distant from life's beginning but nearer its end." Life began on Mars while the earth, formed later as required by the nebular hypothesis, was still molten. Looking sunward from their dying planet, the Martians see "a morning star of hope, our warmer planet, green with vegetation and grey with water, with a cloudy atmosphere eloquent of fertility, with glimpses through its drifting cloud wisps of broad stretches of populous country and narrow, navy-crowded seas."

The convention that Martian civilization must be technologically and scientifically advanced beyond that of the earth is imaginatively developed in the machines brought to earth by the invaders. Unlike his predecessors in the Martian romance, who wrote only of existing inventions, such as the telephone, telegraph, electric motor and dynamo, or inventions that were sure to come in the foreseeable future, such as radio, television, and the airplane, Wells created the incredibly refined machines of the Martians. Their technology had progressed so far that they no longer used the wheel, and on first impression their monstrous metallic walking tripods and spidery handling machines seemed to be living organisms. The Martians employed these devices, which were an integral part of their existence, as naturally as we did clothes. Wells created the devastating Martian heat ray from the idea so often employed in the Martian romances of a spectrum of energy, of which electricity and the strange antigravity force were only two manifestations.

But Welles' greatest transformation of the Martian myth is the Martians themselves. Drawing on his knowledge of biology and the theory of evolution, Wells expands the convention that the Martians must be physically more advanced than man because of the greater age of their species. There had been earlier suggestions, notably in *Across the Zodiac*, that life forms on the older Mars had evolved further than on the earth, but Wells gave to this idea its ultimate development when he cast the Martians as man may be after a million years of evolution. Mechanical appliances have replaced limbs, chemical devices have replaced digestion. Such organs as hair, external nose, teeth, ears, and chin, no longer essential parts of the human being, have disappeared through natural selection. The only parts which cannot be replaced are the brain and hand, which have grown larger and more important. Human reaction to the Martians is horror (as in this often quoted passage):

> The peculiar V-shaped mouth with its pointed upper lip, the absence of brow ridges, the absence of a chin beneath the wedge-like lower lip, the incessant quivering of this mouth, the Gorgon groups of tentacles, the tumultous breathing of the lungs in a strange atmosphere, the evident heaviness and painfulness of movement due to the greater gravitational energy of the earth—above all, the extraordinarily intensity of the immense eyes—were at once vital, intense, inhuman, crippled and monstrous. There was something fungoid in the oily brown skin, something in the clumsy deliberation of the tedious movements unspeakably nasty.[15]

Man on Mars has become a mere brain that never tires and never sleeps. The most terrifying thing about the Martians, however, is not their physical form but their cold, calculating nature combined with extraordinarily great intellect—they have no human emotions because such natural functions as sexual reproduction and digestion have been replaced by inhuman processes, budding and injection of blood from less advanced creatures like man.

And so with these Martians (and three years later with the Selenites in *The First Men in the Moon*) Welles invented the alien whose form is so different from man that he produces a reaction of horror. Something of the extent of Welles' influence is captured in a passage in C. S. Lewis' *Out of the Silent Planet* (itself a use of the Martian myth, as we will see later). Ransom, frightened at the idea of meeting the *sorns*, one of the intelligent species of Mars, can only remember his H. G. Wells:

> His mind, like so many minds of his generation, was richly furnished with bogies. He had read his H. G. Wells and others. His universe was peopled with

> horrors such as ancient and medieval mythology could hardly rival. No insect-like, vermiculate or crustacean Abominable, no twitching feelers, rasping wings, slimy coils, curling tentacles, no monstrous union of superhuman intelligence and insatiable cruelty seemed to him anything but likely on an alien world.[16]

But even the imagined monstrosities—"bulbous eyes, grinning jaws, horns, stings, mandibles"—wouldn't come up to the reality: "...it would be an extraterrestrial Otherness—something one had never thought of, never could have thought of." This Otherness is at the heart of *The War of the Worlds.*

VI

And so by 1898 a major myth of the twentieth century is launched. It would be difficult to assess the separate influence of Lowell's writings about Mars, Lasswitz's *Auf Zwei Planeten,* and Welles' *The War of the Worlds.* Lowell's influence has obviously been very great, as witness Donald Wollheim's dedication of *The Secret of the Martian Moons* as late as 1955: "To the memory of PERCIVAL LOWELL, whose inspired vision of Mars will continue to haunt men's minds until we go there." The myth of the aging Mars with its canals can, I suspect, usually be traced to Lowell. On the other hand, *The War of the Worlds* must be the direct ancestor of all the stories of the invasion of earth by superior aliens, Martian or otherwise. Thus the indebtedness is made explicit in a story as seemingly far removed from Welles' as John Wyndham's *The Midwich Cuckoos* (1957), in which superior aliens impregnate all the women of childbearing age in a little English village, and the golden-eyed, precocious and telepathic Children born of this event are a new species, a threat to the survival of *Homo sapiens.* A chief character, analyzing the situation, compares the threat offered by the Children to the menace of Welles' Martians. Similarly, in Robert Heinlein's *Stranger in a Strange Land* (1961), in which a human raised by the

Martians comes to earth, eventually to found a new religion, *The War of the Worlds* is mentioned in a discussion of a possible Martian invasion. Finally, as for Lasswitz's influence, it would have to be much less, particularly in the English-speaking world, since the work had never been translated into English. But it is obvious in at least one important case, Arthur Clarke's *Childhood End* (1953). In Clarke's novel the Overlords, superior aliens from a distant world who come to earth just in time to save mankind from disaster and to prepare them, by creating a utopian world state, for the next stage in their evolution, are clearly descended from Lasswitz's Martians. And it is unlikely that this is a mere coincidence, for Clarke knew Lasswitz's book, mentioning it in *The Making of a Moon* and elsewhere and speculating at one point that Wells might have gotten from it the idea for *The War of the Worlds.*

After Lowell, Lasswitz, and Wells, the Martian myth flourishes up into the 1930's, when any scientific evidence supporting it had been so discredited that thereafter the myth was no longer viable. From it, though, radiate literally hundreds of stories of other aliens and their invasion of earth (including those who arrive in flying saucers), aliens whose existence can be plausibly posited (a process begun, of course, long before the demise of the Martians). This is an essential point about all such myths of a scientific and technological age: scientific credibility is an essential part of their viability. There has to seem to be a chance, even though an unlikely one, that the myths are true. Up into the thirties, though, the Martians are very much alive in major treatments like Edgar Rice Burroughs' Martian novels, Alexei Tolstoi's *Aelita,* Stanley Weinbaum's "A Martian Odyssey," the Orson Welles radio broadcast, and C. S. Lewis's *Out of the Silent Planet.*

Surely the most spectacularly extensive and the most popularly successful uses of the Martian myth are Edgar Rice Burroughs' Martian novels. His first published fiction was *A Princess of Mars,* which under its original title, *Under the Moons of Mars,* appeared serially in *All-Story* in 1912. It launched Burroughs' career as a writer, and depending on how one counts, he wrote something like eleven more Martian romances. The best were the first three, which formed a trilogy: besides *A Princess of Mars, The Gods of Mars (All-Story,* 1913) and *The Warlords of Mars* (*All-Story,* 1914). There is considerable narrative vigor and imaginative vitality in these three, though even in the later Martian stories Burroughs' imagination never completely failed him. But the first three are particularly outstanding popular literature.

Burroughs' Martian stories are not scientific science fiction in the manner of Welles' *The War of the Worlds* or Lasswitz's *Auf Zwei Planeten:* that is, his stories are not carefully thought out in their technological, scientific detail; there is little stirring of the scientific imagination. Instead, Burroughs' controlling purpose is to use the Martian myth to create an atmosphere of the exotic and strange as a background for incredible adventures. Thus in *A Princess of Mars,* John Carter, a former confederate Army Captain seeking his fortune, is transported somehow supernaturally to Mars—Barsoom in Martian—where he fights under overwhelming odds against all sorts of Martian creatures, has many cliffhanging escapes, and, after leaving behind a trail of gore, wins the Princess of Helium and eventually becomes warlord of Mars.

The myth is present, of course. To begin with, Barsoom is an old dying world, with diminished water supply and thin, depleted atmosphere. A million years ago the highly civilized and dominant white race, the Orovars, ruled the planet in prosperity. But then the seas began to dry up, and in time the advanced civilization collapsed; and the green men, fifteen-foot tall savages who had formerly been under control, overran the Orovars. The few survivors intermarried with a reddish-yellow race and a black one to become the red race that maintains an uneasy and uncertain mastery over the hordes of savage green men. Although not as advanced as the ancient, vanished Orovars, the red Martians have hung on to some science and technology. Here we get all the familiar wonderful devices and inventions of the Martian myth. The red Martians have several kinds of aircraft, instruments to project images of the planets down to blades of grass, houses which are raised on round metal shafts at night (to prevent surprise attack by the green men), and so forth. They maintain the great canals of Mars and also an atmosphere factory which replenishes the air of the planet by utilizing the ninth Barsoomian ray. But with all their aircraft, radium rifles, etc., they mostly ride around on thoats—ten foot high, eight-legged animals—and fight with swords.

Something of the viability of the Martian myth can be seen in its successful transplantation to the Soviet Russia of the period immediately following the Civil War in Alexei Tolstoi's *Aelita* (1923). Here the Martian myth takes the direction of romance, but unlike the work of Burroughs and other such romancers, characters are well drawn, the chief ones being the Engineer Los; the demobilized Red Army man, Gusev; and the beautiful Martian woman, Aelita. Los and Gusev travel to Mars in a rocket built by Los, where they become embroiled in an abortive workers' rebellion. In spite of the sympathy shown for the rebels, the book is not chiefly propaganda in support of communist revolution. Rather, as Gleb Struve points out, there are two other, more important themes. The first, represented by Los, is that of "love being stronger than death or than any sense of revolutionary duty." The second, embodied in Gusev, is that of "elemental, irrational revolt." Gusev is neither proletarian nor Communist, but rather a true Russian.

The details of the Martian myth are skillfully and delightfully handled, and Tolstoi succeeds in creating an exotic and fantastic world, the familiar dying world of the myth:

> 'Long ago the mountains were covered with vegetation,' said Aelita. 'Herds of Khasi used to graze here and waterfalls rumbled in the gorges. Tuma [Mars] is dying. The cycle of milleniums is closing.' [18]

The air is thin and the sun blazes in a "dazzling, bottomless sky, deep blue as the ocean in a storm." Much of the planet is now desert, with great cracks, spindle-shaped cactus, and the dry beds of old canals. Across the desert scuttle bright orange lizard-like animals, and strange prickly-looking balls dart underfoot. At night great giant spiders forage for food, while the two moons, ollo and litkha, race across the sky.

Some of the canals are still in use, and there is a great city,

Soatsera, around the reservoir which forms the hub of one of the networks of canals. The Martians have all the advanced machinery and technology one expects in the Martian romance: viewing screens, aircraft that are mobile and pliant as living beings, singing books, elevated roads on pylons, and so forth.

One of the best Martian stories ever written first appeared in the July, 1934, issue of Hugo Gernsback's pulp magazine, *Wonder Stories:* Stanely G. Weinbaum's "A Martian Odyssey." Its influence on subsequent pulp science fiction has been extraordinarily great, and it is still alive today and very much remembered. The significance of Weinbaum's accomplishment, seen against the impoverishment of most pulp science fiction in the late twenties and early thirties, has been well explained by H. P. Lovecraft:

> Here, I rejoiced, was somebody who could think of another planet in terms of something besides anthropormorphic kings and beautiful princesses and battles of space ships and ray-guns and attacks from the hairy sub-men of the "dark side" or "polar cap" region, etc., etc. Somehow he had the imagination to envisage wholly alien situations and psychological entities, to devise consistent events from wholly alien motives and to refrain from the cheap dramatics in which almost all adventure-pulpists wallow.[19]

"A Martian Odyssey" is also a splendid example of a variety of science-fiction that is characterized by surrealistic images for which willing suspension of disbelief is achieved by the careful working out of scientific plausibility. In the visualization of the exotic and strange creatures Weinbaum's narrator encounters as he works his way back to base camp after his rocket has crashed in the Martian desert, we see this peculiar science-fiction imagination at work. I think this same quality—this blend of surrealism and controlled, scientific imagination—is present in much, though of course not all, of the best science fiction by "professionals" and reaches a kind of apotheosis in Emshwiller's film *Relativity.*

Weinbaum's finest creation is Tweel, a highly intelligent bird-like creature, heir to an advanced civilization (about which we learn nothing), who is rescued from the dream beast by the narrator at the beginning of his odyssey and who becomes the narrator's companion on the 800-mile trek back to base camp. Tweel (his real name is something like "Trrrweerrlll") is alive in his alienness, and part of Weinbaum's success with him lies in portraying the difficulty of communication between minds of such entirely different orders. And there are other equally alien creatures, from the biopods—little walking plants that inhabit the dry canal beds—to the barrel people: no head, just a barrel-like body with four legs and four arms. Perhaps the best, and surely the most surrealistic of the lot, is the silicon beast.

The two travelers come upon a tiny row of brick pyramids, about six inches high, which stretch for miles and miles as the pyramids gradually grow larger. When, after following the line for hours, they come to the end, the pyramids are now ten feet tall. As they watch the last pyramid, its top breaks off:

> 'A long, silvery-grey arm appeared, dragging after it an armored body. Armored, I mean, with scales, silver-grey and dull-shining. The arm heaved the body out of the hole; the beast crashed to the sand.
>
> 'It was a nondescript creature—body like a big grey cask, arm and a sort of mouth hole at one end, stiff pointed tail at the other—and that's all. No other limbs, no eyes, ears, nose—nothing! The thing dragged itself a few yards, inserted its pointed tail in the sand, pushed itself upright, and just sat.' [20]

And then it begins building a new pyramid.

The astonishing creature exists on a silicon life cycle, and already, the narrator estimates, it is half a million years old:

> 'Lord! That queer creature! Do you picture it? Blind, deaf, nerveless, brainless—just a mechanism, and yet—immortal! Bound to go on making bricks, building pyramids, as long as silicon and oxygen exist, and even afterwards it'll just stop. It won't be dead. If the

> accidents of a million years bring it its food again, there it'll be ready to run again, while brains and civilization are part of the past.'[21]

Easily the most literarily felicitous use of the Martian myth is in C. S. Lewis's *Out of the Silent Planet*,[22] the first part of the trilogy whose second and third parts are *Perelandra* and *That Hideous Strength* and which makes extraordinary use of all kinds of myth—not only the Martian, but classical, Arthurian, and—most of all—Christian. The basic myth underlying the trilogy—a *Paradise Lost* written for an unsuspecting, skeptical twentieth century—is, of course, the "silent planet" myth. Since the war in heaven, earth (called Thulcandra in Old Solar) has been quarantined from the rest of the universe to prevent the spread of its spiritual infection. In *Out of the Silent Planet* the barrier is broken when Ransom, the Cambridge philologist, is kidnapped and taken to Malacandra or Mars (an unfallen world) by two men, Weston and Devine, who mistakenly believe a human sacrifice is necessary to further their purposes on that world. A new chapter in the history of the universe is thus begun.

Miss Nicolson is probably right in seeing in Malacandra elements of Keplerian terror, but mostly, I think, it is a representative of the Martian myth. We have Lewis's own admission on this point:

> When I myself put canals on Mars I believe I already knew that better telescopes had dissipated that old optical delusion. The point was that they were part of the Martian myth as it already existed in the common mind.[23]

The interesting thing about Lewis's handling of the Martian myth is that he understands the scientific sensibility very well indeed; and *Out of the Silent Planet* is very much an expression of that sensibility, though ironically the book is anti-science. Lewis has very carefully worked out the ecology and physical details of Malacandra, and in plausibility and vitality it stands with the best of Wells' imagined worlds.

Malacandra, brilliantly the Mars of the myth, is seen through the eyes of an initially frightened Ransom, and at first his perceptions are blurred and unfocused ("you cannot see things till you know roughly what they are") and sees only a bright pale "water-colour world out of a child's paint box." Gradually he masters a few details. The blue was water, the purple stuff vegetation: "...more precisely it was vegetables, vegetables about twice the height of English elms, but apparently soft and flimsy."

Not long after this a group of *sorns* (one of the intelligent species of Malacandra) comes to greet the party; and, overwhelmed with fright, Ransom escapes from his captors. And so, on his own, as the first crushing fear wears off, he begins to discover the true nature of the new world. One of the first things he notices is the theme of perpendicularity, the consequence of the lesser gravitation on a smaller world: ridges, plants, even the waves on the blue lakes display an unearthly vertical elongation. Another early discovery is that the blue water that hisses down streams into the lakes must come from some hotter subterranean source. After spending a day and a night alone, he is befriended by a *hross,* another of the intelligent species of Malacandra; and from then on he quickly sheds his fear and comes rapidly to know the new world.

What he learns is that it is the older, dying world of the Martian myth. The surface is desert and vast red petrified forests—uninhabited because of the cold and the thinness of the air. All of the life of the planet is to be found in or along the great long canals—actually deep canyons (called *handramit*)—where there is warmth, water, and air to breathe. The *harandra*—the surface—is barren and desolate: "jagged peaks blazing in sunlight against the almost black sky." At one point Ransom is taken on a journey near the limits of the atmosphere, in order to cross from one *handramit* to another. It is an awesome sight, but his guide explains that once "there was air on the *harandra* and it was warm." Great forests grew, and "in and out among their stalks" went a people who glided through the air on "broad flat limbs." "It is said they were great singers, and in those days the red forests echoed with their music."

Later, in a last look at Malacandra as the spaceship returns to earth, he sees the Mars of Percival Lowell's drawings:

> Each minute more *handramits* came into view—long straight lines, some parallel, some intersecting, some building triangles. The landscape became increasingly geometrical. The waste between the purple lines appeared perfectly flat. The rosy colour of the petrified forests accounted for its tint immediately below him; but to the north and east the great sand deserts of which the *sorns* had told him were now appearing as illimitable stretches of yellow and ochre. To the west a huge discoloration began to show. It was an irregular patch of greenish blue that looked as if it were sunk below the level of the surrounding *harandra.* He concluded it was the forest lowland of the *pfifltriggi*—or rather one of their forest lowlands, for now similar patches were appearing in all directions, some of them mere blobs at the intersection of *handramits,* some of them of vast extent.[24]

He muses on how much he never learned about Mars, such as about the gigantic feat of engineering involved in the digging of the *handramits* ages before.

In portraying the three rational species (or *hnau*) of Malacandra, Lewis carries the myth of the advanced Martians to its ultimate. He has Wells very much in mind, as is apparent in the famous passage in *Out of the Silent Planet* cited earlier, where Ransom speculates on what the inhabitants of the world to which he is being taken will be like ("He had read his H. G. Wells..."). There are other places where this idea is expressed: "His whole imaginative training somehow encouraged him to associate superhuman intelligence with monstrosity of form and ruthlessness of will." Lewis is remembering not only the Martians of *The War of the Worlds* but also the insect-like Selenites of *The First Men in the Moon.*

In answer to this conception of the inhabitants of another world, Lewis creates his unfallen Malacandra, whose *hnau* (rational beings) are indeed superior as the Martian myth demanded, but with an interesting variation on the convention. They are morally and spiritually superior, not scientifically and technologically.

There are three species of *hnau*. The *hrossa* are tall, thin creatures with "a coat of thick black hair, lucid as seal-skin, very short legs with webbed feet, a broad beaver-like or fish-like tail, strong forelimbs with webbed claws or fingers." The great poets and singers of Malacandra, they lead simple, pastoral lives free from the anxieties of a technologically complex civilization. The *sorns,* the second species, are more grotesque, more like the popular expectations in the thirties of what a Martian would be: they suggest one of Frank R. Paul's covers for the pulp science-fiction magazines. "Stalky, flexible-looking distortions of earthly bipeds," they are two or three times the height of man, "thin and elongated in the leg," "top heavily pouted in the chest." Their faces are long and drooping, their heads narrow and conical, their hands "thin, mobile, spidery, and almost transparent"; and they speak with enormous horn-like voices. They are the intellectuals of Mars. The third species of *hnau*, the *pfifltriggi*, are frog-like creatures who are the artists and craftsmen of Mars. There are also other beings who, though they have a material existence of a sort, are what we would call spirits or angels.

VII

Nineteen thirty-eight is the last and climactic year for the Martian myth. Besides being the year of the publication of *Out of the Silent Planet,* it is also the year of Orson Welles' Mercury Theatre broadcast of *The War of the Worlds*. The extraordinary reaction to the broadcast has been vividly described by Hadley Cantril in *The Invasion from Mars: A Study in the Psychology of Panic:*

> Long before the broadcast had ended, people all over the United States were praying, crying, fleeing frantically to escape death from the Martians. Some ran to rescue loved ones. Others telephoned farewells or warnings, hurried to inform neighbors, sought information from newspapers, or radio stations, summoned ambulances and police cars. At least six

> million people heard the broadcast. At least a million of them were frightened or disturbed.[25]

Cantril's study has little if anything to say about the Martian myth and instead emphasizes other factors: the verisimilitude of interviews and bulletins which made the listener, especially if he tuned in late, think he was listening to actual news broadcasts; the lack of "critical ability" on the part of those who accepted the broadcast as true; the role of individual insecurity and the anxieties produced by the war scare and by years of depression. Although it may be that the Martian myth had nothing to do with the panic, the phenomenon is at least a testament to the vitality of Welles' story.

After 1938, the Martian myth fades away, chiefly because it is, in scientific terms, no longer credible. Martian stories continue to be written, but all are in a sense artificial; the old vitality is gone. A case in point is Ray Bradbury's *The Martian Chronicles* (1950), a collection of stories, loosely strung together, that deal with the theme of the American conquest and colonization of Mars (the Martians are soon killed off by smallpox). As good as many of the stories are, Bradbury's Martians are not imaginatively real, as they are with, say, C. S. Lewis; and he uses the Martian myth in a self-consciously literary way, chiefly as a vehicle for criticism of American civilization and culture. The Americans put up garishly lighted hot-dog stands at the crossroads of centuries-old highways, throw tin cans in the ancient canals, and let discarded newspapers drift across the old Martian sea bottoms. The emigrants cannot understand the beauty and wisdom they are desecrating. Likewise I feel that Heinlein's *Stranger in a Strange Land*—a bible for the hippie subculture—derives its impact not from the Martian myth itself but from the satire and criticism generated as the hero discovers the dimensions of human nature and the values of earthly civilization.

But if the myth of the superior Martians itself fades away, it lives on in all its progeny—the literally hundreds of stories about superior aliens and their invasion of earth. I do not see how there could be much doubt that most of these stories derive ultimately from the Martian myth. Often the indebtedness is explicit and conscious, as we have seen it in Wyndham's *Midwich Cuckoos* and as it is also in Arthur Clarke's novel, *2001*, where an imagined Project Barsoom is conducted by Harvard in 1989 to predict what the effect on the public consciousness would be of the discovery of the existence of extraterrestrials.

Just how alive today is this myth that began with the Martians can be seen in the spectacular, almost overwhelming film, *2001*. At the heart of this twentieth-century epic in a twentieth century medium is our familiar myth: three million years ago, when the man-apes were struggling to survive a great drought, advanced aliens arrived to teach the man-apes the use of weapons and tools, knowledge that would enable them to survive and evolve Mind. At the same time the aliens left a calling card on the moon, whose discovery, when man finally arrived there, would alert the aliens to welcome man on the other side of the Stargate. The essentially religious impulse behind the film's use of the myth has been noted by some reviewers, and Stanley Kubrick has agreed that a "God concept" is at the heart of *2001*: the concept of inconceivably advanced aliens who, in their immortal collective consciousness, stand as gods to man. To Kubrick this is a real possibility in a universe of a billion habitable worlds:

> The important point is that all the standard attributes assigned to God in our history could equally well be the characteristics of biological entities who billions of years ago were at a stage of development similar to man's own and evolved into something as remote from man as man is remote from the primordial ooze from which he first emerged.[26]

From Lowell to Kubrick there must have been a few mythmakers in action.

NOTES

[1] *The Mythmakers* (Athens, Ohio, 1966), p. 181.

[2] See Kenneth Allott, *Jules Verne* (New York, 1941); Leo Marx, *The*

Machine in the Garden (New York, 1964); and Herbert L. Sussman, *The Victorians and the Machine* (Cambridge, Mass., 1968).

[3]*The Origins of Modern Science* (New York, 1962), p. 119.

[4]*Mars,* 3rd ed. (Boston and New York, 1897), p. 122.

[5]*Ibid.,* p. 128. [6]*Ibid.,* p. 209.

[7]See, for example, Henry Gaston, *Mars Revealed; or, Seven Days in the Spirit World: Containing an Account of the Spirit's Trip to Mars* (1880); Anon., *Politics and Life in Mars* (1883); Hugh Maccoll, *Mr. Stranger's Sealed Packet* (1889); Robert Cromie, *A Plunge into Space* (1890); Robert D. Braine, *Messages from Mars by the Aid of the Telescope Plant* (1892); Henry Olerich, *A Cityless and Countryless World; An Outline of Practical, Cooperative Individualism* (1893); William Simpson, *The Man from Mars, His Morals, Politics, and Religion* (1893); and Gustavus Pope, *Journey to Mars, The Wonderful World* (1894).

[8]*Rockets, Missiles, and Space Travel* (New York, 1953), p. 46.

[9]*Die Nation*, xvi (1898-9), 466-469, 480-83.

[10]*Auf Zwei Planeten* (Donnaüwörth, 1948), p. 42.

[11]*Ibid.,* p. 88.

[12]See David Y. Hughes, "*The War of the Worlds* in the Yellow Press," *Journalism Quarterly,* XCIII (Winter, 1966), 639-646.

[13]Details of the Mars from which the invaders come are described in Wells' story, "The Crystal Egg," first published in the *New Review* in 1897. Wells also theorized about Mars and its inhabitants in several articles, most notably in "Intelligence on Mars," *The Saturday Review*, LXXXI (April 4, 1896), 345-6; and "Things that Live on Mars," *Cosmopolitan Magazine,* XLIV (March, 1908), 336-342.

[14]*Seven Science Fiction Novels of H. G. Wells* (New York, 1950), p. 310.

[15]*Ibid.,* pp. 321-2.

[16]New York, 1944, p. 33.

[17]There are dozens of other treatments of the Martian myth in the period 1895-1938, but limitations of space preclude their discussion in this article. Two, however, are of sufficient vitality at least to be mentioned: Edwin Lester Arnold's *Lieut. Gullivar Jones: His Vacation* (1905), which Richard A. Lupoff believes influenced Burroughs' Martian novels; and the episode of the Martian invasion during the era of the Second Men in Olaf Stapledon's evolutionary epic, *Last and First Men* (1930). Stapledon's Martians, clouds of separate cell-entities united by "neural radio," reappear in later science fiction, e.g., Fred Hoyle's *The Black Cloud.*

[18]Moscow, n. d., p. 204.

[19]As quoted by Sam Moskowitz in *Explorers of the Infinite* (Cleveland and New York, 1963), p. 298.

[20]*The Pocket Book of Science Fiction,* ed. Donald Wollheim (New York, 1943), pp. 203-4.

[21]*Ibid.,* p. 206.

[22]For a more extended analysis of *Out of the Silent Planet* as cosmic voyage and Martian romance, see my essay in *Shadows of Imagination: The Fantasies of C. S. Lewis, J. R. R. Tolkien, and Charles Williams* (Carbondale and Edwardsville, 1969). I have used portions of that essay in my discussion of Lewis here.

[23]*Of Other Worlds* (London, 1966), p. 69.

[24]*Out of the Silent Planet,* p. 156.

[25]New York, 1966, p. 47.

[26]*Playboy,* XV (September, 1968), 96.

The Two Whitmans and *Democracy in America*

by

David W. Marcell

Over the past decade a new refraction on the American past has been coming into focus. Partly in response to the anti-intellectual implications of the consensus historians' interpretations of the 1950's, and partly in reaction against the explicit social and economic determinism of the earlier progressive historians, the 1960's witnessed, to paraphrase Daniel Bell, a renaissance of ideology and a new concern for the role of ideas and attitudes in history. Studies such as Stanley Elkins' *Slavery* (1959), William R. Taylor's *Cavalier and Yankee* (1961), Bernard Bailyn's *Ideological Origins of the American Revolution* (1966), Robert Skotheim's *American Intellectual Histories and Historians* (1966), George M. Frederickson's *The Inner Civil War* (1967), together with important articles by Edmund Morgan, John Higham, Gordon S. Wood, John Thomas, and Perry Miller, suggest that in the last ten years intellectual history in the United States has entered a new and vigorous stage. Ideas, attitudes, and intellectual assumptions are once again fair game for the student of social change and historical causality.

Part of this new concern has of course focused on the Civil War and on the role that ideas played or may have played in its inception. In this connection certain ideas and attitudes in particular have caught historians' attention: democracy, individualism, abstractionism, self-reliance, the millenium, perfectionism, the sublime, and especially the rampant anti-institutionalism of certain radical reformers have taken on new importance of causal considerations of what George Frederickson calls "the collective trauma" of the Civil War. But if there is to be an adequate comprehension of the intellectual dimensions of this "trauma," historians must undertake a systematic tracing of what happened to these seminal ideas during, and especially *after*, the war years. Frederickson's study is an excellent beginning, but much work remains to be done.

I want to suggest here only a small part of that task. The Civil War was undoubtedly traumatic for Walt Whitman, and changes in his outlook on many of the pressing questions of the day may give us an important insight into what the war meant to engaged Americans. My hypothesis is that the changing perspective of the pre- and post-war Whitman on several major questions may be regarded as the paradigm for a much larger shift in American attitudes and assumptions. This shift, moreover, can be seen as a kind of shock of recognition, as a rude awakening of Americans to some of the caveats about democracy expressed earlier in the century by that most wordly of commentators, Alexis de Tocqueville. Certainly, at least, this was the case for Whitman, as a comparison of "Song of Myself" and *Democratic Vistas* reveals.

Walt Whitman's accomplishment in *Leaves of Grass,* as Mark Van Doren once observed, was the creation of a legend in which a self-created man became a book by "overflowing into it." But if Whitman overflowed into *Leaves of Grass,* the process was reversed in "Song of Myself," for in that poem all the world and all of history flowed into one inclusive, all-embracing, universal, democratic Self. "Right and left he flings his arms," Whitman wrote in an unsigned review of the 1855 edition, "drawing men and women with undeniable love to his close embrace. . . ." By assuming this stance Whitman's Self achieved both universality and independence, and thus revealed the poet's pre-war perspective on democracy and America. For we can accept Whitman's own judgment that "The proof of a poet is that his country absorbs him as affectionately as he has absorbed it." *Leaves of Grass* and the long, mysteriously unnamed poem which later became "Song of Myself" are Whitman's testimony that by 1855 he had indeed absorbed America and felt himself ready to be absorbed by it.

The Self of which Whitman sang was one whose parameters were limited by neither time nor space. Indeed, Whitman sang as much of what the Self was *not* bound by as what it in essence was. This indirection, in fact, reveals one of the major problems in both writing and reading "Song of Myself," for Whitman was attempting to articulate a limitless, transcendent Self; that he succeeded so well does not obviate the fact that the Self remains throughout the poem mysterious and shadowy, seen, like the wind in the common, ordinary grass, by its almost capricious visitings, by all it touches and is touched by.

Since the poet, as announced in the Preface, is "the president of regulation," his Self can be irregular by ordinary standards. And so can the poem; indeed it has to be. Bounded by neither law nor tradition nor civilization nor nature, the Self requires a poetic form that expresses and evokes but does not delimit. Each line and stanza, consequently, though an organic part of a larger entity, seems a law unto itself. Whitman's Self, the poem suggests, is not part of a genre or class but is, rather, the embodiment of uniqueness and autonomy—and hence also of equality. Initially denying that the Self is confined by any of the ordinary limits of experience and being, Whitman finally comes to reveal that the Self is the "Kosmos," the totality that includes body and soul, day and night, reason and intuition, good and evil, man and God. The Self is, then, the ultimate resolution of all of the dualities that have made up and distinguished Western thought since Plato and before. As such it becomes the surrogate for all other selves, and thus both the celebrator and celebrity of democracy.

Perhaps the most notable quality of the social dimensions of Whitman's Self is its indiscriminacy. In its journeys—one is tempted to say "trips"—the Self associates freely, exuberantly, with all sorts and conditions of men, women and children whose different stations and characters, deliberately juxtaposed, underscore the main point. "Congressman, Cuff," "the youngster and the red-faced girl," the suicide, the criminal, the 28-year-old, voyeuristic maiden, the prostitute, the gigantic Negro slave—all are visited, recognized, embraced and blessed by the poet. His Self, in turn, absorbs them and becomes larger and more multitudinous. Tocqueville observed in *Democracy in America* that "The literature of an aristocratic period is distinguished by its aims at selectness, and the number of things it proscribes; we should expect the literature of a democracy to be remarkable for its comprehensiveness, its acceptance of the persons of all men, its multiform sympathies." Whitman's Self seems the embodiment of Tocqueville's prediction. As Whitman put it in the Preface,

> Did you suppose there could be only one Supreme? We affirm there can be unnumbered Supremes, and that one does not countervail another any more than one eyesight countervails another. . . and that men can be good or grand only of the consciousness of their supremacy within them.

Whitman's Self, then, assumes heroic proportions through this very indiscriminacy. "The messages of great poets," he wrote again in the Preface, "to each man and woman are, 'Come to us on equal terms.' " But by refusing to discriminate among men and things, by embracing all with equal love and affection, Whitman seems to say that evil does not exist; or if it does, that it is simply a necessary part of some larger dialectic within which all shall be eventually justified. Confronted with the agony and horror of the wounded, tortured runaway, Whitman does not judge and condemn, but suffers and becomes. His empathy is loving but paradoxically sterile. In other words, Whitman's transcendent Self is limited by its very transcendence, for it can only *become* all it experiences. The principle of distinction or discrimination is denied to it by definition.

> I am not the poet of goodness only, I do not decline

> to be the poet of wickedness also, . . .
> What blurt is that about virtue and about vice?
> Evil propels me and reform of evil propels me. I stand indifferent,
> My gait is no fault-finder's or rejecter's gait.
> I moisten the roots of all that has grown.

One suspects the wounded slave cannot share Whitman's equanimity.

The Self's definitive transcendence has, of course, large implications for democracy. That which separates the Self from other selves, from other times and places, other categories of experience and being, becomes nothing less than unreal. This transcendence, this cosmic freedom, is what history has been straining to produce, what the universe, as it were, has been waiting for all along. Anything that confines the Self—houses, rooms, clothes, conventions, institutions, gender, age, language, sympathies, accepted truths—all are outmoded, transcended, and thereby ultimately denied. This denial is the basis for the achieved, pantheistic serenity with which the poem ends:

> I depart as air – I shake my white locks at the runaway sun;
> I effuse my flesh in eddies, and drift it in lacy jags.
> I bequeath myself to the dirt, to grow from the grass I love;
> If you want me again, look for me under your bootsoles.

Whitman's poem, then, is a hymn to the universality and sufficiency of the Self. Though the poet recognizes that all is not well in the public, social world of the 1850's, his concerns are basically other. By 1855 Whitman was disengaging from party politics and was denying there was any longer value in an established system of political parties. Though perhaps not a perfectionist in the sense of some American romantic reformers, Whitman nonetheless suggests there is an immanent, indwelling perfection in men which needs only to be evoked by a poet to spiritualize America. All else, one assumes, will follow. The traditional processes and institutions for social transformation and reform are not so much refuted or criticized as they are ignored; given Whitman's mystical, apocalyptic vision of the Self they are merely superfluous. Whitman's Self is not so much anti-institutional as it is supra-institutional. That anarchy or chaos might be implicit in this view is not a concern, for Whitman's exquisite, exhilarating but essentially private exploration of the Self renders these matters as trifles. Writing in "The Eighteenth Presidency," an unpublished pamphlet of 1856, Whitman stated, "We want no *reforms*, no *institutions*, no *parties*—We want a living principle such as nature has, under which nothing can go wrong." That principle is the principle of the transcendent, all-sufficient Self, the basic component of democracy.

By the late 1860's Whitman was older, sadder, and wiser. The war had not become the unifying, uplifting, purifying national experience he had hoped in the early sixties it would prove to be. Instead of sanctifying the Union the war had brutalized it. The achievement of a national, spiritual identity was more complex and elusive than Whitman had envisioned in the Preface to *Leaves of Grass*. Moreover, by the time *Democratic Vistas* was written in 1871 Whitman knew *Leaves of Grass* had not had the spiritualizing effect he had hoped for. Like many latter day Puritan sermons of two hundred years before, *Democratic Vistas* bears the aspect of a jeremiad, of the plaint of the divine who still believes in the democratic gospel but whose congregation is slipping from grace. As Whitman put it bluntly, "genuine belief seems to have left us." The question is, of course, belief in what? In the answer to this question lies the key to Whitman's own changing perspective on democracy and, in turn, to one aspect of what the war may have meant to Whitman and to many of his generation.

Simply put, after this war the American people—and Whitman too—lost their capacity to believe in a certain myth, a myth that had been compelling in the pre-war years and that had been central to Whitman's own achievement in "Song of Myself." The myth was none other than that of the all-sufficient, transcendent Self as the Alpha and Omega of democracy. The dessication and gore of the war and the crudity and crassness of its aftermath had the effect of demythologizing democracy. *Democratic Vistas* is both a lament for a lost faith in democratic immanence and an attempt to refocus the national mythic energies toward the achievement of a true, spiritual democracy in some distant future time.

The dynamics of this achievement, however, are now different and the possibility of failure, unlike 1855, is now real. Rather than celebrating the solitary singer of a transcendent Self as the messenger of democracy, Whitman now calls for a class of "divine" literati:

> Our fundamental want today in the United States, with closest, amplest reference to present conditions, and to the future, is a class, and the clear idea of a class, of native authors, literatures, far different, far higher, in grade, than any yet known, sacerdotal, modern, fit; to cope with our occasions, lands, permeating the whole mass of American mentality, taste, belief, breathing into it a new breath of life, giving it decision, affecting politics far more than the popular superficial suffrage, with results inside and underneath the elections of Presidents or Congresses—radiating, begetting appropriate teachers, schools, manners, and, as its grandest result, accomplishing (what neither the schools nor the churches and the clergy have hitherto accomplished, and without which this nation will no more stand, permanently, soundly, than a house will stand without a sub-stratum), a religious and moral character beneath the political and productive and intellectual bases of the State.

The shift from a preoccupation with the singular though universal Self to a call for a class of poets is basic. The conversion experience necessary for the achievement of true democracy must be vastly more public and pervasive than the extravagant privatism of "Song of Myself." A single poem and a solitary singer are no longer sufficient to the task. Nothing less than an aesthetically induced national conversion is required, and while the lone poet will contribute much to this conversion, he cannot stand alone. The achievement of true nationality, of "the fervid and tremendous Idea," of the true American personality, must be accomplished by an aesthetic elite, by a class of artists and creators whose cumulative cultural achievement will pervade—filter down through—all sectors of American life. Until this happens American democracy will be incomplete; America will remain only a society of scrambling, materialistic "expectant capitalists." The task of conversion has in 1871 hardly begun:

> I say that our New World democracy, however great a success in uplifting the masses out of their sloughs, in materialistic development, products, and in a certain highly deceptive superficial popular intellectuality, is, so far, an almost complete failure in its social aspects, and in really grand religious, moral, literary, and aesthetic results. . . . In vain have we annexed Texas, California, Alaska, and reach north for Canada and south for Cuba. It is as if we were somehow being endowed with a vast and more and more thoroughly appointed body, and left with little or no soul.

The last line of this quotation points up what has happened to Whitman's perspective on democracy. The cheerful, complaisant indiscriminacy of "Song of Myself" has, as it were, come home to roost. Whitman's all-inclusive embrace of the great *en masse* has become selective; it begins, in Tocqueville's terminology, to "proscribe." In *Democratic Vistas* Whitman descries the "flat mean average," and confesses,

> . . . that to severe eyes, using the moral microscope upon humanity, a sort of dry and flat Sahara appears. . . . Everywhere, in shop, street, church, theatre, barroom, official chair, are pervading flippancy and vulgarity, low cunning, infidelity—everywhere an abnormal libidinousness, unhealthy forms, male, female, painted, padded, dyed, chignoned, muddy complexions, bad blood, the capacity for good

> motherhood decreasing or deceased, shallow notions of beauty, with a range of manners, or rather lack of manners (considering the advantages enjoyed), probably the meanest to be seen in the world.

Whitman was clearly in a bad humor when this passage was written; and one can argue that *Democratic Vistas* represents a rather low period in Whitman's life. But it is revealing lowness, for in *Democratic Vistas* he offers a kind of corrective balance to the stance taken in "Song of Myself." The corrective, in Whitman's words, is as follows:

> We shall, it is true, quickly and continually find the origin-idea of the singleness of man, individualism, asserting itself, and cropping forth, even from the opposite ideas. But the mass, or lump character, for imperative reasons, is to be ever carefully weighed, borne in mind, and provided for. Only from it, and from its proper regulation and potency, comes the other, come the chance of individualism. The two are contradictory, but our task is to reconcile them.

Thus speaks the erstwhile "president of regulation." His directive is now down toward the people, not outward from the Self. While spiritualizing the "mass" is still Whitman's goal, this now must be accomplished not from activating some inner popular resource but by an achieved, externally provided "regulation." The people no longer seem to possess, of themselves, the resources necessary for their own fulfillment; those resources must be supplied from without the ranks of the divine average.

It may seem at first unfair to hold Whitman too literally to the inference of selfhood in "Song of Myself" and then to point out how he qualified his perspective in *Democratic Vistas*. "Song" is of course a poem, a work of art, a dramatization, and *Democratic Vistas* is a lengthy, critical, prescriptive essay. Much of Whitman's poetry, however, is prescriptive too, and "Song of Myself" certainly has this cast. It is nonetheless clear that by 1871 Whitman's sense of what was required to achieve true democracy has changed. It is too simple to say that Whitman has reversed himself, for his goal remained the same: a society which celebrated the individual in all his infinite dimensions and which found in that celebration the principle source of national cohesion and wholeness. But the unilateral, solitary singing of Self, however expansive and universal that Self's definition, will no longer avail in the post-war world, and Whitman finds himself forced to seek salvation for American democracy in some larger, more structured and public cultural development.

Moreover, by 1871 Whitman acknowledges the ability and the need to judge and to discriminate; and he has found the standard by which to do so. He has moved away from his simple, democratic posture of total indiscriminate acceptance and toward a still benevolent and charitable selectiveness. But selectivity is positively affirmed. Salvation can obtain for democracies, but only if the people are guided by the better sort, by an aesthetic elite. In the American of the 1870's—of what Parrington called the "Great Barbecue," Twain the "Gilded Age," and Henry Adams, somewhat sarcastically, "Democracy"—much had to be overcome and rejected, and of this Whitman was well aware. What he seemed not to be aware of was that his own pre-war perspective on some of the dominant questions of the day, to the extent that it was shared by others, may have been causal of the very changes in America which troubled him. Whitman failed to see, in R. W. B. Lewis' words, that "the condition prior to conscience might have insidious undertones of the amoral as well as the beguiling naivete of the premoral." The enormities of the Self which so intoxicated the pre-war Whitman blinded him and too many of his contemporaries to the limitations of their view; the paradox contained all the elements of classic tragedy. In the years following the war Whitman had only a fragmented sense of the dialectic his generation had experienced, but it was enough to modify his indiscriminacy and hence his notion of the democratic prospect.

In sum, the change in Whitman's perspective on democracy involved a movement toward selectivity, toward elitism, toward some sort of collectivity of aesthetics and away from solitary, transcendent democratic Selfhood. It also involved a movement away from what Tocqueville called "democracy" and toward its polar extreme: aristocracy. I cannot do more here than suggest this frame of reference, but perhaps it will suffice to recall that Tocqueville's enduring analytical accomplishment in *Democracy in America* was organized around the democratic/aristocratic dichotomy, and that Tocqueville's definition of an aristocracy included refinement, selectivity, proscription, and a class of creators and artists who strove, above all, to objectify and venerate the Ideal in the most skillful and sophisticated way possible. Tocqueville specifically forecast "Song of Myself" when he wrote:

> Amongst a democratic people, poetry will not be fed with legends or the memorials of old traditions. The poet will not attempt to people the universe with supernatural beings, in whom his readers and his own fancy have ceased to believe; nor will he coldly personify virtues and vices, which are better received under their own features. All these resources fail him; but Man remains, and the poet needs no more. The destinies of mankind—man himself, taken aloof from his country and his age, and standing in the presence of Nature and of God, with his passions, his doubts, his rare prosperities and inconceivable wretchedness—will become the chief, if not the sole, theme of poetry amongst these nations.

And Tocqueville forecast specifically the problem Whitman addressed in *Democratic Vistas* when he wrote:

> The social condition and institutions of democracy impart, moreover, certain peculiar tendencies to all the imitative arts, which is easy to point out. They frequently withdraw them from the delineation of the soul, to fix them exclusively on that of the body; and they substitute the representation of motion and sensation for that of sentiment and thought: in a word, they put the Real in the place of the Ideal.

I have tried to suggest here only one aspect of what the war may have meant to Walt Whitman. The topic is certainly worth more exhaustive and comprehensive treatment than it has yet received. While Whitman's perspective on the war was highly personal, his conception of himself as the poet of democracy enhances rather than devalues the significance of his changing attitudes. But scholars have strangely ignored the question. The study of Walt Whitman's Civil War remains to be written.

Mark Twain's *Connecticut Yankee*: The Trouble in Camelot

by

Tom H. Towers

In general, criticism of *A Connecticut Yankee* must come down to a consideration of two closely related matters: the true object of Twain's satire, and the proper understanding of Hank Morgan's apparently ambiguous role in the novel. However, whether critics have made Twain the enemy of the middle ages or of the nineteenth century, whether they have understood Hank as the frustrated prophet of a higher civilization or as the egomaniacal destroyer of primitive innocence, most, I think, have concentrated too exclusively on the explicitly social and institutional materials of the book.[1]

Twain, of course, seems to invite exactly that kind of interest. Most of *Yankee's* most memorable scenes demonstrate the degrading folly of superstition, or the vanity of monarchy and feudalism, or the cynical cruelty of established religion. At the same time though, Hank—and Twain—are concerned with realities more elemental than church and state. I believe that the most basic theme in *A Connect-*

icut Yankee has to do not with institutionalized life in society so much as with the necessary absence of human love and community. It is this sorry fact of the human condition, and not the interdict or Hank's technology, that at last destroys Hank Morgan, and with him Twain's hope for mankind.

When Hank revives after his transforming "misunderstanding conducted with crowbars" (p. 20),[2] he awakens to what seems at first a second Eden. He finds himself in "a soft, reposeful summer landscape, as lovely as a dream, and as lonesome as Sunday." Hank and his captor, Sir Kay, are alone, except for "a fair slip of a girl, about ten years old, with a cataract of yellow hair streaming down over her shoulders." As befits her apparent innocence, the girl is naked except for "a hoop of flame-red poppies" around her head. Hank recognizes in the child "a mind at rest, its peace reflected in her innocent face" (p. 27). But the "peace" of the girl and the blessedness of the landscape itself are more apparent than real. The girl, innocent or not, is naked only because she has the misfortune to be the daughter of a "freeman" too poor to clothe her; and as Hank and Sir Kay continue on their way to Camelot, Hank's sense of the "fair, reposeful summer day" yields to his increasing awareness of human suffering.

The men they encounter "look like animals," and their homes are "wretched cabins" standing in "small fields and garden patches in an indifferent state of cultivation" (p. 28). Camelot itself, Hank discovers, is little more than a "wilderness of thatched cabins," lined by a network of "mere crooked alleys" where "hogs roamed and rooted contentedly about" (p. 28). Arthur's court seems similarly disordered and brutish. It is "a tumultuous chaos," a "storm of howlings and barkings," as the knights and ladies, in the best Arkansas fashion, divert themselves with a dog fight (p. 39). As Hank stands by, waiting his turn with the other prisoners, he thinks of the courtiers as "childlike and innocent" in their "winning naivety" (p. 39). But as he better understands their "guileless relish" in the common talk of "blood and suffering," he perceives that chivalry, in fact, exists without human feeling or real moral knowledge. The nobles go on with their banquet and their boasting, oblivious to the prisoners who stand among them "caked with black and stiffening drenchings of blood" (p. 39), and Hank realizes that his captors—and his fellow prisoners too—are unreasoning savages, "white Indians" (p. 40), or, as he later explains to Sandy, "a sort of polished-up court of Comanches" (p. 178).

Everything in Hank's later adventures bears out the implication of these opening scenes. Virtually every episode in the novel has its trace of gratuitous cruelty or violence. The festive tournament is followed by a night filled with the screams of the dying losers. During his travels with Sandy, Hank finds the idyllic English countryside populated almost entirely by "freemen," whose only expectation is "life-long death from hunger, cold, insult, cruelty and heartbreak" (p. 157). Every castle has its dungeon, and Morgan le Fay's differs from the rest only in being fuller. The comic scene in which Hank liberates the bewitched "countess" and her sister swine is followed at once by the dismal encounter with the slave caravan. Later, during Hank's tour with Arthur, even more striking evidences of "savagery" are commonplace. There is the pathos of the smallpox hut, the horror of the prisoners burned alive in the chapter called "The Tragedy of the Manor-House," and at last, of course, the enslavement and projected execution of Hank and the king themselves.

Hank repeatedly calls attention to the savage, brutish conditions of medieval life. Englishmen are "animals," "white Indians," "big boobies" continuing into "full age and beyond" the mindless cruelties of children (p. 43); they are a "nation of worms" (p. 100), "groping and grubbing automata" (p. 212); they are "barbaric" (p. 191), "juvenile" (p. 467), and perhaps most degrading of all, they are "cow-boys" (p. 176).[3] Appropriately enough, Hank, a civilized castaway in this savage land, thinks of himself as Columbus or Cortez (p. 66), the "champion of hard unsentimental common-sense and reason" (p. 498). Shortly after he has been installed as "The Boss," he says, " 'I saw that I was just another Robinson Crusoe cast away on an uninhabited island, with no society, but some more or less tame animals, and if I wanted to make life bearable I must do as he did—invent, contrive, create, reorganize things; set brain and hand to work, and keep them busy' " (p. 85). But what

Hank, as a later—or earlier—Robinson Crusoe, must at last set his "brain and hand to work" on is not merely superstition, nor ignorance, nor injustice, nor economic and political backwardness, but rather the innate perversity of the "damned human race." Underlying all the suffering and the inhumanity in the novel is a single tragic but simple fact—each man, by his nature, is spiritually alone, imprisoned in a savage self, and cannot be redeemed by love nor ever live in true peace with other men. Thus, there can be no community, no humanity, no real compassion or pity.

When he first reconciles himself to the fact that he is indeed in the sixth century and not the county asylum, Hank exclaims, " 'I shall never see my friends again—never, never again' " (p. 35). The intuition of that cry, of course, is ironically confirmed in the ending of the novel. Hank Morgan eventually dies a stranger, but now a stranger in his own century. And in his final delirium he cries out pathetically to the Sandy of his dream; he has been, he says, " 'set down in that strange England, with an abyss of thirteen centuries yawning between me and you! between me and my home and friends! between me and all that is dear to me, all that could make life worth the living! It was awful—awfuller than you can ever imagine' " (p. 574).

The events of the novel demonstrate that Hank's original fear and the ultimate realization of the dreaded isolation are not agonies special to Hank, but are indeed the common lot of mankind, at least in the savage state of the sixth century. In the dungeons of Arthur's nobles, it is common to separate husbands from wives, allowing each partner to destroy himself in the ordeal of supposing the other dead. Morgan le Fay's most exquisite torture is periodically to allow her most hated prisoner to glimpse from his cell what appear to be the funerals of his family; his greatest pain is his separation from those who survive, the necessity of suffering in solitude the grief that can be assuaged only by being shared. As in *Huck Finn* and *Pudd'nhead Wilson*, the cruelest evil of slavery in *A Connecticut Yankee* is the division of families on the auction block. The keenest anguish of the woman in the smallpox hut is her inability to help or even to see her dying children. And, of course, one of the clearest instances of the inhumanity of the medieval church is the ban which has cast the woman and her family officially outside the range of human sympathy, even in the hour of death itself.

The most fundamental manifestation of the savagery of Arthurian England, then, is not that men must suffer the abuse and injustice of priest and noble, but that in their suffering they must be alone, yearning for the liberation of love, but forever denied it. The separation of families, the casual imprisonments, the universal distrust which makes natural allies betray each other, are all only symbolic of the pervasive spiritual isolation which is the chief characteristic of the savage life.

When the sixth century characters even notice such intolerable conditions, it is to shrug them off as the necessary price that must be paid to preserve the Christian culture. Except for a few nameless slaves and freemen, only Hank recognizes and responds to the human outrage of frustrated love and shattered community. His tour with Sandy, for example, can be seen as a series of confrontations in which he uses his brain and his authority to free prisoners, to restore families, and generally to alleviate the horror of isolation. However, in his more general and programmatic response to this condition, Hank assumes that the agony of isolation, like the discomfort of owning but a single change of clothes, proceeds from faulty institutions and a generally backward idea of society. The trouble, he thinks, is that both noble and freemen accept the established order as divine necessity, and so routinely sacrifice their own humanity and that of others to maintain that order. Consequently, just as Hank sets out to destroy superstition with science, or to relieve poverty through technology, he undertakes to ameliorate the oppression of spiritual isolation by transforming Britains from "worms" to men. In his "man-factory" Hank educates likely freemen in the ways of moral, social, and economic independence. He teaches his candidates to reject the authority of institutions, especially that of the church and the aristocracy, and to rely on their own reason and their own consciences. In addition, he equips them to become the bearers of nineteenth century technology and political economy. The premise, obviously, is that once men are free from the oppression of an established church and a feudal hierarchy, and free also from the even more degrading oppression of physical want, they will be free from the inhuman isolation that Hank assumes to be the direct consequence of poverty and repression. In the new order Hank strives for, men will cease to be "worms"; they will be no longer the victims of brutalizing savagery, but the masters of liberating civilization, no longer a mass of tormented isolatos, but loving members of a truly human community.

As we all know, the culmination of Hank's endeavors is the battle of the sand-belt, and the great wall of corpses within which Hank and his cadets apparently must die. But the reasons for that disaster, I think, have little to do with the destructiveness of what Hank calls his "labor-saving machinery" or with the inadequacy of nineteenth century industrialism generally. I would argue, indeed, that in every outward regard Hank vastly improves the quality of English life. From the institution of the "go-as-you-please" church to the substitution of baseball for the chivalric tournament, Hank has worked to make the lives of most Englishmen, if not perfect, at least much better than they were. Hank's projects fail, in the end, because he has mislocated the origins of human savagery and mistaken the causes of the suffering he hopes to cure.

This point, perhaps, can be illustrated by a brief look at the efficient causes of the division of the round table and the resultant interdict. The catastrophe comes about because of the greed and the selfish ambition of Sir Launcelot. Early in the novel Hank points out that knightly "adventures" were in fact "simply duels between strangers," more appropriate to amoral children than to men of "full age and beyond" (p. 43). After Hank has transformed the round table into the stock exchange, Launcelot transfers his "childish" appetite for violent combativeness from the lists to the counting house. He corners the market in the stock of the London, Canterbury, and Dover Railroad, and by the time he "compromises" with the knights who have been caught short, he has "skinned them alive" (p. 532). The injured parties retaliate by carrying to Arthur the story of Launcelot's long-standing adultery with Guinivere, and the machinery of civil war is set in motion. The "modern," "democratic" state is as susceptible to anti-human ambition and appetite as the age of chivalry. Launcelot's economic savagery is just a newer version of his sexual savagery. Both in his manipulation of the market and in his seduction of Arthur's queen, we see the kind of primal violation of trust and moral sympathy that must culminate in the dissolution of community and in the savage horror of isolation. In short, the men Hank earlier calls "animals" or "Indians" are such, not because of their institutions, but from their natures.[4]

As I have suggested, Hank is virtually alone in his sensitivity to the terror of human isolation and in his efforts to relieve it. But even Hank betrays the very community he apparently strives to establish. The clearest example of Hank's failure is his conduct after he and the king, betrayed first by the freeman, Marco, and later by their "noble" rescuer, have been sold into slavery. Typically, Hank sees in their situation an opportunity to win Arthur over to his own abolitionist position. When the king at last agrees to abolish slavery—if he can only get free from it himself, Hank sets to work on the great "effect" that will liberate them. Like Tom Sawyer "freeing" Jim, Hank devises an elaborate, ultimately destructive scheme; he plans to overcome the slave-master, change clothes with him, chain him to the slave coffle, and march triumphantly to Camelot. Hank admits, "One could invent quicker ways [of getting free], and fully as sure ones; but none that would be as picturesque; none that could be made so dramatic. . . . It might delay us months, but no matter, I would carry it out or break something" (p. 458). When Hank finally sets his plan in motion he bungles it from the beginning. Instead of assaulting the slave-driver, he sets upon a perfect stranger. (Ironically his fight for freedom becomes exactly the "duel between strangers" he condemns in the knights.) The slave-trader, when he discovers Hank's escape, beats the remaining slaves, who, finally provoked too far, turn on him and kill him. In another blunder, deriving again from his desire for "effect," Hank causes himself to be recaptured and sentenced to death, along with Arthur and the rest of the slaves. Before the rescue party can arrive on bicycles, three of the slaves have been hanged. Thus, in his desire to make a grand entrance into

Camelot, Hank has unfeelingly wasted the lives of the very men he hoped to save. Much the same point might be made in regard to the great climactic tournament in which Hank shoots ten knights in order once more to humiliate Merlin, this time in the "final struggle for supremacy between the two master sorcerers of the age" (p. 497).[5] Thus, long before his "death," suffered in pathetic separation from Sandy and Hello Central, Hank yields to his own inveterate savagery, and thereby destines himself to his solitary end.

In *Huck Finn* society is destructive to true selfhood and to human love. We see this most clearly, perhaps, in the final episodes where, once more in society, Huck loses his sense of the free self and becomes a cruder version of Tom Sawyer, while Jim degenerates into the stage darkey.[6] The real and valid community discovered in nature vanishes in civilization. In *Huck Finn*, though, there is always the river, and at the end of the novel, the territory. Huck, in society, may be unable to realize his humanity, but he can "light out for the territory"—he can keep out of the way of society, and hopefully, in the revitalizing benevolence of nature he can attain to what civilization everywhere denies. But in *A Connecticut Yankee* there is no such hope. Nowhere in this novel does Twain suggest any possible life for man outside of society. Hank can turn for spiritual sustenance to Sandy or to Clarence, but not to a primitive, unspoiled nature. For Hank there is no river nor any territory.

In *Yankee*, then, man is condemned to civilization. Filled, as Hank is, with the apprehension of isolation and its agony, man can strive to create a better civilization in the desperate hope that he can thereby attain to genuine community. But in the novel no institution or set of institutions is proof against the innate savagery of men, their essentially inhuman selfishness. Twain's final vision of the human condition in this work shows Hank, who in spite of all his faults, has honestly yearned towards the blessedness, the "mind at rest" of the innocent child, imprisoned by his own benevolent ambition within the great fortress of rotting corpses, destined not to love and the new life of the spirit, but to ages long loneliness and death.

NOTES

[1]For representative discussions of the social ideas in *A Connecticut Yankee*, see the following: Louis J. Budd, *Mark Twain: Social Philosopher* (Bloomington, Ind., 1962), pp. 111-141; Alan Guttman, "Mark Twain's *Connecticut Yankee:* Affirmation of the Vernacular Tradition?" NEQ, XXXIII (1960), 232-237; Henry Nash Smith, *Mark Twain's Fable of Progress: Political and Economic Ideas in "A Connecticut Yankee"* (New Brunswick, 1964); Roger B. Solomon, *Twain and the Image of History* (New Haven, 1961), pp. 95-132; Walter F. Taylor, "Mark Twain and the Machine Age," SAQ, XXXVII (1938), 384-396. Discussions of Hank Morgan's impact on idyllic primitivism appear in the following: James M. Cox, "*A Connecticut Yankee in King Arthur's Court*: The Machinery of Self-Preservation," YR, L (1960), 89-102; Kenneth S. Lynn, *Mark Twain and Southwestern Humor* (Boston, 1959), pp. 249-258; William C. Spengemann, *Mark Twain and the Backwoods Angel: The Matter of Innocence in the Works of Samuel L. Clemens* (Kent, Ohio, 1966), pp. 84-104.

[2]All quotations from a *Connecticut Yankee* are from the following edition; page references appear in parentheses: *A Connecticut Yankee in King Arthur's Court: A Facsimile of the First Edition,* ed., Hamlin Hill (San Francisco, 1963).

[3]Besides the instances cited here, a rough count shows Twain referring to knights and/or freemen as one or another species of animal at least five times; as children, juveniles, etc. at least five more times; and as varieties of Indians or savages at least six times. This count does not include numerous similar references to slaves and prisoners; in those cases Twain obviously intends to suggest the brutality of the masters, not the moral state of the victims.

[4]Lynn, pp. 251-252, makes a similar point when he suggests that in this novel mankind is "degraded beyond the power of any political system to redeem it."

[5]It might be noted that in his increasing identification with the sixth century—shown here by his willingness to consider himself no better than Merlin's rival—Hank becomes less and less the "civilized" man, and more and more the "savage." Speeches like this one prepare the way for his ultimate belief that his "medieval" life is real and his "modern" life a dream.

[6]For a somewhat different statement of this idea, see Ray B. Browne, "Huck's Final Triumph," *Ball State Teachers College Forum,* VI (1965), 10-12.

Henry James and American Culture

by

Peter Buitenhuis

Henry James had little to say about what we normally think of as popular culture—the literature, music, art, and so on, of the people. What he did say of it was usually in accents of the deepest scorn. He did, however, confront culture in its wider, anthropological sense, as well as in the narrower sense of high culture. One should add that this was more true of the work of his later years; in the earlier ones that he spent in the United States, he took a distant view that, by contrast with Europe, most literary expression in the United States was crude and provincial. He at first believed, however, that the American public wanted to and could be educated out of their provincialism by great art. His early reviews reveal this naive belief clearly. In his well-known review of Whitman's "Drum-Taps," in the *Nation,* of November, 1865, he indicates the basis of this belief. "This democratic, liberty-loving, American populace," he wrote, "this stern and war-tried people, is a great civilizer. It is devoted to refinement. It has sustained a monstrous war, and practised human nature's best in so many ways for the last five years, it is not to put up with spurious poetry afterwards." This belief is the *raison d'être* for James's slashing attack on "Drum-Taps," a book, he thought, containing not a single idea, but only "flashy imitations," a book full of extravagances, bald nonsense and dreary commonplaces. "There exists in even the commonest minds," James insisted, "in literary matters, a certain precise instinct of conservatism, which is very shrewd in detecting wanton eccentricities." He worked on this assumption in dismissing, in the name of the American people, Whitman's anomalous style. "[A writer] must have something very original to say if none of the old vehicles will carry his thoughts," he wrote. Needless to say, Whitman had nothing original to say in "Drum-Taps." He was rough, clumsy, grim, an offender against art, but he was *not* original.[1]

For some years, American writing and painting continued to seem impossible to James when it deviated from his view of high art and made claims to originality. Consider, for example, his review of Winslow Homer's paintings shown at the Academy of Design in New York in the Winter of 1874-5. James regarded the paintings as being "not particularly important in themselves," but as representing something "peculiarly typical." "Mr. Homer goes in...for perfect realism," James observed, "and cares not a jot for such fantastic hair-splitting as the distinction between beauty and ugliness...He not only has no imagination but he contrives to elevate this blighting negative into a blooming and honourable positive...We frankly confess that we detest his subjects–his barren plank fences, his glaring, bald, blue skies, his big, dreary, vacant lots of meadows, his freckled, straight-haired Yankee urchins, his flat-breasted maidens, suggestive of a dish of rural doughnuts and pie,...his flannel shirts, his cowhide boots. He has chosen the least pictorial features of the least pictorial range of scenery and civilization; he has resolutely treated them as if they were pictorial, as if they *were* every inch as good as Capri or Tangier." But it seems by this time James was not prepared to be as damning about the Whitman of the painting world as he was about Whitman himself. He praised Homer's honesty and his vigorous way of seeing things, and concluded that if he used "more secrecies and mysteries and coquetries" in his brushwork, he would be "an almost distinguished painter."[2]

James's academic and Ruskinian views of art and life were also responsible for his joining the wolf-pack of critics who took after the Impressionist painters Manet, Monet, Degas and Renoir when they exhibited in Paris in the following winter. According to James "None of [the Impressionists] show signs of possessing first-rate talent, and indeed, the 'Impressionist' doctrines strike me as incompatible...with the existence of first-rate talent. To embrace them you must be provided with a plentiful absence of imagination."[3]

It took James ten years to move away from this normative assessment of art, and he did this by gradually coming to appreciate what the Impressionists were trying to do in painting and the naturalists were attempting in writing. It must be remembered that the two movements were closely associated in their aims. In contrasting his own work and that of his contemporaries with that of the Frenchmen, he condemned what he called the tendency towards "factitious glosses." One of the most interesting signs of this development is the appearance of an Impressionist painter in his own story "A New England Winter," published in 1884. For this painter, Florimond, an expatriate who has lived long in Paris, and who has returned on a visit to Boston, it is not important that things in America should be beautiful; what he sought to discover was their identity—"the signs by which he should know them." At length, he perceives "that even amidst the simple civilization of New England there was material for the naturalist."[4] He sets out to paint Boston just as James soon afterwards set out to write his first naturalist novel, *The Bostonians.* Fiction, as James phrased it in a famous essay published at this time, was to be "a direct impression of life." The critic, he observed, should not attempt to proscribe what kind of life the artist should attempt to represent.

From this time on, James cast his net far more widely into the stream of life, became more of an observer of all kinds of experience that he would earlier have ignored. Let's skip over fifteen years to look at his next encounter with specifically American materials. In 1898, he was asked to write some American Letters for an international periodical called *Literature,* and was sent a pile of books for review on which to base these letters. These included two volumes by Walt Whitman. His reviews of them are a world away from the one of 1865. In his review of the *Calamus Letters,* he called Whitman, "with all his rags and tatters, an upright figure, a successful original." "Vividly American," they contained, "a thousand images of patient, homely, American life." His was "an audible New Jersey voice." "The reader," he added, "will miss a chance who does not find in it many odd and pleasant harmonies."[5] In writing on the letters collected in *The Wound Dresser,* James commented on Whitman's "admirable, original gift of sympathy, his homely, racy, yet extraordinarily delicate personal devotion."[6]

In the early letters in the series, it is plain that James was prepared to listen to voices from all over America. From Rye he looked benevolently westward to "the great common-schooled and newspapered democracy"[7] which exuded, he wrote, in some of its lights,"an element of air and space that amounts almost to a sense of aesthetic conditions."[8] He commented approvingly on how our "predominant and triumphant English"[9] was making a homogeneous American public out of a variety of races and idioms. This seemed to him to provide a fine opportunity, not only for the writer of literature for the billions but also for special publics, or "shoals of fish rising to more delicate bait."[10] He welcomed a new novel by Owen Wister about cow-punchers, and the work of Hamlin Garland, who he called, "with all honour...the soaked sponge of Wisconsin,"[11] so much was he saturated in his mid-western element.

In later letters, however, James's theory of special publics was sorely tried when he reviewed a group of popular novels. One of these was George Eggleston's *Southern Soldier Stories,* a collection of anecdotes about the War. James wondered to what "particular passive public of all the patient publics were these anecdotes supposedly addressed?"[12] Paul Leicester Ford's *The Honourable Peter Stirling,* which had already sold thirty-thousand copies by the time James reviewed it, amazed him even more. In James's view, it was a work, "so disconnected...from almost any consideration with which an artistic product is at any point concerned, any effect of presentation, any prescription of form, composition, proportion, taste, art, that I am reduced merely to noting, for curiosity, the circumstance that it so remarkably triumphs."[13] In a subsequent letter, he tackled an even more popular contemporary author, Robert W. Chambers. He asked in bewilderment of his *Lorraine: a Romance:* "By what odd arrangement of the mind does it come to pass that a writer may have such remarkable energy and yet so little sincerity?" And later: "Why in the world, operetta–operetta, at best, with guns?"[14] After encountering a spate of dialect novels, which left him more than cold, James gave up on popular fiction. He did allow himself one further mention of them in the later *The American Scene.* Commenting on how, in the United States, winter spread in one great wash from latitude to latitude, he saw an analogy between this and the "vast vogue of some infinitely-selling novel, one of those happy volumes of which the circulation roars, periodically, from Atlantic to Pacific and from great windy State to State, in a manner, as I have heard it vividly put, of a blazing prairie fire; with as little possibility of arrest from 'criticism' in the one case as from the bleating of lost sheep in the other."[15]

The American Scene itself is in large part a record of James's disillusionment with the United States he had left over twenty years before. The air and space of democracy, the freedom of movement and development, all the gathered riches that he had seen, in anticipation, gathered in under the wide wings of the English language in the American Letters, were met instead by what he called "the vast crude democracy of trade," in which predominated "the new, the simple, the cheap, the common, the commercial, and, all too often, the ugly..."[16] Freedom, he found, was too often the freedom to grow up to be blighted, especially for the immigrants. Development, he believed, consisted in taking the "large and noble sanities" of nature in America, and converting them "one after the other to crudities, to invalidities, hideous and unashamed."[17] Lastly, English speech, which he had seen as the great homogenizer of all the races, was itself in process of disintegration, particularly in the mouths of the immigrant masses. The cafés of the Jewish east side in New York seemed to him, for example, "torture rooms of the living idiom." "The accent of the very ultimate future, in the States," he concluded, "may be destined to become the most beautiful on the globe and the very music of humanity...; but whatever we shall know it for, certainly, we shall not know it for English—in any sense for which there is an existing literary measure."[18]

The American Scene is James's most comprehensive confrontation of American life and culture, but exigencies of time force me to take knowledge of it for granted and to concentrate the remainder of this brief opportunity on the eight relatively unknown papers that he published in *Harper's Bazar* in 1906 and 1907 on the speech and manners of American women. In these papers he took upon himself not only the role of observer and analyst of human behaviour, but also of its critic and educator. It was, I think, the only time in James's career when he appeared in a mass-circulation magazine, and one can only amusedly wonder what a majority of his readers made of his labyrinthine sentences.

He took as his main axiom that women in America had taken over the social authority which men had all too willingly abdicated. "Women," he wrote, "are encamped on every inch of the social area that the stock-exchange and the football-field leave free."[19] Entrenched in their culture clubs, they alone were in a position to give a tone to the discourse of a society whose English speech was coming under increasing attack. But what a tone the women set! It was, he thought, a mumble, a slobber or a whine, unredeemed by any trouble taken to form words, or any discrimination in the pronouncing of syllables. Conversation was either a continuous yell or a string of linguistic inaccuracies, or both. James's own speech, according to a friend, was "ultra-fastidious, like that of the older University dons."[20] Small wonder that he confronted the speech of American women with such shocked surprise and bent his efforts to bringing to consciousness in his audience the need for reform. One of the four papers is couched in the form of a dialogue between the stately, polysyllabic, analytic and relentless Henry James and a young, artless and uncomprehending American girl. The girl insists that James is making far too much of the value of good speech. James replies:"'Are you sure that *you* don't make too much of the unimportance and of the trouble?...The unimportance, I mean, of missing half the beauty of life. Yes...that's exactly what you do miss. For everything hangs together, and there are certain perceptions and sensibilities that are a *key*—a key to the inner treasury of consciousness, where all sorts of priceless things abide. Access to these is through those perceptions: so don't hope that you can just rudely and crudely force the lock. Everything hangs together, I say, and there's no isolated question of speech, no isolated application of taste, no isolated damnation of delicacy. The interest of tone is the interest of manners, and the interest of manners is the interest of morals and the interest of morals is the interest of civilization...' "

After concluding his case, he leaves the girl, "the pretended heiress of all the ages," as he calls her, locked up in the prison of her inarticulateness along with the rest of her sex 'in perhaps the very best-appointed of all fools' paradises they have ever insidiously prepared for humanity.' "[21]

It was a short step from speech to manners in general, and in the four papers on that subject James pulls few punches in his attack on barbarism. He commented, for example, on the way that shop assistants and customers would stand and bark at each other in the department stores. In Philadelphia, in one immense establishment, he observed "an elderly, grizzled, truculent woman, presiding, with a certain incongruity, over various items of men's 'underwear,' against whose practical defiance of approach, and whose long impunity of insolence, it was inconceivable that any social body coerced to communication with her should *not* have organised for reprisals, for some desperate game of repaying her, horribly, in kind."[22]

James laid much of the blame for this kind of conduct on the women of the United States, who had failed to maintain standards of behaviour for themselves, or to pass them on to their children. Thus he couldn't really censure the conduct of the four adolescent girls who got into a train that was taking him and other passengers from Boston down to the South Shore. The girls proceeded to whoop, holler, caper, flounce, romp and jest through the train with an innocent immodesty that left James awestruck, but left the others in the car, he surmised, silent but unsurprised.

On one fine occasion, James thought that his law of license in the American family had been triumphantly disproved. This time he was in a train from Chicago, and he found himself sitting opposite a family who seemed not only united but animated. It consisted of parents, mature sons and daughters, a presumable son-in-law, and a possible daughter-in-law, all conversing away with spirit. This in itself caused James to rejoice, used as he was to the sterility of silence that usually prevailed in the cars. It turned out that the family was returning from the city, where they had been to attend a number of performances of the opera, to their home town. But as he watched them, he gradually became aware of a fact that dealt him a blow more powerful than any he yet sustained on his American travels. "When I became aware indeed, it was to see *them* all disfigured by their use of their weapon; aware, I mean, that each member of the group, while he or she talked or listened, was primarily concerned after the manner of a ruminant animal. They were discussing Wagner in short under the inspiration of chewing-gum and, though 'Parsifal' might be their secondary care, the independent action of their jaws was the first." "What address," James wondered aghast, "what pleasantness of propriety in general, might be held to consort, for a woman of whatever age, with her having not to 'mind' that her interlocutor, of whatever condition, should chew in her face for sweet freedom or with his having not to mind that she should chew in his?"

The question took James a long way, past the station from which his pilgrims disembarked, and past numberless vast, daubed, signboards, which he came to feel, represented the *"disjecta-membra* of murdered taste, pike-paraded in some September Massacre." Both the hoardings and the ruminant millions were illustrative of a conception of manners, he concluded, that had been sacrificed to keep "the air clear and the ground firm for business transactions."[23] Any analysis of success, or any pleas for discipline, James thought, were held in America to savour of the unholy critical spirit. "What is criticism but pessimism?" he ironically asked, "and where is sacred spontaneity, that of the younger generations in especial, rising and clamoring around us, if we pretend really to analyze or appreciate anything?"[24]

In these papers, James adduced many other examples of the absence of manners and of the critical spirit in the United States, but enough has been given to show the tenor of his views. His final plea was for the use of manners as an indispensable tool of civilization. "Manners are above all," he summed up, "an economy; the sacrifice of them as has always in the long run to be made up, just as the breakages and dilapidations have to be paid for at the end of the tenancy of a house carelessly occupied."[25]

Those words were written sixty years ago, but as we make the jump into the present and look around us, we can see for ourselves the state of the house that James tried to repair, and the mess that subsequent tenants have left it in. For James, with a prescience given to few critics of American life, established the relationship between manners and morals, between the need for articulateness and clarity in speech and that for articulate criticism and clarity of vision about the ugliness of the man-made part of the American environment. He could certainly have seen the connection between what was happening in America in 1904 and 1905 and the smashed and fouled office of the President of Columbia University. Whatever one may adduce about the provocation and justification the students had for their actions, one must ask what they most of all demonstrated. Surely it was nothing so much as a disregard for the economy of manners. We are paying for the tenancy now, and will continue to pay heavily until some organic connections can again be made between speech and civilization, and between manners and morals.

NOTES

[1]*The American Essays of Henry James,* ed. with an introduction by Leon Edel (New York, 1956), 134-7.

[2]*The Painter's Eye, Notes and Essays on the Pictorial Arts,* by Henry James, ed. John L. Sweeney (London, 1956), 96-7.

[3]*Ibid.,* 114-5.

[4]*The American Novels and Stories of Henry James,* ed. with an introduction by F.O. Matthiessen (New York, 1956), 373.

[5]*The American Essays,* 210.

[6]*Ibid.,* 221. [7]*Ibid.,* 198. [8]*Ibid.,* 242-3. [9]*Ibid.,* 198. [10]*Ibid.,* 201.

[11]*Ibid.,*206. [12]*Ibid.,* 222. [13]*Ibid.,* 223-4. [14]*Ibid.,* 230-1.

[15]*The American Scene* (London, 1907), 306.

[16]*Ibid.,* 67. [17]*Ibid.,* 463-4. [18]*Ibid.,* 139.

[19]*French Writers and American Women:* Essays by Henry James, ed. with an introduction by Peter Buitenhuis (Branford, Conn. 1960), 39.

[20]*The Legend of the Master: Henry James,* compiled by Simon Nowell-Smith (New York, 1948), 157.

[21]*French Writers and American Women,* 50-2.

[22]*Ibid.,* 58-9. [23]*Ibid.,* 66-7. [24]*Ibid.,* 69. [25]*Ibid.,* 77.

Little Lord Fauntleroy as Hero

by

Robert Lee White

In the 1880's, many of the books most popular with Americans were "children's books" that turned out to be favorites with young and old alike. Among such books, two that were most successful, and which continue to engage the attention of readers today, were Mark Twain's *Adventures of Huckleberry Finn* and Frances Hodgson Burnett's *Little Lord Fauntleroy.* In the years since their appearance, though, the two books have been absorbed into American culture in quite different fashions. Mark Twain's still affords pleasure to young and old, but Mrs. Burnett's is now read only by juveniles. What is more, the patterns of critical opinion dealing with the two books have been neatly inverted since the 1880's. As all of us know, "Huck Finn" was coolly received by the middlebrow arbiters of public taste, with William Dean Howells singlehandedly attempting to counter the negative opinion voiced, for example, in Louisa May Alcott's observation that "if Mr. Clemens cannot think of something better to tell our pure-minded lads and lasses, he had best stop writing for them." Little Lord Fauntleroy, at the time of his debut, was sometimes guyed at by irreverent wits; he and his creator, though, were warmly commended, on both sides of the Atlantic, by spokesmen for the official culture of the day. William Ewart Gladstone, for example, told Mrs. Burnett that "Fauntleroy [had] charmed him" and that he believed her variation upon the international theme "would have great effect in bringing about added good feeling between [the United States and Great Britain] and making them understand each other."

While discussions of "Huck Finn" comprise a significant portion of contemporary American literary scholarship, today's critics rarely mention Mrs. Burnett and *Little Lord Fauntleroy.* And if they do mention her and her book, they are apt to adopt a tone of sneering disparagement. Witness, for example, Justin Kaplan's remark that William Dean Howells, by praising *The Prince and the Pauper,* assisted in "the transformation of his 'sole and incomparable' Mark Twain into a practitioner of the art of Frances Hodgson Burnett."

Remarks such as Kaplan's are easily explained: they are products of the received adult opinion about *Little Lord Fauntleroy,* an opinion that most educated grown-ups hold as a consequence of the entry of "Fauntleroy" into the English language as a term denoting a particular sort of costume and carrying with it connotations of prissy, sissy behavior. And this lexical charge has been reinforced by characterizations of the book and its hero that have cropped up in print. Frederick Lewis Pattee, for example, in the *D.A.B.* sketch of Mrs. Burnett, asserts that Little Lord Fauntleroy "is an insufferable mollycoddle, and even a prig. Chiefly is he made up of wardrobe and manners." In James D. Hart's *The Popular Book,* Fauntleroy is described, mockingly, in the following fashion:

> ...the novel told about an angelic, blond-haired, lace-collared, and velvet-pantalooned lad reared in New York by his American mother, the widow of a British nobleman's younger son. When little Cedric becomes Lord Fauntleroy and goes to live on his ancestral estate he guides his grandfather, the Earl of Dorincourt, in the ways of *noblesse oblige* by changing this haughty curmudgeon into a kindly

> philanthropist,...while the little Lord himself practices democracy as he makes friends with workingmen and nobles alike. ...The seven-year-old title character became the darling of Anglophile grownups, but he plagued little boys, who were taught to address their mothers as "Dearest" and were forced to walk the streets of Des Moines or Detroit garbed in the fussy costume that Cedric Errol wore at the castle of Dorincourt.

The notion that Little Lord Fauntleroy was a plague to true-blue American youths seems to have been largely promulgated by Thomas Beer's biography of Stephen Crane, which reports that Crane was "enraged" by Mrs. Burnett's book and that once, upon "encountering two small boys who had been tricked out by their mothers in imitation of Reginald Birch's too faithful illustrations, in long curls and lace collars, he coolly gave the sufferers money to have their hair cut." It is certainly true that Crane didn't like Mrs. Burnett's book and so, before going on in my effort to refurbish Fauntleroy's good name, it would be only proper to quote from the angry letter Crane wrote to a reviewer who had likened his "Whilomville" stories to Mrs. Burnett's work: "No thanks. If the Whilomville stories seem like Little Lord Fauntleroy to you, you are demented... See here, my friend, no kid except a sick little girl would like Lord Fauntleroy unless to look at Birch's pictures for it. The pictures are all right."

The points I wish to argue are two: first, that Little Lord Fauntleroy is not a prissy "mollycoddle," that he is, in truth, a small hero possessing characteristics eminently likable; second, that Fauntleroy is, perhaps, a figure more deserving of youthful emulation that Twain's Huck Finn, the fictive hero who has served as a model, admired and commended by adults, for a great many boys who have grown to manhood in the twentieth century. In arguing my brief, I am going to utilize the text of Mrs. Burnett's novel, but I am also, in passing, going to have recourse to reproductions of the original illustrations by Reginald Birch, illustrations which Crane deemed "all right" and Beer considered only "too faithful."

First off, it needs to be made quite clear that Cedric Errol is not a languishing mollycoddle. He has been distinguished, from birth, by a "quantity of soft, fine, gold-colored hair that went into loose rings by the time he was six months old," but Cedric's long hair is no more debilitating than Samson's was—"he had so strong a back and such splendid sturdy legs, that at nine months he learned suddenly to walk." At seven years old, his legs are still sturdy, even though they are usually clad in red stockings, and Cedric is one of the swiftest runners among the neighborhood boys of New York (see plate 1). Cedric's sturdiness is coupled with good looks, but it seems hardly just to complain of such a combination. The English lawyer who comes to New York to inform Cedric of his heritage is not easily impressed, but he is immediately taken with the boy, perceiving that "here was one of the finest and handsomest little fellows he had ever seen. His beauty was something unusual. He had a strong, lithe, graceful little body and a manly little face; he held his childish head up, and carried himself with a brave air."

Cedric, become Fauntleroy, continues to display his plucky nature. In fact, it is his pluck, along with his good looks, that are chiefly responsible for mellowing his irascible grandfather. When Fauntleroy is first ushered into the Earl of Darincourt's library, he marches right up to a "huge tawny mastiff" and puts "his hand on the big dog's collar in the most natural way in the world." When the Earl looks up from his chair he sees a "graceful, childish figure in a black velvet suit, with a lace collar, and with love-locks waving about the handsome, manly little face." And the old Earl is exultant when he sees "what a strong, beautiful boy this grandson was, and how unhesitatingly he looked up as he stood with his hand on the big dog's neck" (see plate 2). The Earl tests Fauntleroy by using him as a crutch to relieve his gouty foot, and is grimly pleased when the young Lord "stiffen [s] his childish muscles, [holds] his head erect, and encourage [s] the Earl as he limp [s] along." Later on, the Earl is even more pleased when Fauntleroy displays an eagerness to learn to ride, and a determination to sit his pony properly (see plate 3).

When Cedric Errol walks manfully up to his grandfather, the old

Earl gets his first glimpse into the fact that "there was no more fear in little Lord Fauntleroy's heart than there was unkindness." Cedric's amiable nature had evidenced itself as early in his life as his manliness: "his manners were so good, for a baby, that it was delightful to make his acquaintance. He seemed to feel that everyone was his friend, and when anyone spoke to him, when he was in his carriage in the street, he would give the stranger one sweet, serious look with the brown eyes, and then follow it with a lovely, friendly smile." As a seven-year-old, Cedric continues to approach everyone in a friendly, disarming manner. He is on good terms with a New York bootblack and a corner grocerykeeper, and when he talks with his grandfather the Earl cannot "help seeing that the little boy took him for a friend and treated him as one, without having any doubt of him at all." It is Cedric's good nature that makes him so ready to help people in need, and it is this zealous kindness that leads him to assume that his grandfather is unaware of the depressed condition of some of his tenants and that eventually shames his grandfather into taking steps to alleviate their plight. Cedric's loving nature is revealed throughout the novel in his relations with his mother, whom he calls "Dearest" in imitation of his dead father's favorite term of affection, but it is also significantly illustrated when he, at an evening party, finds himself attracted to a charming young lady surrounded by older masculine admirers; when she asks him why he is looking at her, Fauntleroy forthrightly tells her: "I was thinking how beautiful you are" (see plate 4).

Huck Finn, while not as forthright, also appreciates charming young girls; in most other respects, though, and not merely in matters of costume and hair style, Huck differs radically from Lord Fauntleroy. Huck has no mother to whom he can pour out his love, he is introspective and leery of human contacts, he is passive and not at all given to philanthropic zeal, and his imagination is morbidly prone to melancholy and visions of disaster. Huck's dark view of human nature and of societal corruption may be, in the long run, *truer* than Cedric Errol's sanguine view of men and of social possibility; it is, though, I submit, an unfortunate model to set before children who must live in society. And I suspect that Huck's dark vision does not really comport very well with the hopes that I think are alive in the breasts of the young people of the 1970's. It seems to me that the Huck Finn model of costume and manners, the model that has for so long effectively controlled the upbringing of so many American boys, is not only archaic but intrinsically pernicious (see plate 5). Such an argument is certainly challengeable, but let me at least suggest it, and let me do so by calling attention to certain aspects of the lives of two of the greatest, but most unfortunate, modern American writers, two writers who were tragically constricted by the Huck Finn model of what an American boy ought to be: Ernest Hemingway and Hart Crane.

Hemingway, of course, as Philip Young made startingly clear in his 1952 study of the author's career, and as Carlos Baker has unwittingly demonstrated in the authorized biography, lived according to the Huck Finn model both as boy and man (see plate 6). It may have provided him with some aesthetic support, but it was not finally consonant with mature self-sufficiency; throughout his adult life, Hemingway's assertions of robust masculinity were frantically shadowed by the repeated slaughterings of the fish and beasts he pursued in a vain effort to recapture his, and Huck Finn's, imagined boyhood (see plate 7). Hemingway was a good writer, but he never grew up, and it is only too bad that most Americans fail to recognize all the ironies implicit in John Berryman's ready epithet, in *The Dream Songs,* for Hemingway: "the shooter" (see plate 8).

While Hemingway may have been crippled by his eager acceptance of the Huck Finn model, it may be that Hart Crane was injured by having the model forced upon him as a child and as a consequence of there being available to him no other personally viable model of American masculinity (see plate 9). Crane's problems were complicated by his homosexuality, and by the responses of his family, friends, and acquaintances to that homosexuality—responses whose general pattern was marvellously prefigured by his family's method of dealing with the three-year-old Hart's desire to dress up in female finery. John Unterecker's biography of Crane notes how

> His Aunt Bess still wonders if she was right to forbid

> him to play in the big bandboxes of dressmaking materials that filled an under-the-stairs closet of his parents' home. He had just turned three, when suddenly all his energy seemed to go into decoration. For days he played with the bright materials, amusing his mother by trimming and modeling her wide hats in most ingenious ways. Feathers and buttons, velvet and lace were arranged and rearranged on the broad hat brims. Soon he began to collect discarded hats from other ladies in the family. It was all right, Bess felt, for a very young boy to play with dolls, but this seemed too much—the boy playing alone in the big house, sorting through box after box of buttons and bows, watched only by an indulgent mother. When one day Harold set to work on his aunt's new hat, he sealed his doom. Bess convinced Grace that such effeminate amusements were not in the boy's best interests. "He cried for two days," she recalls; and she wonders now if "getting it out of his system" might not, after all, have been best for him.

Crane, it seems, was never comfortable in Huck Finn's tattered hat and overalls, and he was not much attracted to the rough camaraderie and bluff virtues of the sportsman; the only other model of American masculinity available to him was that of the American businessman, the model exemplified for him by his father, C.A. Crane, the successful Ohio candy manufacturer. It was in the garb and stance of the businessman that Crane most frequently comported himself (see plate 10). The midwestern businessman's nondescript costume, however, is apt to denote a would-be Huckish personality within; as Sinclair Lewis' *Babbitt* perceptively noted, when the American businessman relaxes from hustling, his notion of the good life is an unbuttoned retreat from civilization, into the he-man's campfire world of smoking, drinking, and cussing. If there had been other options open to Crane, if he could have worn dandiacal clothes or sported a Whitmanian beard, if he could have worn beads north of the Rio Grande, then maybe his poetry wouldn't have been choked off–and maybe he wouldn't have had to kill himself (see plate 11).

Five years after Hart Crane leaped from the Orizaba, death came, also by water, to Vivian Burnett, who as Mrs. Burnett's younger son had been the chief model for Little Lord Fauntleroy (see plate 12). Vivian's death, of a heart attack after his rescue of a sailing party capsized in Long Island Sound, seems to have been the direct consequence of the last of a long series of strenuous efforts to live down his childhood notoriety. The *New York Times* account, on July 26, 1937, of the rescue and death, portrays Vivian Burnett as having lived a life devoted to the attempt to free himself from his mother's hurtful image; the news story, which refers to the "saccharine romanticism" of his mother's book, naturally assumes that the fictional Fauntleroy was nothing other than a sissy. On the following day, the *Times* editorially, but not at all critically, observed that "after the turn of the century public opinion was not kind to golden-haired mothers' darlings in velvet breeches" and warmly commended Vivian's "brave struggle to live down a painful past."

While Vivian Burnett's gallantry is commendable, the grounds for the editorialist's smug applause are not; it is more than unfortunate that so many American males, Crane and Hemingway among them, have been born into a culture that has defined manhood so narrowly and been so preternaturally harsh with "golden-haired mothers' darlings in velvet breeches." It may be that the American culture is presently revising its notions of what constitutes, for men and boys, masculinity; if so, then maybe Mrs. Burnett's youthful hero will not continue to be misrepresented and put down. It may be, even, that Cedric Errol will be viewed a precursor to such American males as Allen Ginsberg and Arlo Guthrie.

Plate 1. Reginald Birch illustration for first edition of *Little Lord Fauntleroy*.

Plate 2. Birch illustration for "Fauntleroy."

Plate 3. Birch illustration for "Fauntleroy."

Plate 4. Birch illustration for "Fauntleroy."

Plate 5. E.W. Kemble illustration for first American edition of *Adventures of Huckleberry Finn.* Twain checked and approved all the Kemble illustrations.

Plate 6. Ernest Hemingway at age 5, fishing for trout in Horton's Creek in northern Michigan. From the Family Collection of Mary Hemingway. Used by permission of Mary Hemingway. Copyright © 1969 Mary Hemingway.

Plate 7. Ernest Hemingway and friend, with porcupine trophy. Reproduced by permission of The World Publishing Company, from Leicester Hemingway's *My Brother, Ernest Hemingway* (1962)

Plate 8. Ernest Hemingway and Idaho friend Taylor Williams, near Sun Valley in 1940. Reproduced, by permission of The World Publishing Company, from Leicester Hemingway's *My Brother, Ernest Hemingway* (1962).

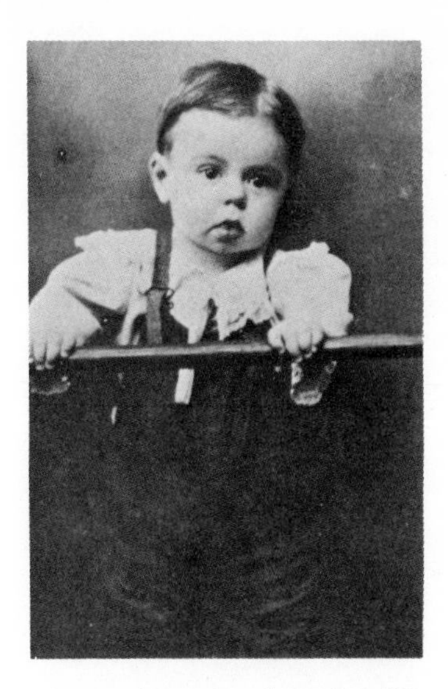

Plate 9. Earliest surviving photos of Harold Hart Crane, approximately 18 months old. Reproduced by permission of the Columbia University Libraries.

Plate 10. C. A. Crane and son, in Chagrin Falls, Ohio, December 1930. Reproduced by permission of the Columbia University Libraries.

Plate 11. Hart Crane in Mexico, two months before his death. Reproduced by permission of the Columbia University Libraries.

Plate 12. Vivian Burnett, nine years old. Photo used by Reginald Birch in preparing illustrations for *Little Lord Fauntleroy*.

Mrs. Johnston's *Little Colonel*

by

Elizabeth Steele

"If America ever writes a woman's name in her temple of fame, that one should be the name of Lloyd Sherman—*The Little Colonel*!" dreams twelve-year-old Lloyd in the book *The Little Colonel's Hero* (1902). I need hardly tell any of you that this daydream did not come true.

Yet go to Pewee Valley, Kentucky, as I did this autumn, and you will find yourself crossing the tracks of the L and N railroad and confronting the pale-stuccoed facade of a small theater building with the sign *The Little Colonel Players* strung across its front in big block letters.

Later that day I was told, by the present owner of the Little Colonel's "own" mansion (named The Locusts), about a local chapter of the recently formed International Reading Association: this chapter calls itself The Little Colonel Reading Circle. Nor does The Little Colonel live on in Pewee Valley only. Mrs. Carl Martin, present owner of The Locusts, gets scores of letters every year from interested readers throughout the United States—mostly *former* readers, to be sure, reliving their childhoods; but also from young readers just discovering The Little Colonel. The day before I met Mrs. Martin, she'd received a letter from a subteen in Nebraska who said that she and young friends of hers in Nebraska and Kansas "just loved the books."

Since the series has been out of print for some time, young readers must either get them from the library, have recourse to an older relative's treasured set or make lucky contact with a used-book dealer. Placed as she is, Mrs. Joseph Mudd, owner of an antique shop in Pewee Valley (called Lloydsborough Valley in the books), is widely recognized as the best source for second-hand copies of all Annie Fellows Johnston's works. She has constant calls for complete sets of *The Little Colonel*–mostly from grandmothers and mothers who want to give their daughters the pleasure they once enjoyed. Whether the daughters always respond like the subteen in Nebraska, is dubious, but meanwhile Mrs. Mudd's business is good.

In the context of the Second Annual Meeting of the American Studies Association, I feel justified in considering the Little Colonel books from three standpoints: as Americana, as popular art, and of course as children's literature.

As children's literature, their earlier popularity is well attested to. In 1955 Alice Payne Hackett, in her *Sixty Years of Best Sellers,* gave sales figures of "around the 2,000,000 mark" for the Little Colonel series. The first five volumes were also published in England; and some titles are reputed to have been translated into 14 foreign tongues, including Japanese.

Let me discuss two realms in which it seems to me Mrs. Johnston made her greatest impact: (1) that of middle-class moral values; and (2) that of culture –not only the "culture" involved in knowing about music, painting, and literature, but the broader culture relating to history, geography, folklore, even games.

What were the middle-class moral values advocated and illustrated in the Little Colonel books? First, that home relationships should be close. No generation gaps, if you please! "I always tell mothah everything," says the Little Colonel (though not prissily or smugly) in *House Party.* And she is as much at ease with her grandfather, Colonel Lloyd, and her father, "Papa Jack."

Not that adults are pictured as perfect. Fathers may be, for instance, generous with money but not with time; mothers may be beautiful, charming and sweet to their children when at home, yet still be away from home too much. This is not true of the Little Colonel's parents, but some of her friends suffer from these situations.

Even outside the various family circles there is constant emphasis on the generations' enjoying and needing each other.

Peer relationships within the younger generation are just as fully explored, but no more so. Naturally, perhaps, there are greater storms: girls are jealous of one another, boys bicker, boys tease girls, girls think they "hate" boys, and so on. Even true-love affairs have their swirls and eddies. The two main characters in the series, Lloyd and, in the last three books, Mary Ware, both almost miss marrying their man. This was heady reality for the young reader.

Throughout the series, scorn is heaped on girls who flirt with boys and vice versa. The highest terms of mutual commendation between the sexes are friend, pal, companion. School-girl crushes with faint Lesbian overtones are sympathetically handled in *Boarding School, Maid of Honor* and *Mary Ware.*

To move on to caste relationships, especially black ones—servants are described condescendingly. Even the names assigned them are sops to white prejudice. Thus normally democratic Mary Ware is able to speak about "Waffles, the old colored cook on the train, you know," who "just laid himself out to please" her brother Jack. All servants, black and white, domestic and foreign, are eager to please in Little Colonel land. The few exceptions occur in households where the mistress is slack and doesn't know how to "manage" her servants.

In the books with Western settings, the place of blacks is filled by Mexicans. Their differentness is exploited at the same time they are being scorned for being different. Although Jack Ware works with Mexicans at the mines and even saves the lives of two of them, thus sustaining a serious injury himself, he won't let his young brother play with Mexican boys.

The attitude toward poor Anglo-Saxon whites is more ambiguous. The Ware family themselves are poor, after all; and so is Mrs. Sherman's god-daughter, Betty Lewis (who later marries Jack Ware). Lloyd in *Holidays* is allowed to "learn" that some poor people are never grateful, no matter how much you do for them; and her "dainty" distaste for the dirty surroundings of the poor is commended. But by the last half of *Promised Land,* written eleven years later, Mary Ware is not allowed to criticize the poor for being dirty: their few chances of keeping clean, at least in city slums, are explained, and the onus is heaped on their landlords. It is worthwhile to recall here that the author's sister, Albion Fellows Bacon, was a zealous housing reformer who pushed important anti-slum bills through the Indiana legislature in the years before women had the vote. To her, Mrs. Johnston's later books undoubtedly owe some of their growing humanity.

And what of the relations with the very rich? Only two families described in the books fit this description. The typical Valley families, one understands, are very comfortably off but nothing more.

An interesting sidelight here is Mrs. Johnston's use of jewelry, shaped in symbolic forms and/or engraved in meaningful ways, that figures throughout the series, rewarding promises made or kept, betokening affection, etc. The metals are always pure, not alloyed, and the jewels are always real, never fake. While the ring of money is seldom heard in Mrs. Johnston's pages, this recurrent introduction of jewels provides an aura of ample wealth.

Now for hints as to general manners and morals. (a) One answers letters promptly and as entertainingly as possible. (b) One—whether male or female—does not drink. (Other than unfeeling landlords, the only real villains in the books are those men who because of "drink," drag their wives and children down to near-annihilation.) Mrs. Johnston believed that alcoholic tendencies were inherited.

(c) One admires and praises our armed forces and our policemen. (d) Boys can't fight with girls, even their sisters. (e) One should not eavesdrop or gossip (though Mrs. Johnston, with her plots in mind, sometimes excused both). (f) Don't chew gum. (g) Young ladies always wear a hat, even to the Post Office of Lone-Rock,

Arizona.

About chaperons Mrs. Johnston seemed of two minds. In *Christmas Vacation* (1905) the Little Colonel will not attend a matinee with two girlfriends and a boy she doesn't know, unless they have a chaperon. But three years later, in *Mary Ware,* the author lets Mary exclaim, "One must feel like a poodle tied to a string—always fastened to a chaperon. As for me give me liberty or give me death."

Of course, Kansas-born Mary Ware is not Lloyd Sherman and Mrs. Johnston was consistent in depicting character. But in books as didactic as these, though subtly so, such changing attitudes are significant.

As for the other half of Mrs. Johnston's message: the "cultural" aspects of life she tried to impart to young readers; of these literature is far and away the most pervasive. Other creative arts such as painting and music are barely touched on; and when they are, it is in their practical, immediate aspects. Will this painting or drawing or piece of music move its viewer or listener toward action? Mrs. Johnston was interested in affective art.

This is rather less true of her literary allusions, an impressive array. If the author really kept in her head, as apparently she did, the varied key words and phrases, and much longer quotations that stud her pages, it is a tribute to the wide range of reading, memorizing, and reciting encouraged in the schools and enlightened homes of the American Midwest during the late 19th century. Such ecleticism may be directly traceable to the McGuffey Readers. And much like them, the Little Colonel books are almost a graded series of literary selections. The first volume (1898) contained nursery rhymes, lullabies, old-timey Southern songs. With each succeeding volume the tempo and complexity increased, till by *Knight Comes Riding* (1907) the pace was at white heat.

Above all, Mrs. Johnston knew her Tennyson; Kipling was another favorite. But these two names suggest really nothing of the range and aptness of literary quotation employed by her throughout the series. Furthermore, she expected the reader to identify the allusions as well as she and supposedly her characters do. The Little

Colonel and her friends of all ages, male and female, delight in word games and word play, tossing quotations back and forth, proposing conundrums, finishing out famous lines, even satirizing normally "sacred" passages (for the author had a good sense of humor).

Incorporated into the books are several cautionary playlets and tales written by Mrs. Johnston and later published individually as keepsake books. Her favorite backgrounds for these were medieval England a la Tennyson, and the Near East (from Omar Khayyam?). Both models encouraged her, in these special tales, to employ archaic diction and maintain an atmosphere of prophetic utterance rather distasteful to the modern ear.

But were they effective at the time? Yes indeed. The most appealing tale was "The Three Weavers," from *Boarding School,* which sparked a nation-wide chain of girls' clubs, called The Order of Hildegarde after its protagonist.

History and geography play their parts in developing the series as a whole. Texas, Arizona, New York City and Europe transcend and expand the Kentucky scene. But (and here is where the study of the Little Colonel books as Americana comes in) Mrs. Johnston never forgets the Upper South. Despite her Hoosier birth and bringing-up, books about Southern authors are glad to claim her. She downplayed the Civil War–making Papa Jack a Northerner named Sherman was a good start–, but Grandfather Lloyd's establishment was as antebellum as the O'Hara plantation in *Gone with the Wind.* Along with this environment went the proper trappings: snatches of folklore or "voodoo" attributed to the "darkeys"; the Little Colonel's accent (she's the only white character in the books who drops her "r's"); allusions to early Kentucky history; the fondness of the characters for horse-flesh; word pictures of the Kentucky landscape as the mild seasons come and go. In *Maid of Honor* a Boston man appears (his name is Miles Bradford) and is treated to some "real Southern life": a realistic coon hunt, complete with its bloody kill.

Another kind of culture exploited by the author, however, seems more country Indiana than subplantation Kentucky: the books are full of how-to-do-its. Usually it's how to give a party, from invitations to costumes, games, and food. Every volume features at least one party-occasion. And there are other feminine how-to's: how to trim a hat, make a pie, decorate a cottage. Practical details are given for the young reader to follow.

To encourage such readers to create their own good times and then enjoy them, in 1909 Mrs. Johnston published *The Little Colonel Good Times Book.* After a friendly, fairly long preface, its elegant pages were left blank for young readers to record their "shining hours."

So in her own way Mrs. Johnston tried to keep her readers happy and busy. Her tools were a pretty heroine who had a few problems but not many; plenty of other characters of all ages who did have problems and usually solved them; a romantic Southern setting, veering sometimes to the wild and woolly West (about which, however, Mrs. Johnston was careful to explode the cliches); a parade of high ideals expanded through supplementary, sweetly noble tales; several chaste love stories; literary allusions by the score; practical instructions on how to stretch your dollars and yet have a wonderful time; plenty of laughs and good humor—plus a Good Times Book, whose pages you filled to prove you had learned your lessons well and were having a good time, just like the Little Colonel.

The first volume stayed in print longest, prolonged by the Shirley Temple edition issued after Miss Temple made her popular film in 1935. It appears frequently on television, though sometimes as a symbol of unpraiseworthy attitudes toward blacks, I'm afraid.

If the other books have been out of print longer, one can see why, especially from a topical viewpoint: the last current event they mention is the Spanish-American War. On the other hand, there's that enthusiastic young reader in Nebraska Mrs. Martin heard from recently. . . .

In any case, as children's literature, as popular art, as Americana, Mrs. Johnston's Little Colonel still deserves, as they say, to be studied. And among scholars there is no greater praise.

The Gangster and the Drama of the Thirties

by

Alan Casty

In the serious melodramatic and tragic plays of the Thirties, the face of the evil in the world was most frequently the face of the gangster—in all of his disguises. The strength and prominence of this popular stereotype were obviously the result of contemporary events—prohibition, the depression, labor busting and racketeering, public enemies. But they were clearly also the product of the popular arts of the detective story and the motion picture.

It was the motion pictures most of all that furnished the models and transformed the gangster into the mythic figure that would become one of the basic cultural symbols of an era. As Clifford Odets commented, the movies were to be praised for getting the folk material of the times to the people. But he criticized them for misusing it, for lying with it. "It is about time," he said, "that talented American playwrights began to take the gallery of American types, the assortment of fine vital themes away from the movies," to start, "where the movies left off."

Gangsters had been a part of the motion pictures from their infancy, D. W. Griffith's one-reeler, *Musketeers of Pig Alley* (1912), was one of their earliest appearances. But the genre of the gangster film did not take hold until late in the twenties—with Joseph Von Sternberg's *Underworld* (1927), the best of this early group. In these, neither the films nor the gangsters developed the heroically doomed, wise, flamboyant winningly vicious style of the gangster films of the thirties. *Walking Back* of 1929 did, however, feature the kind of staccato interchange (in silent film titles!) between two paid killers that was to become a part of the convention. Its debt to Ernest Hemingway's "The Killers" (first published in 1927) is further revealed by its recurrent use of "Bright Boy."

It was *Little Caesar, The Public Enemy* and *Scarface* (released in 1930, 1931, and 1932, respectively) that crystallized the genre and its style. There were, however, many other films in those years that included some of the same elements, fifty in 1931 alone, according to Arthur Knight. In these films brutal violence, callousness, and corruption were conveyed as the natural, seemingly the inevitable, ambience of life. Within it, accepted and even glorified on their own terms, the gangsters exhibited a daring, a courage, a loyalty to a personal code that contrasted oddly with the surface condemnation in the messages of the pictures. In *Little Caesar,* directed by Mervyn LeRoy, and *Scarface,* directed by Howard Hawks, the central figure was modeled after Al Capone and played by Edward G. Robinson and Paul Muni, although Robinson became the popular image for the type. He was an Italian, working at the highest level of organized crime, with a satanic drive for power, an insatiable ego that raised him, aloof and mysterious, beyond normal human relationships. At the end of *Little Caesar,* Robinson, dying says, "Mother of God, is this the end of Caesar?" Here he establishes the kind of mythic conception of himself that he continued to embody and established as well the kind of operatic, pseudo-poetic dialogue that was his trademark. In *Scarface,* the romanticized irony of the gangster's dream is suggested by the neon sign seen through the window of Scarface's bulletproof apartment: "The World is Yours," a sign that is again seen when he is lying shot to death in the street. In both were established as well the conventions of the cross-section of types in the gang, each with his own mannerisms of size, dress, and action:

George Raft in *Scarface* always flipping his quarter, even as he is shot.

In *The Public Enemy*, directed by William Wellman, James Cagney established the other basic and more influential, type of gangster. He was the young man up from the streets, with an energy and vitality that were typically American, with nothing but crime to put them to. In his case the pressures of his environment (as in the early scenes of *The Public Enemy*) were given more prominence: He had been made what he was. Jaunty and agile, with a quick, brash smile and a ready wisecrack, Cagney was hard and cruel and self-absorbed. He was always springing off his heels as he walked or stood, always clenching his fists, stabbing with his index finger as he talked. Yet for all his violence, even sadism, there was a touch of charm, even a rueful boyishness gone bad. As Otis Ferguson commented about him in a later film, he was "all crust and speed and sap on the surface," but underneath there was a "quick generosity and hidden sweetness, straight, anti-fraud, native humor, feckless drive."

The tough-guy persona of Humphrey Bogart wasn't shaped until his appearance in *The Petrified Forest* in 1936. In Bogart this American hero-villain was to become more world-weary, less ebullient. His sardonic surface hardness obviously became a shield for some inner spirit that had been hurt and warped. And in the roles of John Garfield, beginning with *They Made Me a Criminal* and *Dust Be My Destiny* in 1939, the transformation was to be completed. The tough guy came to be seen as victim of the system, driven, often desperate but with a dignity and sensitivity that somehow endured.

From the start, these gangster films of the thirties popularized a jargon—part gag and wisecrack, part philosophic bon mot, part folk-poetry—that became a consistent ingredient of the stereotype on both stage and screen. Some examples: "So you can dish it out but you can't take it!" "I wanna be somebody." "Don't be a sucker." "Take him for a ride!" "You're so strong, but you're just a boy, you want what you want." "How much (whiskey)?" "Oh, about two ounces, one for each kidney." "Chaser?" "Always have been." "Put that away or I'll jam it down your throat." "Cut me in and I'll up your take." "Smart little guy, aren't you?" "I've been around."

"Take a gander at her." "I wonder how she'd go for a goose."

The basic materials of the popular stereotype of the movie gangster served a variety of functions within the predominant theatrical conventions of the time—which were fundamentally the conventions of social realism. In brief, the chief features of this drama were a realistic social environment, the use of representative social types, the strength of the influence of social causation, and the equal possibilities of the individual will that did not deny the forces of the environment. Character was thus derived from the full interaction of the individual will and its environment: character growth was associated with the possibility of social reform.

The greatest number, and least complex, of the stage gangsters were labor-busting goons or racketeers in the more obvious plays of social protest. In these, they were in close partnership with the capitalist businessmen and their corruptions. They served to furnish the specific acts of evil that produced the greatest awareness of the down-trodden (or occasionally the middle class) and led them to act for reform and change. To cite just three examples from many:

In George Sklar and George Peters' *Stevedore*, gunmen are hired to break a longshoremen's strike. When Lonnie, a negro stevedore, becomes a militant leader in the strike, he is framed on a rape charge. The gunmen then help incite and lead a lynch mob into the negro district, but are met in pitched battle by the aroused negroes, who, in an application of class unity, are joined by white workers to rout the mob.

This pattern is given a more complex development in Lillian Hellman's *Days to Come.* Although it is not among her better plays, it is a far cry from the propagandic protest plays. Miss Hellman is concerned with the emptiness and futility in the lives of the capitalist family that owns a brush factory in a small midwest town. The deceits and confusions of the personal lives are paralleled by the situation of a strike at the factory. The indecision of Andrew Rodman—estranged from his wife, trapped into deadly routine by family pressures—is indicated by his allowing strike-breakers to be brought into the town, but not allowing them to take their usual measures in inciting the strikers to violence so that reprisals can be taken. The usual connection between gangsters and leaders of the economic system is established. Samuel Wilkie, the gang leader, calls himself a business man: "I come in to break strikes. That's my business." His two chief henchmen, Massie Powell and Joe Easter, are typical movie gangsters; one is thin and dour, the other fat. Massie always nervously cracks his knuckles: Easter always toys with some object, a lighter, a knife, a deck of cards. These gangsters precipitate the violence of the play, and from the violence Andrew and his wife gain a greater understanding of their lives.

Probably the most famous and theatrically successful of the plays that employed the labor gangster and the pattern of growth of awareness in response to the actions of the gangster was Odets' *Waiting for Lefty,* first produced by members of the Group Theater at the New Theater League early in 1935. In *Waiting for Lefty,* the racketeer Fatt is the corrupt head of the union. His gunmen are used, in collusion with the bosses, to enforce his own selfish purposes. At the play's climax, as Agate exhorts the men (and audience) to turn against Fatt and strike, he is manhandled by Fatt and his gunman. But this only makes the men more militant. When the shooting of Lefty by the labor gangsters is revealed, all take up Agate's cry, shouting "STRIKE, STRIKE, STRIKE!!!" at the curtain.

In a reverse pattern, in a number of plays the gangster was seen as a tragic, and even romantic, product and victim of the evils of society. Two contrasting views of this function of the gangster can be seen in John Howard Lawson's *The Pure in Heart* and Sidney Kingsley's *Dead End.* In 1934 Lawson's *The Pure in Heart* depicted the destruction of romantic idealism and individualism by the times and system. Annabel comes to the big city mistakenly seeking something grander in life in the theater. Annabel falls in love with Larry, a parolee, who is blocked from making a new start by society. He gives in to one more robbery, kills a man and is hunted down and shot, along with Annabel, by the police. Larry is full of the Cagney-like wisecracks of the movie gangster, but underneath he is an idealist. Typical of his repartee: "I'd like to get you in a dark corner and squeeze you till you'd burn up and scream for more." "That's me, hot, cheerful, and full of spinach." "I been in cold storage and it takes a little while to warm up." "You look good, you look like Broadway after dark."

Baby-Face Martin, in Kingsley's *Dead End* (1935), is no such doomed idealist, but figures as the negative example of what the economic system—particularly the slum environment—can produce. Kingsley's play is a unique example of the interplay between film and theater. Itself influenced by earlier movies, it in turn became a Humphrey Bogart movie vehicle in 1937 and then spawned a whole series of Dead End Kid and Bowery Boys movies. Martin, in the standard double breasted pin stripe, tight at the waist, has the cocky swagger and underlying nervousness of the movie gangster. When anxious, he "sucks his teeth." When asked if he is ever scared, he typically replies, "Me? What of? What to hell, you can't live forever. Ah, I don't know, sure sometimes I get da jitters." When he slaps Gimpty and is asked what's the idea, he replies, "Dats ee idea for shootin off yer mout. I don like guys at talk outa toin. Not tuh me!" Other typical bon mots: "Listen, kid. Ere ain't no fair, and ere ain't no square. It's winnah take all." "Dose dames are pushovers, fish fuh duh monkeys."

In another group of plays, the gangster is treated less literally, not as the actual gunman of the bosses, nor as the victim of the system. Rather, he is seen as a symbolic parallel to the system's emphasis on money, as an exaggerated personification of the evils of the profit system and the values it induces.

In Lawson's *Success Story,* produced by the Group Theater in 1932, the gangster figure is an offstage parallel to the destructive greed of the young advertising executive, Sol Ginsburg. Sol, up from the slums, gives himself to making money; his brother had tried for success in the rackets and had been shot in a gangland feud. Sol has vowed to do better: "This is a gangster's world and I'm out to beat it...I swore at the funeral—to get what he was after and to get it respectable." And in typical gangster jargon: "I'm going some place; anyone stands in my way I'll smash 'em—." To complete the parallel Sol, too, is finally killed with a gun.

In a lighter vein, Maxwell Anderson uses a trio of petty and inept gangsters as a parallel to the selfish and destructive values of the modern business world in his fantasy comedy of 1937, *High Tor.* Buddy, Dope and Elkus are a typical movie set of two underlings and a boss:

> *Buddy:* We'll get four hundred years for this. *Elkus* [the boss]: What do you think you are, a chorus? Go on back to St. Thomas's and sing it to the priest. You're about as much help as a flat tire.

In Irwin Shaw's *The Gentle People,* the protection racketeer Goff has the ruthless violence, the wise talk of the movie gangster. This time, however, in 1939, he not only is the symbol of economic oppression, he is also representative of the forces of brutal authoritarianism and facism. Still, the most frequent references are to business and its relationship to the injustices in American society.

The people's responses to this force of evil vary. The daughter of one of the men being extorted is infatuated by the lure of the glamor and excitement Goff can bring her. The men at first are passive, then unsuccessfully try legal means. Finally they realize they can stand up to Goff and kill him. Again, the gangster has precipitated the resurgence of the will and action of the people.

The most popular and subsequently influential of symbolic patterns is set by Odets in *Golden Boy,* written after two years of working in Hollywood. Joe Bonaparte has the energy, the same "feckless drive," the same aura of potential of many of the slum boys of the films who turned to crime as their outlet. As was the case in a number of subsequent Hollywood products (and most effectively in Robert Rossen's *Body and Soul* and *The Hustler*) the sports world is used as the microcosm of the society and the gambler-promoter version of the gangster as the personification of capitalist corruption. Joe's impelling need for success as the illusory symbol of his identity is enunciated in the typical fashion of the movies of the thirties: "When a bullet sings through the air it has no past—only a future—like me! Nobody, nothing stands in my way!" He spurns the values clustered around the violin—family, art, love, integrity—and chooses the values offered by Fuselli, the racketeer, those clustered around the boxing gloves—success, power, money, excitement, speed, loss of self, death.

Even when Joe recognizes, too late, what has happened to him, the romantic allure of the world of the gangster is too much for him. For the thrill of speed, he drives off in the Dusenberg that his fighting has bought him and is killed. It is an accident that is more than an accident—an almost intentional completion of the self-destruction that the trap of his false values has created.

In three of the most significant plays of the decade, the gangster has a broader symbolic context. In varying ways, he provides the situation in which the dramatists attempt to affirm the possibilities of the individual will as well as the possibilities of tragic drama. In Robert E. Sherwood's *The Petrified Forest* and Anderson's *Winterset* and *Key Largo* the gangster represents the more universalized force of evil and power in the world that the tragic heroes must finally come to terms with, in one way or another.

Duke Mantee, in *The Petrified Forest,* is a romanticized, tragic figure of a brute man; he first supplied Humphrey Bogart (in both the stage and screen versions) with the combination of traits that became the Bogart image. Mantee is world-weary, cynical, with a stoic impenetrability, a hard defiance that still reveals an inner core of dignity. His speech is laconic but forceful: "Let's skip it, here's happy days." "Maybe you're right, pal." "I got to think about my health, pal." "It was a bad shot, pop. But I had to get it off fast...I let that mugg make a mugg out of me." "Can't say, pop. Maybe we'll decide to get buried here." And when he shoots Alan Squires, "Okay, pal, I'll be seeing you soon."

Mantee provides Squires with a sense of the energy and vitality of life that he has irretrievably lost. But for the disillusioned, alienated, hopeless intellectual Squires, Mantee provides a last, romantic means of melancholy self assertion. Duke Mantee becomes the means for Squires to sacrifice himself for the future (and for the insurance policy he can leave the young waitress, Gabby). Thus, in this inverted assertion of will, he does not act against evil, but senses his kinship with it and in unholy alliance can use it to assert his identity in the only way left for him, or at least the only way Mr. Sherwood, none too convincingly, has insisted is left for him.

For Mio, the gang leader Trock in *Winterset* provides a slightly different final moment of truth. Trock represents a more malicious form of evil. He resembles more the Italianate, Edward G. Robinson gangster image, larger than life, but unsentimentalized. He is the high level racketeer boss, driven to kill anyone who threatens his obsession with the maintenance of what freedom is left him by his fatal illness. His speech has the pseudo-poetic loftiness of the gangster genre without the youthful brashness of the Cagney type: "Because I'm cold, punk. Because I've been outside and it's cold as the tomb of Christ." "I say it is, see? You wouldn't want to let the judge walk, would you? The judge is going to ride where he's going, with a couple of chauffeurs, and everything done in style."

Although allied with the evil of political injustice and corruption, Trock and his obsession go beyond the limited symbolism of the political protest plays. He is that force of evil that must be routed if Mio is to find the truth and justice that will restore meaning to his life. Mio's quest becomes a tragic dilemma, however, when the assault on Trock and injustice becomes also an assault on Miriamne's brother Garth and thus a violation of the new value of love that Mio has discovered. Torn between his two warring desires, Mio delays too long. Thus he allows himself to be killed by Trock when Miriamne mistakenly says the way is clear. He has chosen not to destroy evil if it means violating love, but implacable evil still destroys him.

In *Key Largo,* Murillo is only a small time gambler, and is allied with a local brand of injustice and police corruption. But again he represents the pervasive universal evil that the hero, King McCloud, must finally come to terms with if he is to regain the meaning of his life that he lost when he fled from the parallel evil of the facists in the Spanish Civil War. Murillo too speaks the conventional movie argot: "Anytime you want to start more trouble, baby, just put in your nominations." "We're going to get that thirty out of him if we have to melt it out of his teeth."

When, finally, the alliance of police corruption and the brutal selfishness of the gangster threatens two innocent Indians, King takes his stand against evil. His gun against Murillo's stomach, he carelessly allows Hunk, the henchman, to shoot him. Then before he dies, he shoots Murillo. For it was not only the destruction of evil that was important to him, it was the acceptance of the facing of death. "I knew you couldn't stand it," he says to Hunk. "You must be shooting. I counted on you, and you did it."

In the last four plays discussed (certainly among the most important of the period) the gangster has provided the dramatists with a tangible representation of evil and a credible contemporary situation of heroic crisis. Yet in all four the form of action taken by the hero, when face to face with the force of the gangster, has been a kind of heroic suicide. This response to the gangster rises, it seems to me, from the difficulties encountered by the playwrights of the thirties in carrying out their assumptions about the possibilities of asserting human will without falsifying the pressures of the environment.

These difficulties are especially noticeable in plot resolutions. In the plays discussed earlier, the final assertion of will, as catalyzed by the gangster, was based on ideals of political commitment and possibility and produced actions of political resurgence. In seeking to go beyond the simplifications of this affirmative pattern and into the area of traditional tragic assertion of human dignity and will, Odets, Sherwood and Anderson all chose an interesting form of romantic masochism that violates the logic and inevitability of the dramatic and tragic stoicism they sought. In each case the hero has had chosen for him a purifying martyrdom that resembles the masochistic alternative defined by Theodore Reik in his *Masochism and Modern Man.* When faced with the insurmountable difficulties of direct fulfillment within the environment, Reik explains, the masochist intentionally provokes the environment to do its worst and only then can he find some sort of twisted victory, as if to say, I can take whatever you can give, even death, and still find my triumph. In one way or another this was the stance of Joe Bonaparte, Allan Squires, Mio, and King McCloud. In the world of the gangster, and all he represented in the theater of the thirties, this posture of romantic masochism seemed to be all that remained once the gesture of political idealism was refused.

The Hardy Boys Revisited: A Study in Prejudice

by

Gerard O'Connor

"Luke Jones don't stand for no nonsense from white folks.
Ah pays mah fare, an' Ah puts mah shoes where Ah please."

Luke Jones sounds like a Nat Turner of the Pullman. But he isn't. "He hastily restored his feet to their proper place whenever the conductor came through the car."[1] Luke Jones is no revolutionist, no leader of the people. Luke Jones is simply the "big black fellow" who "done stole de money" in The Hardy Boys story *The Hidden Harbor Mystery.*

Written in 1935 and read by millions of American kids since, *The Hidden Harbor Mystery* is a microcosm of the whole Hardy Boys series. The world of *Hidden Harbor* is that of the Hardys: a world of gross prejudice, of insulting stereotypes, of crude caricature. In this world, where you come from determines what you become; and how you spell your name determines how you speak. If you are fresh off the gondola, then you try to "sella da good fruit at da good price." If a potato famine has driven you here, then you walk a beat, dreaming of corned beef and cabbage dinners. If you are black and know your place, then you become a "shining-faced servant" who dutifully says "Good mawnin', gen'mun" to the teenage Hardys. If you are black and do not know your place, then you become a Luke Jones and bluster that you won't "stand for no nonsense from white folks." But like the guilty Luke, who "cringed and hung his head when he saw his master," you will end up captured by the Hardys, howling for mercy, and headed for jail.

Polarizing this world of prejudice is the Hardy circle. The family itself and most of the close friends are unobtrusively but unmistakenly WASP. (Aunt Gertrude's suggestion that Frank and Joe spend Sunday afternoon discussing *Pilgrim's Progress* is the exception rather than the rule.) Of the Hardy chums only Tony Prito and Phil Cohen are not WASP.

There is little doubt about Tony Prito's ethnic background. His "dark hair, olive skin, and sparkling eyes indicated his Italian parentage, even more emphatically than his name." Characteristically, Tony still stumbles over shibboleths. He says "What's the mattah?" and "I wish is was mine" because "he had not yet been in America long enough to talk the language without an accent." But compared to Rocco the fruitman, Tony is very much assimilated: his father is "one of the most respected citizens in the Italian colony of Bayport," and Tony has his own speedboat, the Napoli. In contrast, Rocco talks like Vanzetti and still lives in fear of "da Blacka Hand." Faithful to his stereotype, Rocco serves as the butt of the vaudevillian jokes. In one episode in *The Tower Treasure* he is duped by the Hardy boys and chums into thinking that a package containing an alarm clock is a time bomb. The high point of the comedy is Rocco "dancing about in the middle of the street, yelling, 'Bombs! Police! Da Blacka Hand!' " Rocco's performance is only natural, however, for "like most of his countrymen, he was of an excitable nature."

Phil Cohen is the most obscure of the Hardy chums. "A diminutive black-haired Jewish boy," Phil is accepted by Frank and Joe for the apparent Some-Of-My-Best-Friends reason. Occasionally Phil will play the comic role, and with unmistakenable idiom: "Oy! what a fine day you pick for your trip!" But for the most part Phil functions simply as the Resident Jew.

However, the acceptance by the Hardys of a Phil Cohen does not preclude a Charlie Hinchman or a Moe Gordon. Charlie, "a small beady-eyed man with a pointed goatee," owns a candystore in *The Clue of the Broken Blade*. When a car crashes through his store window and Joe Hardy asks him if he's hurt, Charlie answers:

> "No matter about me. Look at my shop! The big sedan–she run right through the window! Oh, oh, she is owing me ten thousand dollars' damages!"

Faithful to the mold, Charlie immediately threatens to get a lawyer and sue the driver who has "ruinated" his shop. But Charlie is not really the avaricious Jew candystore owner of tradition. He is actually an avaricious Jew crook of the 1930's. Charlie specializes in hijacking, but he is not above murder, if there's a profit in it.

Even more rapacious than Charlie Hinchman is his cheese-eating cousin Moe Gordon. For in addition to his hijacking, Moe deals in extortion, knives, and poisonous snakes. Like Luke Jones in *The Hidden Harbor*, Moe preys on a wealthy WASP family. Where Luke steals a diamond ring from his "master," Moe extorts cash from a "friend." Where Luke smashes old people over the head, Moe plants a viper in their room. Each in his own stereotyped way is after WASP money, and both try to destroy WASP families to get it. But criminology not crime pays in The Hardy Boys; the WASP money circulated is always reward money for Frank and Joe.

The blatant Jewishness of Hinchman and Gordon is an exception to the general rule in The Hardy Boys that criminals are ethnically amorphous. Spike Hudson, Taffy Marr, Gus Montrose, Duke Beeson *et al* are names apparently derived from American criminal mythology and given a slight Dickensian twist. Baldy Turk, Trett Rangle, and Ganny Snackley are more strongly Dickensian, but still cannot be identified ethnically.

Similarly, Bayport's constabulary, Chief of Police Ezra Collig and Detective Oscar Smuff, are Dickensian caricatures. Infallibly fatuous, they read the comics, play checkers, and use "ain't" habitually. To the Hardys and, particularly, Chet Morton they are objects of ridicule—detectives who, according to Chet, can't catch the proverbial cold. If the internationally famous detective Fenton Hardy were not always getting captured by ignorant mobsters, then the disrespect for the law which The Hardy Boys inculcate would be the most amusing irony in the series.

However, Detective Oscar Smuff looks like Alec Leamas compared to Constable Con Riley, Bayport's only visible patrolman. For Con Riley is "thick-headed," very thick-headed. He walks his beat dreaming of the corned beef and cabbage dinner that Mrs. Riley is cooking. As a result he does not notice a pickpocket lifting his handcuffs and nightstick. In the series he suffers every indignity from having his helmet knocked off by a Chet Morton snowball to having his "who done it' corrected to "who did it" by the same Chet. Con naturally speaks with a brogue, and this sometimes creates problems in communication:

> "From what I can learn," said Riley with a severe glance at Chet, "the whole business was a food."
> "A what?" said Frank puzzled.
> "A food. One of them foods among Chinamen. You know."
> "Like chop suey?" inquired Chet, interested.
> "A food, I said," declared Riley. "A battle. A war. A food."
> "A feud!" exclaimed Joe.

Con Riley is the Stage Irishman, the butt of all the jokes. Con Riley is the man for whom the NINA signs of the nineteenth century were invented. He is Mike of Pat and Mike.

And as painfully as Con Riley is the Stage Irishman, MacBane is "Sandy MacPherson" of Can You Top This immortality; Louis Fong is the No-Tickee No-Shirtee Laundryman gone bad; and all the blacks are Rastus, Remus, or Uncle Tom. A janitor at Bayport High, MacBane is, predictably, "cantankerous" and "dour." When Jerry Gilroy badgers him in *The Secret of the Old Mill*, MacBane lapses into "broad Scotch. . . spluttering unintelligible phrases that could only have been understood in the remotest reaches of Caledonia."

Louie Fong is the most villanous-looking Oriental this side of Fu Manchu:

> His head was pointed and almost bald, while a cruel mouth was partly concealed by a dropping wisp of mustache. His eyes were as cold and glittering as those of a snake.

In *Footprints Under the Window*, Louie proves that "his evil yellow face" is no lie: he throws around, liberally and accurately, his "long, sharp evil-looking knife"; and he dispatches, frequently and indiscriminately, his "enormous dog, lean and ferocious, with slavering jaws." When Louie Fong is after you, as Tom Wat tells Frank, "Alee samee dead man now."

Louie Fong is not, however, "the worst scoundrel Frank and Joe have ever come across." That distinction goes to Luke Jones. To be a worse scoundrel than Louie Fong, to say nothing of Baldy Turk and Ganny Snackley, is no small achievement. But Luke Jones is actually less interesting psychologically than he is historically and sociologically. For Luke is a nearly perfect example of the Brute Negro stereotype. As Sterling A. Brown described him, the Brute Negro is vicious, ignorant, swaggering, revengeful, gaudily dressed, and–most important–dissatisfied with his place in life and somewhat eager to improve it.[2] First appearing in Reconstruction literature, especially that of Thomas Nelson Page, the Brute Negro is most familiarly, and perhaps most sensationally, illustrated by Silas in *The Birth of a Nation.* The only difference between Silas Lynch and Luke Jones is that the proprieties of the Hardy Boys preclude the raping and the gin-drinking.

For the "black rascal" Luke manifests all the other characteristics of the stereotype: he wears a "suit of extreme collegiate cut, a pink shirt with violet necktie," shiny patent leather shoes, and he flashes a big roll and a sparkling diamond (both stolen). He is always "swaggering," "insolent," and "arrogant." In addition to knocking old Mrs. Rand and old Mr. Blackstone over the head, Luke attempts to murder both Ruel Rand and Chet Morton. This viciousness is not the "motiveless malignity" that Coleridge ascribed to Iago. Luke has his motives, and they are made incontrovertibly clear by his father, an Uncle Tom figure:

> "Evah since he's been up No'th with Massa Blackstone he thinks he's smart. Fine new clothes, big diamon' ring an' he swaggers 'roun' heah lak he own de place."

In fact, so much has Luke been corrupted by the taste of the good life up North that he organizes a Secret Society that out-KKK's the whites. Only the courage, cleverness, and daring of the Hardys prevent these black, "rather stupid looking" rebels from effecting a social coup d'etat.

The message of the *Hidden Harbor Mystery,* 1935, is as self-evident as it is self-condemning; blacks should be kept in servitude because they are an ignorant, violent, immoral people who are as incapable of understanding freedom as they are of fulfilling the responsibilities concomitant with it. Blatant in the *Harbor,* this message is reinforced over and over in the other Hardy Boys stories. All blacks speak in Uncle Remus dialect, all hold menial jobs, all are anonymous. No black is accorded any respect, no black is entrusted with any responsibility, no black is accepted as a human being.

And the case of the black in the Hardy Boys, as we have seen is an intensification of that of every minority group. Irishmen pound beats, Scotchmen sweep floors, Italians sell bananas. The Applegates and Websters have the money, the Blackstones and Rands have the tradition, the Hardys have the brains. This is the world of the Hardy Boys. This is the American Dream of Franklin W. Dixon.

The influence of the Hardy Boys stories on American thought is as inestimable as their readers are incalculable. Both are enormous. Millions of minds, my own included, have been irrevocably warped by the taken-for-granted caste system. Re-reading the series now, twenty-five years after I grew up with it, is an experience as traumatic as it is embarrassing. For I probably read *The Hidden Harbor Mystery* a half-dozen times in the early 1940's, but I never really saw Luke Jones until two months ago. I know now that I would have accepted it as perfectly natural then if Chet Morton had ever suggested, one day at a carnival, a little eenie-meenie-meinie-moe to see who would throw first in the Hit-the-Coon, Get-a-Cigar game.

Today the Hardy Boys are as popular as ever. Now the stories are being read the world over, from England and France to Iceland and the Argentine. But there is a little hope. For many of the original stories, including the *Hidden Harbor Mystery* and *Footprints Under the Window* now bear the following note on the title page verso:

> In this new story, based on the original of the same title, Mr. Dixon has incorporated the most up-to-date methods used by police and private detectives.

The note is slightly misleading. "Mr. Dixon" died about thirty years ago in the person of Edward Stratemeyer; the revision is largely the work of the Stratemeyer Syndicate. Secondly, and far more significant, in the *Harbor* and *Footprints* new "methods" means new book. That is, Louie Fong and Luke Jones have disappeared. There is little, if any, connection between the revised plot of these two stories and the original.

Now it is certainly good and proper that someone in the Syndicate has finally realized that these two stories were extremely bigoted in the original. One only wishes he could be more enthusiastic about the revisions. For although Luke Jones and Louie Fong are gone, and Rocco has become Mr. Rocco, and Con Riley is now Patrolman Riley, the essential nature of the Hardy Boys world has not really changed at all. Mr. Rocco is still selling fruit and he still has an accent. Patrolman Riley is still an Irish cop pounding a beat. And in the revised *Hidden Harbor Mystery*, Mr. Blackstone's door is now answered not by old Uncle Tom Jones but by Minnie, a "young Negro maid."

It is clear that The Hardy Boys are rooted in what Gordon Allport calls "culture-bound traditions." That is, the hierarchic structure of the society and the set of values implicit in it constitute *de facto* prejudice of the worst—because it is so taken-for-granted—kind. Thus, calling the fruit peddler "Mr. Rocco" is about as effective as putting a band-aid over a cancer. Substituting Minnie the Maid for the Brute Negro is removing the cancer and replacing it with a tumor. The Hardy Boys are sick, very sick. In fact, the Hardy Boys are so sick that I doubt that even a heart transplant could make them well.

NOTES

[1]My quotations are all from the original Hardy Boys Series, Grosset & Dunlop Publishers.

[2]Sterling A. Brown, "A Century of Negro Portraiture in American Literature," *The Massachusetts Review*, Winter, 1966; reprinted in *Black Voices,* ed. Abraham Chapman, New York: Mentor, 1968.

Theodore Dreiser and Music

by

Neil Leonard

A good deal has been written about Theodore Dreiser's interest in the different arts. Aside from the large amount of material on his fiction, we have studies of his concern with painting, with the theater, with the film, and several scholars have commented on his poetry. But we know little of his interest in music. This is scarcely surprising in view of his small contribution to that field. Yet music held an important place in his sensibility, and this is worth exploring. While making no claims for the validity of Dreiser's ideas about music, I want to trace his interest in it and to suggest some of its connections with his writing.

In her biography of Dreiser, Dorothy Dudley pointed out that he had "an imperfect ear,"[1] a fact evident in the shortcomings of his fictional dialogue as well as in his musical taste. His faulty ear, however, did not noticeably dim his enthusiasm for music. "All my life I have had a feeling for music," he told an interviewer in 1928.[2] His secretary and friend, Margaret Tjader, called him "inordinately susceptible to emotion coming through music" and recalled how his head seemed full of it:

> There was always a musical quality about Dreiser himself, if it was only the vibration of his extraordinary soft, low and harmonious voice, when he spoke. He was also capable of making sounds in his speech, between words, or to emphasize words, to envelop them in a deeper, sardonic or affectionate meaning. There were *Ahh's* of surprise or *Baah's* of scorn, or sounds, sighs, or purrs, too subtle to correspond to letters.
>
> He had a way of humming, a sort of running accompaniment to happier thoughts and moods. A low, harmonious undercurrent which bore his restlessness smoothly along. Sometimes he would follow some old melody or refrain of the day; at other times, it seemed as if he were making an indistinguishable murmur, like the noise of bees on a summer afternoon, usually in a minor key.
>
> I can remember particularly how Dreiser used to hum when he was riding along in a car, after a happy day in the country. His low voice would fit into the purr of the motor, or rise above it, in some favorite old musical comedy number or verse for which he knew the words. . . . And the night would have a wholeness and a beauty around his humble song.[3]

As a young man growing up in Indiana he heard music from several sources. One important one was his brother Paul. Older than Theodore by fifteen years, his influence on the future novelist was enormous. At the age of sixteen, unable to stand his father's strictness and plans for him to enter the priesthood, Paul ran away from home to join a medicine show selling Hamlin's Wizard Oil. Later he changed his last name to Dresser and became a successful songwriter, publisher and celebrity on Tin Pan Alley. As Dreiser described it,

"His world was that of the popular song, the middle-class actor or comedian, the middle-class comedy [of] Bill Nye, Petrolium V. Nasby, the authors of the Spoopendyke Papers and 'Samantha at Saratoga' . . . . I say this with no lofty condescending spirit by any means—he was entirely full of simple middle-class grossness, all of which I am very free to say won me completely and kept me so much his debtor."[4] Dreiser loved him not simply as the "ballad maker of a nation," but as a *bon vivant* and *raconteur* who supported the family in times of need and introduced him to the glamorous world of show business in New York. After Paul's death Dreiser wrote a touching reminiscence of him, which, in its final form, appeared as "My Brother Paul" in *Twelve Men.* It was Paul who owned part of the music publishing house which brought out the magazine *Ev'ry Month* and gave Theodore his first editing job (1895-97). The two brothers collaborated on the song, "On the Banks of the Wabash," Theodore contributing the verse and first chorus of the lyrics. He was impressed with Paul's melodies, many of which were popular hits of the day, including "On the Bowery," "My Gal Sal," and "Just Tell Them That You Saw Me," and believed that, if Paul had had more formal musical training, he might have written symphonies and operas for which his friend and admirer, the composer Louis Gottschalk felt his talents were suited.

Before he had fully felt Paul's influence, however, young Theodore had grown fond of the music played in small towns in Indiana. He was charmed by the conventional romantic music of his boyhood days, just as he was by the romantic theater, and enjoyed a Warsaw theater orchestra's renditions of "La Paloma" and fragments of *Carmen, The Poet and the Peasant,* and *William Tell* which evoked "the contemplation of perfections which had no relation—or small, at least, to the shabby world of fact before me." As a teenager he enjoyed standing on the lake shores in the evening and feeling "a spirit of romance" while listening to a guitar or mandolin played offshore.[5] Later he learned to appreciate academic music at concerts conducted by Theodore Thomas in the Chicago Auditorium. Upon going to St. Louis, he enthusiastically played the banjo and sang at parties with his young friends on the *Globe-Democrat*.

In the nineties he had plans to use his knowledge of the music business to write a novel about a composer of popular songs, but changed his mind and began *Sister Carrie*. He did, however, do three articles on aspects of Tin Pan Alley as well as one on Theodore Thomas and others, mainly women who were successful musicians.[6] His travel writings, too, reflected his musical interests. In *A Traveler at Forty* he recounted his experiences with a temperamental pianist and remarked on the musical street cries of Venice.

He also liked negro music and what passed for it, minstrel songs and the music of the negroes themselves, partly because he believed that "the poor and the ignorant and the savage are great artistically."[7] In St. Louis he visited a negro brothel where he liked the wild music and dancing of the inmates, and later in New York he took special pleasure in introducing into one of his parties an African dance troup, "discovered" in Harlem, which performed in mask and loincloth, responding to wild rhythms with abandoned shrieks and leaps. He also enjoyed ragtime and later became interested in jazz and spirituals, such as "Sometimes I Feel Like a Motherless Child." As the theater critic for the St. Louis *Globe-Democrat,* he had lavishly praised a recital of similar songs sung by one "Black Patti" and had been rebuked for breaking the St. Louis custom of withholding appreciation of Negroes in newspapers.

Among his favorite composers were Beethoven, Tchaikovsky and Grieg. "It was in the province of the tragedian—tragic music—that he came nearest to understanding the art," wrote Margaret Tjader, who also said that he was a thorough-going "sucker for program music,"[8] a characteristic not surprising in a man whose imagination worked so strongly in visual terms. In connection with a piece by Grieg, he wrote, "at once I see Fjords and ice-capped horns, bleak winter light and buxom peasant girls in bright dresses. As a matter of fact it takes very little material for Grieg to create a mood, compared to hundreds of words Ibsen has to use to say the same thing." Furthermore, he believed that music could convey the effects of painting: "The delicacies of Debussey seem to epitomize the light idealistic temper of the French. Often enough he says the same pastel and lovely things that you find in phases of Watteau's work."[9]

With some exceptions Dreiser disliked opera and regarded its dramatic structure ill-suited to music. He was troubled when the tenor, sword drawn and fire in his blood, stormed to the footlights only to have to wait for his introductory music before he could express himself. But Dreiser had no such reservations about the ballet, which he enjoyed perhaps more for its "mass movement, mass color, mass spirit, and . . . concerted and unified action" than its music.[10] In 1928-29 he helped to organize and finance the American visit of the Russian ballet which had captivated him in Russia the year before, and for a time he became a self-styled balletomane. As for contemporary music, Dreiser felt that it lacked harmony and proportion as well as "poetry and dreaminess" thereby making "a harsh cynical business of life, overlooking its beauties." Traditionalist critics of his day had said that his novels cynically portrayed the harsh business of life, overlooking its beauties, and possibly he sensed his weakness when he acknowledged that, "Our music standards are still traditional ones. We aren't prepared for the things that are being put before us as modern music. For that reason, there may be more beauty in them than we can see." Still, he argued that contemporary composers lacked genius and that only Debussy qualifies as a giant comparable to Dostoevsky or Freud in their fields. "Music," he concluded, "is behind the other arts—notably writing and sculpture—in finding modern forms in which to express the modern mind."[11]

Whatever his doubts about modern music, he sometimes saw modern life in musical terms, often with bizarre results. "Life orchestrates itself at times so perfectly," he wrote in *A Hoosier Holiday.* "It sings like a prima donna of humble joys, and happy homes and simple tasks. It creates like a great virtuoso, bow in hand, or fingers upon invisible keys, a supreme illusion." Elsewhere, he said that New York is the most beautiful city; it "sings, it plays, it's symphonic."[12] On another occasion, he wrote of Chicago; "How I loved the tonic note of even the grinding wheels of the trucks and cars, the clang and chatter of the electric lines, the surge of vehicles in every street! The palls of heavy manufacturing smoke that hung over the city like impending hurricanes; the storms of wintry snow or sleety rain; the glow of yellow lights in little shops at evening, mile after mile, where people were stirring and bustling over potatoes, flour, cabbages—all these were the substance of songs, paintings, poems."[13] On still another occasion, Dreiser suggested that prose could resemble music when he spoke of an editor on the St. Louis *Globe-Democrat* whose paragraphs "ended like music, the deep sonorous bass of an organ."[14]

He believed popular songs were good indices of "the reactions and aspirations" of the people, and mentioning the nature of the songs and their enormous popularity he observed, "what other than an innocent-minded and deeply illusioned democracy could this indicate?"[15] More significant were his comments about the ideal nature of music. He spoke of it as a "mystical realm" adding, "I have no quarrel with idealism as such. It is altogether lovely. I could not love music as much as I do and not find a place for the emotional ideals of man."[16] That idealism applied to his thoughts about popular, as well as academic, music is clear from his assertion that, "We Americans have home traditions of ideals created as much by song and romance as anything else: 'My Old Kentucky Home,' 'Swanee River.' "[17] His poem, "Music" (presumably referring to academic music), bespeaks an ideal realm of perfection which we associate with the Genteel Tradition, a world of the spirit transcending the physical. It goes in part:

> Music, how subtle!
> Like a liar, you lie, and like truth, uplift!
> As one broken-hearted, you speak of the unattainable.
> There is in you a sway and sweep drawn from the eternity of motion.
> From the spheres a voice,
> From all outer certainty, meaning.
> Even of the infinite is your strain.[18]

Dreiser strongly felt the tie between music and poetry. Sometimes his comments about music contain cliches of romantic verse. In *A*

Book about Myself he told of being in a blue mood, torn between love and ambition, and of "an ache that rivalled in intensity those melancholy moods we sometimes find interpreted by music." Peering soulfully out of the window, he pondered the significance of his all-too rapidly passing life and concluded, in words suggesting Grey's "Elegy," that "only silence and the grave ended it all."[19] This thought occurred at twilight, the time of day that Dreiser tended to poetize and Paul was accustomed to brood poetically on the piano keys. Sister Carrie, too, had a poetic moment at twilight as she responded to the sounds of a piano in a neighboring apartment "much as the strings of the harp vibrate when a corresponding key of a piano is struck." Dreiser went on to describe how "she was delicately moulded in sentiment and answered in vague ruminations certain wistful chords." She looked longingly out of the window as the music sounded "in a most soulful and tender mood. . . . It was that hour between afternoon and night when. . . things are apt to take on a wistful aspect."[20]

Music has a significant place in some of Dreiser's other writings as well. His dramatic fantasy, *The Spring Recital* (which Ivan Boutnikoff adapted for orchestra and ballet in 1941), is partly in verse and calls for selections by Bach, Grieg, Chopin and Mozart along with delirious dancing by fauns, nymphs, "newly dead spirits" and "Three Priests of Isis," among others. Several of Dreiser's poems have musical titles, including "Song," "Zither–Spring," and "Fugue," and these, like much of the rest of his poems, contain musical figures of speech.

In his brother's songs he heard some of the very things that touched him most deeply and are prominent in his writing, no matter how commonplace and sentimental they may seem in the music. "What pale little things they really were," he wrote of Paul's songs, "mere bits and scraps of sentiment and melodrama in story form, most assinine sighings over home and mother and lost sweethearts and dead heroes such as never were in real life, and yet with something about them, in the music at least, which always appealed to me intensely. . . . They bespoke, as I always felt, a wistful, seeking, uncertain temperament, tender and illusioned, with no practical knowledge of any side of life, but full of true poetic feeling for the mystery of life and death, the wonder of the waters, the stars, the flowers, accidents of life, success, failure."[21] In varying degrees the feelings expressed in Paul's songs are those of Dreiser himself and the heroes of his novels, Carrie, Jennie Gerhardt, Eugene Witla and even Frank Cowperwood. Such feelings, from the romantic or ideal side of his nature, provided evocative power for his writing. Fusing them with material from the hard-boiled part of his nature, he invested them with an intensity far beyond that found in contemporary popular music and gave them dramatic significance above the commonplace sentimentality of Tin Pan Alley.

NOTES

[1]Dorothy Dudley, *Forgotten Frontiers* (N.Y., 1932), p. 78.

[2]R. H. Wollstein, "You Know Mr. Dreiser," *Musical America,* XLIX (February 25, 1929) 36.

[3]Margaret Tjader, *Theodore Dreiser* (Norwalk, Conn., 1965), pp. 18-19.

[4]Theodore Dreiser, *Twelve Men* (N.Y., 1919), p. 78.

[5]Theodore Dreiser, *Dawn* (N.Y., 1931), pp. 186, 361.

[6]The three articles on Tin Pan Alley were: "Birth and Growth of a Popular Song," *Metropolitan Magazine,* VIII (Nov., 1898), 497-502; "Whence the Song," *Harper's Weekly,* XLIV (Dec. 8, 1900), 1165-1166A; "Who Was King of Tin Pan Alley in the Gay Nineties," *The Gallery of Stars,* I (Winter 1941-42), 31-32, 48. The other articles mentioned appeared in *Success* in 1898 and 1899.

[7]Theodore Dreiser, *A Traveler at Forty* (N. Y., 1913), p. 40.

[8]Tjader, *Dreiser,* p. 17.

[9]Wollstein, "You Know Mr. Dreiser," p. 36.

[10]Tjader, *Dreiser,* p. 18.

[11]Wollstein, "You Know Mr. Dreiser," pp. 37, 55.

[12]Theodore Dreiser, *A Hoosier Holiday* (N.Y., 1916), p. 38; Konrad Bercovici "Romantic Realist," *Mentor,* XVIII (May, 1930), 40.

[13]Theodore Dreiser, *A Book about Myself* (N. Y., 1965), p. 22.

[14]*Ibid.*, p. 99.

[15]*The Songs of Paul Dresser* (N. Y., 1927), Introduction by Theodore Dreiser, p. 1x.

[16]*Letters of Theodore Dreiser,* ed. Robert H. Elias (Phila., 1959), Vol. I, p. 205; Vol. II, p. 646.

[17]Dreiser, *Book About Myself,* p. 354.

[18]Theodore Dreiser, *Moods, Cadenced and Declaimed* (N.Y., 1926), p. 312.

[19]Dreiser, *Book about Myself,* p. 110.

[20]Theodore Dreiser, *Sister Carrie* (New York, 1927), p. 114.

[21]Dreiser, *Twelve Men,* p. 97.

The Wild and Woolly World of Harry Stephen Keeler: Scenes From the Last Act

by

Francis M. Nevins, Jr.

Who has not read, with delight and stupefaction, the wild and woolly writings of Harry Stephen Keeler? Unfortunately, the truth is that no more than a handful of mystery readers over the last twenty years have had that pleasure. But though he is all but forgotten today, Keeler was in his time and still remains the sublime nutty genius of crime fiction. He specialized in monstrously long and involuted intrigue-farces, whose thousands of bizarre plot-pieces he would invariably weave together by means of a galaxy of eyeball-popping coincidences. With full consciousness and malice aforethought, he produced dozens of gargantuan burlesques of conventional mystery fiction, each one spiced with the fruitiest narrative and dialogue conceivable.

Keeler was born in Chicago in 1890 and lived there most of his life. His education was somewhat spotty: he once said that on the day they taught grammar and rhetoric he played hooky and caught perch at the foot of Superior Street, and judging from his rather idiosyncratic notions of English prose, he never spoke a truer word.

He obtained a degree in electrical engineering from the old Armour Institute of Technology and went to work in 1912 in a steel mill.

He had begun writing short stories in 1910, but the first major step in his literary career was not taken until 1914. In that year he made his first sale in the mystery field, a short story about the life and death of a professional strangler, entitled "Victim No. 5," which appeared in *Young's Magazine.* During the following ten years he turned out a stream of stories, novellas and booklength magazine serials. In 1924 Hutchinson, the British publisher, issued between hard covers one of these serials, *The Voice of the Seven Sparrows,* followed by *Find the Clock* (1925), *The Spectacles of Mr. Cagliostro* (1926), and *Sing Sing Nights* (1927). It was also in 1927 that E. P. Dutton published Keeler's first book in this country, *Find the Clock,* and followed it with a host of others. *Sing Sing Nights* (Dutton, 1928) and *Thieves' Nights* (Dutton, 1929) were the first novels in which Keeler employed his uniquely wacky Arabian Nights structure of stories-within-a-novella-within-a-novel in order to incorporate his earlier magazine fiction within an expanded framework.

With the turn of the decade Keeler escalated his verbosity and his zany theories of construction: *The Amazing Web* (Dutton, 1930) fills more than 500 pages with superbly screwy plotting, and is a pure joy to read. His next works were even longer and more luscious: *The Matilda Hunter Murder* (1931) and *The Box from Japan* (1932) each runs well over 700 closely printed pages, and each plunges its boyscoutish hero into endless ridiculous dilemmas. With *The Marceau Case* (1936) and its sequels, Keeler escalated the outrages once more by breaking up a 1500 page meganovel into four separate volumes published a year or so apart. Five more such series-novels appeared during the late Thirties and early Forties, but during the war years it became sadly apparent that Keeler's audience had dried up. A small publisher continued to issue his novels in the U. S. until 1948, and his British publishers offered a handful more from 1949 to 1953; but thereafter Keeler could not find a publisher in his native tongue.

Any readers who still cared must have concluded at that point that Keeler had retired or died. In reality, he remained as active as before, writing twenty or more new novels directly for translation into Spanish or Portuguese editions before he died in frustration and obscurity on January 22, 1967. The rest of this paper will be devoted to brief accounts of a few of these late novels, which may give some idea of the screwball delights which English-speaking readers have been denied.

The Circus Stealers, written about 1956 and published in Spain in 1958, is another adventure of kindly old Angus MacWhorter and his Biggest Little Circus on Earth, which Keeler first introduced in *The Vanishing Gold Truck* (Dutton, 1941). As usual in late Keeler, most of the book consists of conversations recounting action that has occurred offstage, and most of the conversationalists speak in one or another outrageous dialect. As the book opens, MacWhorter's circus has reached a burg called Pricetown, in some unspecified state in the Bible Belt. Its itinerary then calls for it to cross the desolate and dangerous Idiot's Valley, which is traversed only by one winding dirt road, known as Old Twistibus and likened "to a giant strand of boiled spaghetti tossed down by a super-giant." The first third of this delicious valley, filled with scrub oak and cactus-studded loam, is locally referred to as The Land the Lord Forgot. The middle third is the only inhabitable part, but every single dweller therein is a mental defective, and most of them tote guns. The final third is the famous Poison Swamp, passable only by way of a narrow sandstone ridge-road and filled with horrible man-eating Starky Fish. At the far end of the valley lies the town of Foleysburg, whose founder believed that electricity was the devil incarnate and made it impossible for any electrical device (including radios, telephones and telegraph lines) to be brought into or near the town. Checks are not legal tender in Foleysburg; the United States Supreme Court has just decided (Earl Warren dissenting I trust) that in Foleysburg "midnight" means 6:01 P.M.; and there is a local ordinance making it a crime to bring a prehistoric animal within the city limits. Out of these and other elements, a villainous rival bigtop entrepreneur named Wolf Gladish has hatched a diabolic scheme to snatch the entire MacWhorter circus out from under its owner's nose. MacWhorter learns of the plot, and Gladish finds out that MacWhorter has found out, and the rest of the book is move and countermove, thrust and parry, until the last-minute arrival of a truck-driving skeleton saves the day and the circus for our hero.

Keeler's dialogue and characters are as dizzying as his plot. "Don't corrugate your young cerebellum about what might happen," an evil magician advises an idiot boy. Earlier the same illusionist, while waiting for a phone connection, says out loud to himself: "Why the hell doesn't that lank, ugly-looking freckle-faced female with the big ears, who was pointed out to me earlier today as manning the phone exchange in this town, answer the (telephone)?"; which, if not the worst piece of exposition in the history of world literature, is topped only by other gems from HSK's pure poetic pen. There can be little doubt that the officials of Foleysburg are in Wolf Gladish's pocket after we learn that their names are Mayor Akers Mull, Sheriff Pike Hussbottom and Judge Fishkins Dollarhide.

Although the elements of *The Circus Stealers* are as fruity as ever, Keeler does not, as he did in his prime, shape and reshape them into fireworks displays of stupefying coincidence. But the book is still so much more blissfully nonsensical than what passes for humorous crime fiction nowadays that I believe its rejection by English-language publishers can only be described as dumb.

The title page of a Keeler manuscript from 1958, when the bottom had virtually dropped out of the fantastic-fiction market, mirrors much of the author's frustration in his last active years. It reads:

THE CASE OF THE TRANSPARENT NUDE
(*Not* a science fiction or fantasy novel)
A Crime Enigma Laid in Chicago
by
HARRY STEPHEN KEELER

> Author's note: The author's *Sing Sing Nights,* when movieized, had three—3!—separate and distinct motion pictures made from it. His *The Spectacles of Mr. Cagliostro* is now currently being filmed. Other books by him will be conveyed, as to titles, upon request.

Most of the first half of the book takes place 25 years before the present, and recounts how Helmon Hobersteed, the lecherous chief of Chicago's Homicide Investigation Division, and Blackaby Oxnard, the young Cook County coroner and Hobersteed's sexual rival, investigate the "accidental" death of a young woman in a steam vapor cabinet. When they open the cabinet, they find to their dumbfoundment that the woman is not there. Her head is sticking out of the cabinet top and her toes out of the bottom but the rest of her is, to use a Keelerism, "non-esty." It is not until a quarter of a century later, after Hobersteed has developed the illusion that he too is transparent and been retired to a funny farm, that Chicago's greatest unsolved murder is cleared up. At that point Jonathan Paley—antivivisection crusader, true crime writer, and the present head of Chicago's H.I.D., receives a strange letter from a circus fat lady, and finally hears from her lips the story of the unlucky butcher Carl Schliefgeisser and of his entanglement with the transparent nude.

The fat lady's story forms the second half of the book, and no man but Keeler could have concocted it. Its ingredients include a house that lies half in Pennsylvania and half in Ohio, a whorehouse of physical freaks, a religious sect that believes the legal punishment of murderers to be against God's will, the old reliable twins who don't know of each other's existence, an unnamed South American country which does not recognize U. S. marriages as legal, and a boarding-house keeper who throws out all her roomers at regular intervals. The whole thing is tied up into a wild but, within Keeler's wacky terms of reference, neat package with the help of two whopping surprises in the last five pages of text.

The Case of the Transparent Nude is overflowing with the customary Keeler coincidences, grotesquerie, and mathematically constructed madness. It also contains a full measure of Keeler's unique brand of racism, which is so gratuitous, so completely unconnected with anything else in the book, that its effect is to make itself and all racism ludicrous. Thus we find casual sentences like: "[A] couple of pickaninnies standing in front of the two [buildings] showed Negro infiltration of this once-fashionable region." My favorite Keeler comment on race occurs when he takes us inside the troubled mind of Carl Schliefgeisser, who has just found a body: "And the landlady. . . would call the police–if not that, maybe some Negro burglar climbing up to the window tomorrow would see [and] tip the police off." I have a feeling that this approach, similar to what the film *Dr. Strangelove* did to the military with Generals Buck Turgidson and Jack D. Ripper, could be fruitfully explored by other writers.

Keeler's most extensive work on the white man's image of the black man was completed a year later, in 1959. *The Man Who Changed His Skin* is almost devoid of crime and detection but is rich in puzzlement, coincidence, dialect, and bizarre plot elements. Its setting is not the present or near future like most of his other novels, but the past: specifically, Boston in April 1855. And it may very well be the funniest historical novel anywhere.

The white knight in this game is Clark Shellcross, instructor at a Boston boys' school and a fanatic English history buff. Poor Clark has the misfortune to be deeply in love with beautiful Vernice Treves, who makes her 80-year-old grandmother scrub floors and chop wood, and who refuses to marry Clark unless he gives up the teaching he loves and gets a well-paying itinerant job that will allow her to move to a new place every week. When Clark suggests that her wanderlust will vanish when the first baby comes, she replies: "Mister–Shellcross!. . . In all my life, I never heard of a gentleman making remarks like that. . . Since the conversation has now descended, at least on your part, to sheer gutter-talk, I must leave the room. You–know the way out, I presume?" When Clark reminds her that he has no training for any kind of on-the-road job, she counters with supreme imperiousness: "You'll succeed–because you have *me* as your stimulus."

On his dejected way home, Clark encounters and gives a dollar to a bum eating scraps from a garbage heap. Jeb Polliver gratefully bestows on Clark a wad of black gum he claims to have gotten from a unique tree in Africa years before. When swallowed the gum transfers one's mind into somebody else's body, and vice versa–or so Jeb claims. This tale is a bit much for a trained historian to swallow, but Clark swallows the pellet that night, just to prove that the old bum was lying. Immediately, he finds himself inhabiting the body of Sam Brown, who lives in the Negro rooming-house across the street. And, nature abhorring a vacuum, Sam Brown's mind is transferred to Clark's body. Unhappily, Sam before retiring had determined to kill himself upon waking, unless he thought up an answer to a woman problem that had been bedeviling him. Failing to do so, he shoots himself in Clark's bedroom, leaving Clark's mind no Shellcrossian body to return to. Clark comments to himself on hearing this piece of news: "I–I–Clark Shellcross–am now confined for life–in the body of a nigger!"

One need not have read much Keeler to guess that a Keeler hero will not be too happy in the body of a "nigger". But, amazingly, the rest of the book is concerned with the hero's gradual realization that Clark Shellcross and Sam Brown shared very similar problems in their lives. And at the end of the novel, thanks to an assist from the Reverend Doctor Callixtus Fearnought, President of the Baptist College of Theology and reluctant harborer of runaway slaves (and from a few well-timed Keeler coincidences), Clark Shellcross winds up with all his problems solved, and damn glad that he is black.

Even when his subject was one of the central problems of our time, Keeler remained Keeler, the coiner of such mad similes as "It was like trying to think about the square root of minus zero" and "He looked like a man who had been flung atop a hot plate." Keeler's treatment of racial themes was uneasy and ambivalent to say the least: he seems to use the terms nigger, Negro, black boy, and black man almost interchangeably. But I think anyone personally or professionally concerned with what whites have thought (and sadly still do think) about blacks could learn much from this book. And who but Keeler would dare to make racial strife funny?

In these days of black humor, camp, and the Absurd, it is amazing that there has been no renaissance of interest in Keeler. Fortunately there are some signs—this paper is one of them—that such a movement may be in the offing. For Keeler was beyond dispute the great wack of American letters, and today's readers should be given the chance to decide for themselves whether they can't stand HSK, or like me, can't live without him.

Popular Culture as Cyclic Phenomenon in the Evolution of Tennessee Williams

by

John J. Fritscher

In a wagon so newly painted as Popular Culture, every ride we take is—like the Popular Culture Association—to our Traditionalist critics, whether we like it or not, a kind of defensive apologia for the premises, principles, and relevancy of the new discipline of Popular Culture. Not only has the sense of what ought to be considered "cultural" widened, but so have the ways changed to get into, inside, the old traditions. The reality is that the new novel, the new theatre, the new film are arrived. Let's face it: Traditionalists have very few real issues still to be ascertained. But in the now-moment relevancy of Popular Culture VERDICTS ARE CONSTANTLY IN THE MAKING. It's traditionally safe to talk of Jamesian attitudes of America, just as it is traditionally safe to say "1492." But to be so untraditionally openended as to say, "Wait, America still hasn't been discovered" plays serious fun with uptight tradition, opens up the relevant now moment into which art gives insight, especially if the moment be as now revolutionary.

In art forms of human concern, We are Curious (Popular). Our style may be new, our forms different, but yet the hearttransplant of our matter is solidly from Sophocles and Thomas Mann and Dostoevsky. Our heart is the universal same. Our massage is new and now. Myra Breckinridge compared, to, say the women of Butch Hemingway and Sundance Capote, is the New American Woman, William Buckley notwithstanding. At first glance, she's far from Phaedra or Juliet because she is popcartoon. Her dialog is written in over-head balloons. And just as looking at Claes Oldenburg's Giant Pool Balls or Giant Raisin Bread sculpture causes us once seeing so large, to perceive the small real thing afterwards ever so differently, so does billboardsize Ekberg-like Myra cause us to look into the human male-female character with new eyes.

Post Pollock, post Williams Burroughs, post the destruction of form into formlessness concealing form, we cannot validly monitor the current human condition through traditionalist form and matter. This we accept; but to rap with Traditionalists we ought to be able to show them that oftentimes their very terms are in fact evolvable. Tennessee Williams, saint-dramatist in the Traditionalist canon, is excellent case in point.

Williams' career began in the late Thirties/early Forties, coincidental with that time when, so Myra Breckinridge claims, the movies of the Forties were the highpoint of Western Culture. Back in those Forties, Tennessee Williams hired himself out to MGM; the Studio wanted him to knit plots for Lana's Sweater Flicks. Instead he wrote a screenplay called *Girl in Glass.* He was fired. Six years later MGM was outbid by Warner Bros. for screenrights to *Glass Menagerie,* a vehicle conceived on their time.

The flowing form of this Forties' stage play is owed to the story's filmic conception. In fact, *Glass Menagerie,* a drama of gapping generations, was conceived by Williams for the stage as a Mixed Media Production using slides, filmed words, and taped music. Producer Eddie Dowling refused to humor Williams whom he considered eccentric rather than in advance of his time.

1945's *Glass Menagerie,* therefore, while it was a huge financial and critical success was less than the plastic organic futurentity

Williams had conceived. Because the forward-looking Mixed Media Ideas were dropped, Williams was given a safe Establishment production. In turn, he was lauded for singing to days gone by. The Establishment saw it as Amanda's play about the lost pastness, not Tom's play about the raw future. Chagrined Williams has since all but set himself afire to destroy the Establishment image that he is not avantgarde.

Williams' work currently is out of vogue. Small wonder; after all, he's in his fifth decade of production; yet if his plays have shorter runs, Williams as personality garners more publicity; jumping into Catholicism when everyone short of the Pope is jumping out, being chased by Mafia hoods, doing his own version of Judy Garland's Final Show, himself bedded, however, hospital-safe and covered well with *TimeLife* reporters. He knows a good show in times when it is the personality as much as the art product that counts. Faster than you can say Jacqueline Susann he keeps himself in the news.

The fact is neither he nor the theater would be today the same without the other. In direct reciprocity Williams has both created and been created by the theatricality which ingests Everything in Every American Subculture: Our mass media are voracious to raise or lower everything to the middle-class consumer level. April 1969 *McCalls* published a chapter of *The Love Machine* and editoralized how it cleaned up the language for its consumers.

Raquel's Myra seems a long way from Williams' bitches, but the mold is the same. Williams, like Myron, like their American context, has been movie-bred. He writes, as did the classical dramatists, using the cultural mythology at hand: Hollywood Goddess or Super Stud. He takes the measure of the popular archetypes of our time—exactly the way Hemingway's Old Man and Simon/Garfunkel look at Joe Dimaggio. His characters talk so much about the movies in plays that have in turn been made into movies that watching his films talking about the movies is (if not coincident with a form of absurd drama) at least like the Op Experience—known to every little boy in his first barbershop—of sitting between two facing mirrors whose images curve off to infinity.

Williams adapts well to the screen (despite an occasional fiasco like Burton-Taylor's *Boom* or an elaboration like Natalie Wood's *This Property Is Condemned.* This, because he is basically cinematic. When I interviewed Mr. Williams two years ago in Chicago at the world premiere of *Eccentricities of a Nightingale,* he said that he intended to write no more three-act plays. He prefers now to compose a 70-80 page script divided like *Suddenly Last Summer* into six or seven scenes which slide easily into one another like overlap dissolves of the movie camera. The stage length he intends approximates the length of the feature film. This evolution in his form to scenes commanding shorter attention spans shows him picking up on the pacing that TV, segmented by commercials, has given to American audiences. Thus he has become one of the umbrella contributors to *Oh Calcutta,* that TVlike review which sees that movies in the 40's style (confer Joshua Logan directing anything) are no longer really simpatically with-it, that movies stylized after TV dramas (confer Otto Preminger directing anything) are a cross-media mistake. What films, what plays need now is the spirit of the TV commercial; short attention demands, with visceral point.

Williams grew up in movie theatres much like his shortstories' Joy Rio and Delta Brilliant. Small wonder, then, he has always employed materials popular in the period his plays were conceived or set. Many Williams women are associated with a particular Tin Pop Alley song. Alexandra del Lago, Chance Wayne, Sissy Goforth, and *Camino Real's* Street People are all turned on to, are all well linked and lettered into the American drug scene. His attitude toward Blacks has always been well tempered and surprisingly Afro in orientation as in *Battle of Angels/The Fugitive Kind.* (Attention to folk heritage and pop culture often overlap.) The combined image of Brando/Kowalski which Brando careered into the seminal Stanley Kramer motorcycle film *The Wild One* produced the exclusively American phenomenon, the blackleather motorcycle outlaw (now under contract to American-International Films), the motorcycle easyrider, independent as Natty Bumppo and the Marlboro TV cowboys worshipped enviously by the highly urban males of *Period of Adjustment.*

Brando, in fact, is a good point of real reality and reality of the movie reel overlapping. Just as Brando engineered the torn Tshirt image out of *Streetcar* and the Williams motorcycle stories, so have Paul Newman, Rip Torn, Geraldine Page, Elizabeth Taylor, Anne Meacham, and Shirley Knight all to greater than lesser extents gratefully allowed the Williams characters to tub off on their own pop marquee images. And Williams has certainly, too, been proliferated upon by protege William Inge tonally in any play and Mart Crowley in *Boys in the Band* where Sebastian Venable is recalled as martyr-saint in the gay camp canon.

Williams has always had touches of madness about him. But since the Andy advent of the Warholed Sixties, he has gotten even wilder. His characters like Chance Wayne (whose chances are waning) and Sissy Goforth (who is afraid to go forth to die) often have names Ian Fleming's Pussy Galore or Al Capp's Moonbeam McSwine would envy. Just as many of his later characters, so are his plays of the Sixties littered with Roy Liechtenstein dialog-for-Comic-Strip-Balloons as he animates characters like *Kingdom of Earth's* Chicken and the superbly lithographed Molly-Polly, Fraulein, and Hollywood Indian Joe in 1966's *Gnadiges Fraulein*. Is Latter-day Williams one gross put-on? He recently claimed *The National Enquirer* to be the only honest, real literature being printed in the USA. He appears in the December '69 *Playboy* between Tiny Tim and Raquel Welch with his newest horror story: "A Recluse and His Guest." The stage and film versions will undoubtedly follow.

His latest novella, *The Knightly Quest,* is in fact pop paraliterature in the same outrageous vein of Gore as *Myra Breckinridge.* Williams has always been poetic social observer, but with the best or worst of them he can leave subtlety behind (should the *Laugh-in* times not favor Amanda-like gentility of statement.) He satirizes in the New American Scene the plastic fantastic chromium American drive-ins, the stuffed levi codpieces and stuffed silicone bosoms, the Detroit City cars parked next to moonlaunch pads, the eternal American Question: not "To be or not to be?" or "Do I dare?" but "Is it Clean?"

Such Comic Book Panels are a decade or two this side of *Menagerie* and *Streetcar Named Desire* (a title sufficiently pop-mythological for Volkswagen to borrow this year to billboard its product.) But such Comic Book Panels he has long signaled. In the mid-fifties Williams' only published filmscript was an excellent animated Cartoon Panel of Chaucerian bawdry. Mating the child-bride folklore of his native South to the child-bride of *The Canterbury Tales,* he created a Classics Comicbook pair of young lovers who end up a tree while the young girl's old husband searches for the pair in the dark. The Oldenburg pop exaggeration of this was lost on the late Cardinal Spellman and the Traditionalist Legion of Decency who pressured Warner Bros. to the extent that no one will ever see *Baby Doll* on TV's late show. Southern writer Reynolds Price, close friend of "Baby Doll" Carol Baker, disclosed recently in a conversation with a fellow Southerner, Professor William Combs at Western Michigan University, that Warners destroyed all the prints except for three: one owned by director Kazan, one by Miss Baker, and one by co-star Eli Wallach.

Williams' latest play *Two Scenes in the Bar of the Tokyo Hotel* opened in May for a six weeks run to mixed-to-unreceptive reviews. Two points here: Pinter producers Richard Marks and Henry Jaffe opened *Tokyo Hotel* off-Broadway, this new location of great significance to the new Underground Williams; and secondly, the play, regardless of its reviews has gone into almost immediate film production, much like the immediate stage-to-celluloid transferral of Crowley's current hit *Boys in the Band.* Williams is a prime example of a certain American pop mystique: we don't consider a play or novel complete until it is movified.

And mystically when pop astrology and *Hair* are pumping this as the Age of Aquarius when Eastern culture will suffuse Western, then look to the waterfloods of *Kingdom of Earth* as well as to Williams' knowledgeable use of Eastern Mysticism in *Night of the Iguana* and of the Nōh Theatre in *The Milk Train Doesn't Stop Here Anymore.* He is that much into McLuhan's Global tribe, pop united by Lennon-McCartney's Iamheandyouaremeandweareal ltogether raga blues.

In conclusion, a quote from *Period of Adjustment,* spoken by the Jane Fonda character, gives not only, I think, Williams' view of himself as tuned-in artist, but also defines the role of any visionary critic examining the human condition by taking the now-pulse of his popular culture.

> The world is a big hospital, a big neurological ward
> and I am a student nurse in it.

Analogically Williams is both measurer and matter of the American pulse. He has a where-it's-at mythic pop capacity: every artist starts out as seer then becomes sayer for his culture. When the culture in turn picks up on his work and takes it into its mythology like Leonard Cohen's Suzanne or Charles Webb's Mrs. Robinson, the circle is complete; for Mrs. Robinson herself is created in the image of Williams' almost-menopausal American women who stay their *Roman Springs* by vamping confused but hot young boys.

Thus the artist who comes out of his culture takes that culture's disparate ends, pulls them together, and in-forms (that is, gives new form) to that culture. In this doublefeed, Tennessee Williams—so long *in, of* and *with* the Popular Culture—offers himself out of the Old Traditions to new consideration by Popcultists. For us to know where Popculture is, it's imperative to know where it has been. For Popculture is an elusive quicksilver discipline at any given moment. Popculture is, in fact, like that bit of Labrador Spar Emerson talked of: you hold it, turn it, the facets flash by, each relevant for its *moment* of view, the effect *cumulative* and *insightful.* Tennessee Williams has had and is giving yet his facet for us.

A Critical Dilemma: J. F. Powers and the Durability of Catholic Fiction

by

David M. La Guardia

In chapter twelve of J. F. Powers' novel, *Morte D'Urban,* the ever-wordly Father Urban ponders a regretful reality of his vocation: "You never knew what people were thinking–only that you lost or gained ground fast the moment it was known you were a priest."[1] Father Urban's position as priest is ironically applicable to J. F. Powers' position as artist: he either loses or gains ground fast the moment it is known that he is a Roman Catholic artist who writes fiction that is Roman Catholic in orientation. But he is more than mere Catholic writer. There exists a shadowy area in his fiction which involves universality and durability but which hinges on his Catholicity.

Powers' problem is not an uncommon one. He is not unique because he is a Catholic writer, since there are plenty of these, and he is not unique because he chooses to write from a point of thematic reference that is essentially Catholic, though in this area he is more unusual. We think immediately of Graham Greene, Flannery O'Connor, and Morris L. West as other successful modern fiction writers who use Catholicism frequently as their thematic medium. Powers is unique, however, in the extent to which he uses Catholic materials. His characters are not simply Catholic in the general sense of religion and philosophy; rather, they are most often Catholic priests or Catholic nuns or Catholic laymen who operate in direct relation to Catholic goals in a Catholic parish or diocese for Catholic bishops under a Catholic Pope. It is this extremity of Catholicity in the fiction of Powers that bears investigation.[2] Nor should we concern ourselves with "Catholic" only. What we say about the Catholic themes and subjects of Powers should apply from a critical standpoint, to the Jewish themes and subjects of Bernard Malamud and, on a different level, to the Negro themes and subjects of James Baldwin.

In one respect, the problem is more a matter of personal prejudice than one of aesthetic principle: Powers (and Greene and the others) can expect to lose the interest of readers whose personal religious feelings would be antagonized by Catholic or simply religious themes; and he can expect to gain the unqualified enthusiasm of those readers, especially those Catholic readers, who would welcome any modern literature that ignores violence, perversity and agnosticism and that conforms to their personal philosophy and background. But Powers or Greene or O'Connor should not care about losing the former or gaining the latter; both groups, in fact, would be very much shocked if they came to these writers with such predispositions.

The ambiguities involved in evaluating artistic worth are great enough. But when the wrench of religion is thrown in, new problems, which ordinarily would not be pertinent to an aesthetic discussion, suddenly become very pertinent. Sister M. Bernetta Quinn illustrates the perplexities involved.

> Unambiguously the term *Catholic* before physician, teacher, butcher, engineer, refers to the fact that each of these persons belongs to the Catholic Church. Yet if the adjective *Catholic* is prefixed to *writer* ambiguity immediately results. Does the speaker mean someone who, whether a Catholic or not, presents a

> view of reality similar to or identical with that held by those within the Church, or a writer who happens to be a Catholic and who may or may not let his commitment be evident in what he writes.[3]

Sister Bernetta takes special offense to a comment made by Robert Bowen in his review of a collection of Powers' short stories: "J. F. Powers is probably best thought of not as a Catholic writer, but as a writer who happens to be a Catholic." "No writer," retorts Sister Bernetta, " 'happens' to be what he is...."[4] She elaborates upon the effect on him, and on all writers, of providentially arranged matters such as native environment, specialized talents, etc.

We cannot argue with Sister Bernetta on such elusive matters—matters based more on faith than aesthetics. Like so many of the religious—priests, nuns, and brothers—who review the writings of J. F. Powers, she is in the peculiar position of being somewhat blind to the totality of an artistic dilemma because, ironically, she sees too much of the problem from a Powers'-eye-view. As critic she must disengage herself from specifically Catholic theology, from specifically Catholic terminology, and, to whatever extent it is possible, she must try to confront him simply as an American fiction writer whose art should be appealing to an audience of *human beings,* not an audience of Catholic beings or human beings who conform to the theological or philosophical tenets of the Roman Catholic Church.

I do not suggest that Sister Bernetta, or any member of a religious order who confronts J. F. Powers as artist (or any writer as artist), is herself unaware of these critical principles. But I do suggest that the fiction of J. F. Powers, by the nature of its subject matter, may exclude her from legitimate critical comments, just as the political propensities of a news analyst might naturally inhibit his political evaluations despite his conscious desire for objectivity. She must, in short, become a critic who "happens to be" Catholic and not a Catholic critic; and to the extent that she is unwilling or unable to do this, she must not criticize. It is evident that Sister Bernetta recognizes the problems involved when *writer* is prefaced by *Catholic,* but it is not so evident that she recognizes a related problem for critics.[5]

On the other hand, any critic, of whatever denomination, is faced with special problems when confronting the art of Powers. The one question that is, and must be, of uppermost importance, is—is this Catholic art only? Is it too local, too specialized, too irrelevant to too many readers? If the answer is in the affirmative, then it is only proper that Powers be left to the Catholic nuns and Catholic priests and Catholic laymen who find his fiction so entertaining. This would make him a lesser artist. But there are many who do not see Powers as a lesser artist, and certainly Powers does not see himself as such: "I am not just writing to get this stuff published, or even to make a living. I quite often look at it from the point of view of posterity. I suppose that's a kind of pride. Everything I write now I hope will stand up, become part of my little canon."[6]

To confuse the critical dilemma, Powers tries to solve his own problem in a quite off-hand way, in fact in the very way that Sister Bernetta Quinn so strongly denounced, when he comments: "To say Mauriac is a Catholic writer, or Graham Greene is a Catholic writer—I suppose that's true; but, more than that, they are writers."[7] In his most serious moments of critical reflection, Powers intimates that he is quite concerned with the problem of achieving fictional universality despite thematic specificity. "I want to deal with things that I regard as important, like life and death," he asserted in one interview, "...but I write about priests for reasons of irony, comedy and philosophy. They officially are committed to both worlds in the way that most people officially are not. This makes for stronger beer...I just start with a priest, with a man with one foot in each world. It's as simple as that."[8] In the same interview he agreed when his questioner suggested that his fiction treats "real human situations that are only incidentally contemporary."[9] Powers was greatly annoyed by the reception *Morte D'Urban* got in some places: "It was presented as a book about priests, about Catholics, for Catholics. After the National Book Award, a reviewer in Denver said that *Morte D'Urban* was a book for Catholics, and I wrote and asked: 'Would you say that *The Wind in the Willows* is a book for animals?' "[10] He readily admits that he has enjoyed a lesser following due to the subject matter of his work. He laments to having "suffered in the market place" and realizes that "I have a kind of readership, but I would have a much greater readership if I had followed the pattern of Catholic romance."[11] To the question, "You don't want to have only a strictly Catholic posterity?" he answers emphatically, "No, I don't."[12]

All of this information adds to an aesthetic quandary that grows as we learn more about it. Although it is important to know that Powers himself is annoyed with those who would question his artistic relevance because of a limited thematic scope, it is likewise important to reassess that scope in terms of its durability and universality. And although it is important to enter him into a context of literary controversy, it is likewise necessary to note that an alarming number of the critics who are sympathetic to the fiction of Powers happen to be priests and nuns. (I might add that many of those most heatedly opposed to him are also priests and nuns.) In itself, this latter point is significant only insofar as it suggests, with questionable relevance, granted, that those who most strongly identify with the Catholic conflicts in the stories of J.F. Powers are often *very* Catholic. We admit to a certain cynicism when we note that the most significant critical articles and reviews on the writings of Powers have appeared in such religiously oriented journals and magazines as *The Catholic Messenger*, *The American Benedictine Review*, *Commonweal*, *Catholic Worker*, *Our Sunday Visitor*, *America*, *Review of Religion*, *Blackfriars*, *Homiletic and Pastoral Review*, *Worship*, and others. This is not denying the appearance of criticism in the *Yale Review*, the *Kenyon Review*, the *Atlantic Monthly*, *The New York Times Book Review*, etc., but, significantly, the presence of Powers in these less partisan journals is more often in the context of a brief book review than an elaborate critical discussion.

Again, we confess to the somewhat irrelevant nature of any conclusions drawn on the basis of where articles on Powers appear or have appeared. We acknowledge that there would be a natural tendency for one eager to publish an article on Powers to go to a publication which attracts an audience naturally sympathetic to that article. Also there would be a natural tendency for a priest or a nun directly involved in literature to prefer to become enmeshed in a problem or controversy involving a discussion of J. F. Powers than in one considering Henry Miller, Gore Vidal, or even D. H. Lawrence. Religious predispositions do dictate literary preferences. More and more religious writers are producing more and more good articles and books on the great figures of modern literature, and this is as it should be. Nevertheless, the fact that a slight imbalance seems to exist with regard to the decidedly Catholic character in the criticism of Powers might suggest, however slightly, a limitation in Powers' literary appeal–not simply his popular appeal, but his critical appeal too.

There is another approach to Powers' fiction that must be evaluated. Evelyn Waugh considers J. F. Powers as a writer whose "whole art is everywhere infused and directed by his Faith."[13] But Peter De Vries, who affirms that it would never have occurred to him to put it that way,asserts that, "Mr. Powers does not seem to me a religious writer at all. He is undoubtedly a religious man, but that is something else entirely."[14] What makes De Vries' comments important is the fact that he writes not as a Catholic nun, priest, or layman, but as one who during his lifetime has confronted both the legend and the fact of Roman Catholicism from the point of view of the outsider. ("When I was 10, I was the only Dutch Reformed boy in a solidly Irish Catholic parish...."[15]) We are interested in the non-Catholic critical view of Powers in the same way that we are interested in D. H. Lawrence's or Heinrich Straumann's comments on American Literature. The bird's eye view often has a distinct advantage over a more earthly one. Like many outside the Church, De Vries confesses to a puerile infatuation over what goes on inside it: "Conformity soon had me tipping my cap as I passed in front of St. Leo's; curiosity soon had me peering past its portals into the glimmering gloom of the interior, then venturing forward for closer scrutiny."[16] He imagines himself confessing ("those dark boxes") and he realizes that "I had more curiosity about my playmate's religion than they had about mine."[17] He notes, too, that "there was one building of which the mystery remained total. I mean the rectory. Its doors were closed to me. Now at last they are open. It has remained for Mr. Powers after all these years to fling them wide.

In [his] stories we are inside the rectory as we have always wanted to be, with no advance notice to the housekeeper that we are coming or to the priests that we would stay to dinner. This is the Church in dishabille."[18]

We have noted the subtleties and pitfalls involved in the Catholic criticism of the fiction of J. F. Powers. We have said that the Catholic critic must disengage himself from strictly Catholic theological and philosophical premises; he must objectify his criticism. The comments of Peter De Vries suggest that there are just as many subtleties and pitfalls involved for the non-Catholic reader of Powers as for the Catholic one—and more and more the painful truth of an earlier statement is emphasized: when religion becomes entwined in an aesthetic discussion, problems which ordinarily would not be pertinent suddenly become very pertinent.

De Vries' statements hint that as much as a non-Catholic reader might attempt to respond simply and humanly to the work of Powers, he still very often succumbs to a specifically *non-Catholic* reading, a reading influenced by the effects of Protestant rumors about Catholic ritual, by the effects of adolescent and adult prejudices about Catholic practice, and by the effects of irrelevant and irreverent gossip about the habits of priests and nuns behind those cloistered walls. De Vries dramatizes the possibility of this point by emphasizing his early fascination with what went on inside the Catholic Church—"including, of course, the basement where I was sure the rifles were stashed in preparation for the revolution that would seat the Pope as temporal head of the country."[19] In his adulthood, De Vries, of course, does not have such an imaginative vision of the Church, though it is safe to say that his adolescent misconceptions of the Church were instilled in him by well-meaning adults who *still* have their doubts about Catholic political motives, and who might be among those who come to read Powers as a means of substantiating or validating what they have secretly always known to be true about priests, nuns, etc.

The point of this over-elaboration upon De Vries' comments has been to demonstrate that just as Catholic and especially religious readers and critics might be too close to the thematic frame in the fiction of Powers to make wholly valid aesthetic and human judgments about it, so might many non-Catholic readers and critics be too distant to do the same thing: their human response is often in danger of deflection by their non-Catholic response; and their non-Catholic response is dictated, in many cases, by influences and causes outside of the realm of literary consideration. Most importantly, to the extent that these hypotheses are true must we judge the universality of the fiction of J. F. Powers. If he appeals by the nature of his themes and subjects to a limited audience, for extra-literary and extra-human reasons, then his literary significance is limited proportionately.

A sizeable portion of Powers' critics recognize in him a talent for artistry and a sense of humanity deep enough to make him a great American fiction writer. But many of these also recognize that he may be placing too great a burden upon his readers; he expects them to divest themselves of philosophical tenets and theological leanings, Catholic or not, so that they may enjoy a fiction that concerns itself with human foibles and human conflicts, but a fiction which, at the same time, contains in the very core of its artiface, those philosophical and theological tenets and leanings which many of his readers cannot deny or ignore. It is not simply a question of whether Powers is a propagandist. He is not. Nor is it a question, simply, of whether he is allegorical, which he sometimes is. Rather, it is a question of whether Powers, by this ambiguous demand he places upon those readers who want only to digest good fiction, alienates many Catholics and non-Catholics alike who are unable to see through the *frame* to get to the art, which, once achieved, is well worth the effort, a fact that will not be denied in any case.

I doubt that the Jewish reader can enjoy J. F. Powers in the same way that the Christian and even Catholic reader can enjoy Bernard Malamud, and this is upsetting from a critical point of view insofar as Powers is in potential as good a writer as Malamud. True, Malamud treats Jewish situations in a philosophical context that is primarily Jewish. But he does not take us into the rabbinical school or even into the synagogue, while Powers takes us into the Catholic Church, the parish house, the convent, etc.

Powers makes his priest-protagonists exceptionally *human* human beings. As a group, they are beer-drinking, cigar-smoking, pseudo-saints, replete with weird sexual submersions and other celibate eccentricities. But the characters who are exposed by Powers and the society he places them in remain very priestly and therefore very restricted. Sister Kristin Malloy posed to Mr. Powers a significant question the answer to which he somewhat evaded: "Is it wise to let the world know that priests and religious are this human?"[20] The point is well taken and should be considered. Will the non-Catholic totally unfamiliar with clerical life—or even the Catholic, who is as much disposed to imaginative wonderings concerning what goes on behind mysterious convent and/or parish house walls as his Protestant friends—will these in their respective states be able to respond in a totally human and unbiased way to the situation, for instance, of the housekeeper and Father Firman in the popular story, "The Valiant Woman"? Will the readers of this wonderful story be able to adjust to the fact of a priest living alone in a house with a woman who not only launders his underwear and darns his socks and admonishes him to "cut your toenails, why don't you? Haven't I got enough to do?" but with whom he shares his bathroom and plays a nightly game of "honeymoon bridge," and because of whom one priest friend hums to himself the tune of "Wedding Bells are Breaking Up That Old Gang of Mine"? Is it possible that the parochial understanding required for full appreciation of the nuances and subtleties of this story is too much to ask of the non-parochial reader? I wholeheartedly agree with John V. Hagopian when he states that Powers is able to shape "highly charged human situations out of parochial material,"[21] but I wonder if the parochial material does not often stand in the way of universal human response.

It is not the business of the student of literature to judge the worth of art in terms of popular response. However, it is legitimate to ask, Will the reader unfamiliar with, but open to, the religious themes and settings in Powers have sufficient understanding to delineate fictional situations and conflicts? To every great work of art each individual brings his own particular complexity of emotions. Each responds in his own way on his own level of understanding and in proportion to his own capacity for feeling. The great work of art has something to offer to all. If Powers is limited as an artist; if he is a "lesser artist," it must be because the nature of his work precludes this possibility of universal human response. In answer to the question "Have you read J. F. Powers?" too many reply, "Is he the one who wrote all those priest stories?" Such a response suggests that Powers might be facing a dilemma which James Fenimore Cooper seems to have faced, a dilemma of limitation. As Cooper concerned himself with one character named variously Hawkeye, Natty-Bumppo, Leatherstocking, Deerslayer, Long-Rifle, so Powers, to those readers who through no fault of their own lack sufficient religious understanding to delineate situations and conflicts—to these readers—Powers likewise has created one character named Father Urban-Udovic-Burner-Firman-Eudex-Etc. Cooper was more at home in the wilderness as Powers is more at home in the rectory. "Greatness" in the art of both is limited by this provincialism.

There is one other way of looking at the priest-stories of Powers, a way that Powers would prefer, and even, perhaps, the right way. In several instances the religious setting or the clerical theme tends to create fictional electricity where it might not otherwise have existed. Powers is primarily interested in the complexities of good and evil at work in the hearts of individual men. His perception of these complexities is of the deepest and most significant kind. In choosing priests as protagonists, Powers is able to avoid the major issues of evil in the world, those involving extreme violence, hatred and passion; he can substitute in their place the common and often comic foibles of the human condition, the hidden vanities, the concealed prejudices, the camouflaged hypocricies of the man in the street. When these sins are dressed in clerical garb and imbued in the context of a total commitment to God and fellow man, they assume an awesome ugliness more dramatic in its effect than murder, rape, or incest. Like Fra Lippo Lippi, the artist in Browning's famous monologue, Powers realizes that the complexities of life cannot be embodied in an art which concerns itself with "saints, and saints, and saints again."[22]

This discussion of the Catholicity in the art of J. F. Powers ends in a paradox, a critical dilemma which involves, however remotely, the marriage of aesthetic principles with religious controversy. The dangers involved in confronting the paradox include the tendency to generalize to such an extreme as to suggest that fiction of a provincial setting can never have a universal import. It has not been the purpose of this paper to even hint at such a misconception, nor to suggest that Powers' art specifically is of no import—literary or otherwise. His fiction is important to twentieth century American literature and especially to the short story. The problem involved is one of durability and universality in the context of specific Catholicity. The facets to the problem are not wholly aesthetic, not wholly religious. Hagopian notices that "readers who do not personally believe in Catholicism *must* at least see it at work in even the most casual details of a Powers story."[23] (Italics mine) I suppose this paper has been concerned with the MUST in that statement. If there exists a slice of sensitive humanity which CANNOT adjust itself to the Catholicity at work in Powers' stories, then I suggest the existence of a problem that is artistic in repercussion if not in substance.

NOTES

[1]J. F. Powers, *Morte D'Urban,* p. 271.

[2]It should be pointed out that not all of the fiction of Powers concerns itself with specifically Catholic situations. But the work for which he is best known does. I cannot agree with John V. Hagopian when he remarks concerning Powers' non-clerical fiction: "Had Powers never written a story about a priest, some of these pieces [stories with secular themes] would alone ensure his status as a distinguished writer." John V. Hagopian, *J. F. Powers.* p. 37.

[3]Sister M. Bernetta Quinn, O. S. F., "View from a Rock: the Fiction of Flannery O'Connor and J. F. Powers," *Critique* II (Fall, 1958), 19.

[4]Quinn, p. 23. (The quote from Bowen is also from Quinn's article.)

[5]The irony involved in this entire paper is that I, as writer, am Catholic, and I have had to confront constantly the fact that my religion is more a hindrance than a help in making aesthetically competent evaluations of the art of

J. F. Powers.

[6]J. F. Powers, "The Catholic and Creativity," as interviewed by Sister M. Kristin Malloy, O. S. B., in *The American Benedictine Review,* XV (March, 1964), 74.

[7]Powers, interview with Sister Malloy, p. 64.

[8]*Ibid.,* p. 69 and p. 70.

[9]*Ibid.,* p. 68. (This statement is Sister Malloy's.)

[10]*Ibid.* [11]*Ibid.,* p. 71. [12]*Ibid.,* p. 75.

[13]Evelyn Waugh, "Scenes of Clerical Life," *Commonweal,* 63 (March 30, 1956), p. 667.

[14]Peter De Vries, "Introduction" to *Lions, Harts, Leaping Does and Other Stories,* by J. F. Powers, Time Reading Program Special Edition, p. xv.

[15]*Ibid.* [16]*Ibid.,* p. xvi. [17]*Ibid.,* pp.xvi-xvii. [18]*Ibid.,* p. xvii. [19]*Ibid.*

[20]Interview with Sister Malloy, p. 71.

[21]Hagopian, p. 15.

[22]Robert Browning, "Fra Lippo Lippi," 11. 48-49.

[23]Hagopian, p. 121.

List of Contributors

Esther K. Birdsall is on the faculty of Maryland University, College Park.

Joel H. Bernstein is on the faculty of the University of Montana.

Peter Buitenhuis is on the faculty of McGill University.

Neal Canon is on the faculty of Indiana State University, Terre Haute.

Alan Casty is on the faculty of Santa Monica City College, California.

John Fritscher is on the faculty of Western Michigan University, Kalamazoo.

Michael Gordon is on the faculty of the University of Connecticut.

Francis S. Grubar is on the faculty of George Washington University.

Mark R. Hillegas is on the faculty of Southern Illinois University, Carbondale.

Irma B. Jaffe is on the faculty of Fordham University.

John Lachs is on the faculty of Vanderbilt University.

David M. La Guardia is on the faculty of John Carroll University.

Neil Leonard is on the faculty of the University of Pennsylvania.

David W. Marcell is on the faculty of Skidmore College.

Paul R. Messbarger is on the faculty of St. Mary's College, Notre Dame.

Francis M. Nevins, Jr. is an attorney in East Brunswick, New Jersey.

John W. Nichol is on the faculty of the University of Southern California.

Gerard O'Connor is on the faculty of Lowell Technological Institute, Mass.

John W. Rathbun is on the faculty of California State College, Los Angeles.

Elizabeth Steele is on the faculty of the University of Toledo, Ohio.

Elmer F. Suderman is on the faculty of Gustavus Adolphus University.

Tom H. Towers is on the faculty of Wisconsin State University, Whitewater.

Eckard V. Toy, Jr. is on the staff of the library, University of Wyoming.

Wilcomb E. Washburn is on the staff of the Smithsonian Institution.

Robert Lee White is on the faculty of York Univeristy.

Editors

William K. Bottorff is associate professor of English, University of Toledo.

Ray B. Browne is Director of the Center for the Study of Popular Culture, Bowling Green University, and Editor of the Bowling Green University Popular Press.

Larry N. Landrum is on the staff of the Center for the Study of Popular Culture, Bowling Green University.